MEDIEVALISM

Volume XIII

William Morris and the Icelandic Sagas

ISSN 2043–8230

Series Editors
Karl Fugelso
Chris Jones

Medievalism aims to provide a forum for monographs and collections devoted to the burgeoning and highly dynamic multi-disciplinary field of medievalism studies: that is, work investigating the influence and appearance of 'the medieval' in the society and culture of later ages. Titles within the series will investigate the post-medieval construction and manifestations of the Middle Ages – attitudes towards, and uses and meanings of, 'the medieval' – in all fields of culture, from politics and international relations, literature, history, architecture, and ceremonial ritual to film and the visual arts. It welcomes a wide range of topics, from historiographical subjects to revivalism, with the emphasis always firmly on what the idea of 'the medieval' has variously meant and continues to mean; it is founded on the belief that scholars interested in the Middle Ages can and should communicate their research both beyond and within the academic community of medievalists, and on the continuing relevance and presence of 'the medieval' in the contemporary world.

New proposals are welcomed. They may be sent directly to the editors or the publishers at the addresses given below.

Professor Karl Fugelso
Art Department
Towson University
3103 Center for the Arts
8000 York Road
Towson, MD 21252–0001
USA

Dr Chris Jones
School of English
University of St Andrews
St Andrews
Fife KY16 9AL
UK

Boydell & Brewer Ltd
PO Box 9
Woodbridge
Suffolk IP12 3DF
UK

Previous volumes in this series are printed at the back of this book

William Morris and the Icelandic Sagas

Ian Felce

D. S. BREWER

© Ian Felce 2018

All Rights Reserved. Except as permitted under current legislation
no part of this work may be photocopied, stored in a retrieval system,
published, performed in public, adapted, broadcast,
transmitted, recorded or reproduced in any form or by any means,
without the prior permission of the copyright owner

The right of Ian Felce to be identified as
the author of this work has been asserted in accordance with
sections 77 and 78 of the Copyright, Designs and Patents Act 1988

First published 2018
D. S. Brewer, Cambridge

ISBN 978 1 84384 501 0

D. S. Brewer is an imprint of Boydell & Brewer Ltd
PO Box 9, Woodbridge, Suffolk IP12 3DF, UK
and of Boydell & Brewer Inc.
668 Mt Hope Avenue, Rochester, NY 14620–2731, USA
website: www.boydellandbrewer.com

A CIP catalogue record for this book is available
from the British Library

The publisher has no responsibility for the continued existence or
accuracy of URLs for external or third-party internet websites referred
to in this book, and does not guarantee that any content on such
websites is, or will remain, accurate or appropriate

This publication is printed on acid-free paper

Printed and bound in Great Britain by
TJ International Ltd, Padstow, Cornwall

MIX
Paper from
responsible sources
FSC
www.fsc.org   FSC® C013056

For my parents and grandparents

Contents

Acknowledgements

Many people have given me invaluable help in writing this book, particularly Marcus Waithe, Florence Saunders Boos, Emily Lethbridge, Judy Quinn, Matthew Townend and Richard Dance. I am also grateful to Helen Cooper, John Kerrigan, Clive Wilmer and Dunstan Roberts. Caroline Palmer and Rob Kinsey have provided excellent advice during the final stages of preparation.

I am especially indebted to Andrew Wawn for his expert guidance. A number of the points that I make in Chapter 4 began as his suggestions.

For their support and encouragement, I would like to thank my parents, my sister Clare and her family, Paula Buttery, Duncan Pritchard, Jane Hill, Craig Kilvert, Sarah Weaver, Željko Jovanović, Susan Currie, Sally Gibbs, Philip Prager, David Webb, Stefan Szwed, Caroline Seymour, Elizabeth Mackay, Philip Sidney and Simon Morley.

Finally my thanks to the Dorothea Coke Fund for their financial assistance towards publication.

Author's Note

In order to show how the Old Norse literature of medieval Iceland inspired William Morris, it is necessary to explain a little about the terminology and method that I have used. 'Old Norse' is an umbrella term that refers to the language spoken in Viking Age and later medieval Scandinavia. The vast majority of the extant texts in Old Norse were originally written between the twelfth and fourteenth centuries in Iceland, which was settled by Old Norse speakers who emigrated across the North Atlantic from the west of Norway in the second half of the ninth century. In recent years, scholars have begun to describe the medieval literature written in Iceland as 'Old Norse-Icelandic' so as to distinguish it from Old Norse literature written elsewhere that might be, for example, 'Old Norse-Norwegian'. At the risk of being imprecise, throughout this book I have used 'Old Norse' to refer to both the language of the relevant editions that I cite (nearly all of which derive from manuscripts written in Iceland) and to the literature that they constitute. In addition, I have used the term 'Norse' occasionally to describe the literary culture of the medieval Icelanders; for example, when referring to Morris's 'Norse-inspired' poems, such as *Sigurd the Volsung*, which were partially based on texts written in Old Norse in Iceland and partially inventions. Though 'Norse' is also an inexact term, it avoids others that are potentially vaguer such as 'Nordic', 'Northern' and 'Old Northern'.[1]

'Old Norse literature' comprises chiefly medieval Icelandic prose and poetry, although some of the stories (such as those relating to the Sigurðr cycle) were known elsewhere in Scandinavia, probably even before

---

[1] For discussions of the terms 'Old Norse', 'Old Icelandic', 'Old Norse-Icelandic', etc., see Margaret Clunies Ross, *The Cambridge Introduction to the Old Norse-Icelandic Saga* (Cambridge: Cambridge University Press, 2010), pp. 13–14; Heather O'Donoghue, *Old Norse-Icelandic Literature: An Introduction* (Cambridge: Blackwell, 2004), pp. 7–8.

Iceland was settled.[2] The prose stories known in English as the 'Icelandic sagas' or 'Old Norse sagas' (which are frequently interspersed with poetry) have conventionally been divided by scholars into several subgenres. In the broadest terms, these are: the *Íslendingasögur* ('sagas of Icelanders', sometimes also called 'family sagas' in English), such as *Laxdæla saga* and *Njáls saga*, which often centre on feud and were mostly composed during the thirteenth century, despite portraying characters typically living in Iceland during the ninth, tenth and eleventh centuries (a period also known as the 'Saga Age'); the *konungasögur* ('kings' sagas'), which recount the lives of legendary, semi-legendary and real-life Scandinavian kings, and were mostly composed in the twelfth and thirteenth centuries; the *fornaldarsögur* ('sagas of ancient times' or 'legendary sagas'), such as *Völsunga saga* and *Ragnars saga loðbrókar*, which recount legendary or mythological stories set more loosely in Scandinavia before the Icelandic settlement and were composed in the thirteenth and fourteenth centuries; the *samtíðarsögur* ('contemporary sagas'), which portray characters who live mostly in Iceland during the twelfth and thirteenth centuries, and were composed shortly after the events they portray; the *riddarasögur* ('knights' sagas' or 'chivalric sagas'), which are courtly stories composed from the thirteenth century onwards; the *heilagra manna sögur* ('saints' sagas'), which are saints' lives from Scandinavia, composed in the twelfth, thirteenth and fourteenth centuries; and the *biskupasögur* ('bishops' sagas'), which are mostly thirteenth- and fourteenth-century accounts of the bishops of Iceland. In addition, the *skáldasögur* ('poets' sagas') are a subdivision of the sagas of Icelanders whose heroes are Icelandic poets during the Saga Age, and the *þættir* ('short tales', singular *þáttr*) recount briefer narratives that usually centre on Icelanders, or other historical or legendary characters from elsewhere in Scandinavia.[3]

By contrast, Old Norse poetry has conventionally been divided by scholars into two types: the first type, known in English as 'eddaic' or 'eddic' poetry, includes poems written in a range of comparatively simple verse forms, the most important of which are the mythological and heroic poems contained in the *Poetic Edda* (also called the *Elder Edda*), which is the modern English name for a collection of poems in a thirteenth-century Icelandic codex referred to as the *Codex Regius*, *Konungsbók* (the 'King's Book') or GKS 2365 4to, now at the Árni Magnússon Institute

---

[2] See Clunies Ross, pp. 14, 22.
[3] See Clunies Ross, pp. 27–36; O'Donoghue, *Old Norse-Icelandic Literature*, pp. 22–24.

for Icelandic Studies, Reykjavík; the second type, known in English as 'skaldic' poetry, consists of verses often attributed to named skalds that are written in a highly complex form known in Old Norse as *dróttkvætt* ('lordly metre' or 'court metre') and have mostly survived as quotations interspersed amongst the prose of the sagas (especially the kings' sagas), as well as in the thirteenth-century Icelandic mythological and poetic treatise known in Modern Icelandic as *Snorra Edda* ('Snorri's *Edda*', also called the *Prose Edda* and the *Younger Edda* in English).[4]

In considering Morris's engagement with Old Norse literature, I have included only those of his works that are based directly on editions of the Old Norse texts or otherwise inspired by his work with Eiríkur Magnússon. This includes all the translations from Old Norse that they made together, as well as Morris's long poems that arose from their translation work. It also includes Morris's short poems that were inspired by his reading of the sagas with Eiríkur or his trips to Iceland, his Icelandic journals, and the lectures of the 1880s in which he talks about his earlier response to Icelandic culture. It does not include poems, such as 'The Fostering of Aslaug', which are likely to have been based on epitomes of the sagas in translation and may have been conceived before Morris met Eiríkur.[5] Nor does it include Morris's 'Germanic' romances of the late 1880s, which, as I show in Chapter 6, present a vision of early Germanic culture that was not directly inspired by Old Norse texts.

Throughout the book, I have used Modern Icelandic spellings of male names ending in *-ur* to refer to scholars, except when referencing

---

[4] See O'Donoghue, *Old Norse-Icelandic Literature*, pp. 62–93.

[5] May Morris believed that 'The Fostering of Aslaug' (published in Part IV of *The Earthly Paradise*) was primarily based on the epitome of *Ragnars saga Loðbrókar* in Benjamin Thorpe's *Northern Mythology* rather than on the saga itself, which Morris owned in C. C. Rafn's 1829 edition. See Introduction *CW*, v, pp. xxi–xxii; William Morris and May Morris, 'Partial Catalogue of William Morris's Library', 1876, MS 860, Library of the Society of Antiquaries, London, p. 19; 'Catalogue of A Portion of the Valuable Collection of Manuscripts, Early Printed Books, etc. of the Late William Morris' (Sotheby, Wilkinson & Hogg, 1898), BIBL/SOT(O), William Morris Society Library, London, p. 84. The 1876 catalogue is a facsimile of a manuscript now held at the Yale Center for British Art, New Haven, CT. For the fullest catalogue of Morris's library over his lifetime, see https://williammorrislibrary.wordpress.com. For further evidence of the potentially early date of 'Aslaug', see J. N. Swannell, *William Morris & Old Norse Literature: A Lecture Given by J. N. Swannell on 18th December 1958 in Prince Henry's Room Fleet Street London* (London: William Morris Society, 1961), pp. 6–8; *TEP*, ii, pp. 451–52.

publications in the apparatus that give a different spelling, i.e. 'Eiríkr Magnússon' or 'Gudbrand Vigfusson'. I have not normalised the spelling of any of the Old Norse passages that I quote, although I use normalised spellings of Old Norse names whenever I refer to literary characters more generally in the body of my argument. I also use 'ö' rather than 'ǫ' in relevant words in my argument, i.e. *Völsunga saga* rather than *Vǫlsunga saga*. I have referred to each saga that Morris translated by its full name initially and by a shorter name thereafter, except where clarity calls for the full name to be repeated. Hence, *Grettis saga Ásmundarsonar* becomes *Grettis saga*, *Gunnlaugs saga ormstungu* becomes *Gunnlaugs saga*, and so on.

Whenever I have quoted from one of Morris's and Eiríkur's translations, I have provided the relevant section of the Old Norse edition on which it was based. In ascertaining which editions the collaborators are most likely to have used, I have referred to the partial catalogue of Morris's library from around 1876; the 1898 catalogue of the sale of his books conducted after his death; Karl O. E. Anderson's 1940 doctoral thesis; Andrew Wawn's chapter 'William Morris and the Old Grey North'; and William Whitla's list of Morris's Old Norse translations and related materials.[6] When Morris is known to have had access to two or more different editions, and it is not certain which one he used (in the case of the *Poetic Edda*, for instance), I have followed Anderson's opinion.[7] I have also attempted to quote from literary editions that we know Morris used, even when they are not of texts in Old Norse such as Robert Southey's edition of *Le Morte d'Arthur*.

I have included my own translations of the Old Norse passages in question, in addition to those of Morris and Eiríkur. In arriving at these translations, I have consulted the following works: Gwyn Jones's translation of 'Þorsteins þáttr Stangarhöggs' in *Eirik the Red and Other Icelandic Sagas* (1980; repr. 1999); Jesse Byock's translations of *Grettis saga* (2009) and *Völsunga saga* (1999); Anthony Faulkes's translation of the *Prose Edda* (1987; repr. 2002); Carolyne Larrington's translation of the *Poetic Edda* (1996; repr. 1999); Rory McTurk's translation of *Kormáks saga* in *Sagas of Warrior-Poets* (2002) (supplemented by O'Donoghue's partial

---

[6] Andrew Wawn, *The Vikings and the Victorians: Inventing the Old North in Nineteenth-Century Britain* (Cambridge: D. S. Brewer, 2000), pp. 245–82; William Whitla, '"Sympathetic Translation" and the "Scribe's Capacity": Morris's Calligraphy and the Icelandic Sagas', *The Journal of Pre-Raphaelite Studies*, 10 (2001), 27–108 (p. 60).

[7] See Note 3 in Karl O. E. Anderson, 'Scandinavian Elements in the Works of William Morris' (unpublished Ph.D., Harvard University, 1940), pp. 111–12.

translation of the saga in *The Genesis of a Saga Narrative: Verse and Prose in Kormaks Saga* [1991]); Robert Cook's translation of *Njáls saga* (2001); Lee M. Hollander's translation of *Heimskringla* (1964; repr. 1977); Hermann Pálsson's and Paul Edwards's translation of *Egils saga* (1976); Katrina Atwood's translation of *Gunnlaugs saga ormstungu* (also in *Sagas of Warrior-Poets*); Martin S. Regal's translation of *Gísla saga Súrssonar* and Judy Quinn's translation of *Eyrbyggja saga* (both in *Gisli Sursson's Saga and The Saga of the People of Eyri* [2003]); and the translations of *Laxdæla saga* by Magnus Magnusson and Hermann Pálsson (1969), and by Keneva Kunz (in *The Sagas of Icelanders: A Selection* [2001]). I have referred regularly to Richard Cleasby's and Guðbrandur Vigfússon's *Icelandic-English Dictionary* (1874), as well as to Geir T. Zoëga's *A Concise Dictionary of Old Norse* (1910; repr. 2004). In translating skaldic verse, I have also been guided by the prose word order given in the three Íslenzk fornrit volumes that contain *Grettis saga*, *Gunnlaugs saga ormstungu* and *Kormáks saga* (published in 1936, 1938 and 1939 respectively, and edited by Guðni Jónsson, Sigurður Nordal and Guðni Jónsson, and Einar Ól. Sveinnson).

I realise that my translations are yet another subjective description of what the Old Norse 'means', and are themselves affected by my identity as a British English speaker in the early twenty-first century. I have included them, nevertheless, in an attempt to achieve two things: first, by following the syntax of the Old Norse reasonably closely I hope to give a reader who is neither fluent in Modern Icelandic nor proficient at reading the medieval language some help in picking out what Morris would have recognised as 'similar to English' in the editions in front of him; second, by presenting a translation that is more idiomatic than that of Morris and Eiríkur, I hope to show how radical many of their linguistic choices were.

Abbreviations

CW   *The Collected Works of William Morris*, ed. May Morris, 24 vols (London: Longmans, Green, 1910–15)

EDD   *Sæmundar Edda hins fróða. Den ældre Edda*, ed. Svend Grundtvig (Copenhagen: Gyldendal, 1868)

GRÁ   *Hin forna lögbók islendínga sem nefnist Grágás: Codex juris Islandorum antiqvissimus, qvi nominatur Grágás*, ed. Johan Frederik Vilhelm Schlegel and Jean-Marie Pardessus, trans. Þórður Sveinbjørnsson, 2 vols (Copenhagen: Thiele, 1829)

GRE   *Grettis saga*, ed. G. Magnússon and G. Thordarson, Nordiske oldskrifter udgivne af det Nordiske Literatur-Sámfund, 16 (Copenhagen: Berling, 1853)

GUN   *Saga þeirra Hrafns ok Gunnlaugs Ormstúngu*, in *Íslendinga sögur, udgivne efter gamle haandskrifter af det Kongelige Nordiske Oldskrift-Selskab*, ed. Carl Christian Rafn, Jón Sigurðsson and Finnur Magnússon, 2 vols (Copenhagen: Möller, 1847), II, 189–276

HEI   Snorre Sturlassøn, *Heimskringla eller norges kongesagaer*, ed. C. R. Unger (Oslo, Brøgger & Christie, 1868)

KOR   *Kormaks saga: sive, Kormaki Oegmundi filii vita*, ed. Finnur Magnússon and Þorgeir Guðmundsson (Copenhagen: Thiele, 1832)

LAX   *Laxdæla-saga: sive, Historia de rebus gestis Laxdölensium*, ed. Gunnlaugur Oddsson and Hans Evertsson Wium, trans. Þorleifur Guðmundsson Repp (Copenhagen: Popp, 1826)

LOT   Fiona MacCarthy, *William Morris: A Life for Our Time* (London: Faber and Faber, 1994)

LWM   J. W. Mackail, *The Life of William Morris*, 2 vols (London: Longmans, Green, 1899)

SEM   Stefán Einarsson, *Saga Eiríks Magnússonar* (Reykjavík: Ísafoldarprentsmiðja, 1933)

SOH   Snorri Sturluson, 'Story of Olaf the Holy', trans. Eiríkr
       Magnússon and William Morris (Leeds University Library, 1891),
       MS C19 Morris, Brotherton Collection
SoK   *The Story of Kormak the Son of Ogmund*, trans. William Morris
       and Eiríkr Magnússon (London: William Morris Society, 1970)
TEP   William Morris, *The Earthly Paradise*, ed. Florence Saunders
       Boos, 2 vols (London: Routledge, 2002)
TSL   The Saga Library, ed. William Morris and Eiríkr Magnússon, 6
       vols (London: Quaritch, 1891–1905)
VÖL   *Völsúnga saga*, in *Fornaldar sögur Nordrlanda*, ed. Carl Christian
       Rafn, 3 vols (Copenhagen: Popp, 1829), I, 113–234
ÞOR   'Þáttr af Þorsteini stangarhögg', in *Vápnfirðinga saga; Þáttr af
       Þorsteini hvíta; Þáttr af Þorsteini stangarhögg; Brandkrossa þáttr*,
       ed. G. Thordarson, Nordiske oldskrifter udgivne af det Nordiske
       Literatur-Sámfund, 5 (Copenhagen: Berling, 1848), pp. 48–63

Introduction

THIS BOOK IS about what the sagas and poetry of medieval Iceland meant to the poet, novelist, designer and political campaigner William Morris (1834–96). Today, Morris is best known for his abundant textile and wallpaper patterns, revolutionary socialism, and pioneering influence on the Arts and Crafts Movement. Alongside this, he is celebrated as one of the forefathers of modern environmentalism and twentieth-century fantasy fiction. What, then, could Old Norse literature possibly have to do with him? Well, in fact, rather a lot. Renowned foremost in his lifetime as a poet and novelist, for the eight years between 1868 and 1876 when he was aged thirty-four to forty-two, Morris became utterly consumed with Iceland and its medieval poetry and prose. In these years he based two of his most famous poems on Old Norse literature: 'The Lovers of Gudrun' on *Laxdæla saga*, and *The Story of Sigurd the Volsung and the Fall of the Niblungs* on *Völsunga saga*, the *Prose Edda* and the *Poetic Edda*. With his collaborator, the Icelander Eiríkur Magnússon (1833–1913), he translated and published several Old Norse sagas, most of which had never appeared before in English. Iceland and its literature also inspired some of Morris's most moving short lyrics, including sonnets written to Grettir Ásmundarson, the iconic hero of *Grettis saga Ásmundarsonar*. Further, in the summers of 1871 and 1873 he travelled to Iceland to undertake demanding journeys on horseback across its interior, during which he kept the only extensive journals that he ever wrote. Subsequently, in the final years of his life in the early 1890s, Morris again turned his attention seriously to the sagas, publishing translations of five more of the sagas of Icelanders, as well as the monumental collection of kings' sagas known as *Heimskringla* ('The Circle of the World').

Old Norse literature and Iceland became so important to Morris between 1868 and 1876 that one of his most popular biographers, Fiona MacCarthy, has called them a 'central obsession' in his life (*LOT*, p. 709). This book considers the nature of that obsession. By looking closely at the translations from Old Norse that he made with Eiríkur, the journals that he wrote during the Icelandic treks in which he matched his knowledge of the sagas with the surrounding landscape, and his Norse-inspired long poems and lyric poetry, we come to see that in his middle years he developed a more nuanced ideal of heroism through his involvement with medieval Iceland. Strongly attracted in the 1850s and early 1860s to Arthurian narratives that portrayed the possibility of transcending the earthly, such as the quest for the Holy Grail, as he began to read Old Norse literature in earnest Morris perceived, and then increasingly celebrated, an ideal of tenacious commitment to the here and now that held worldly transcendence as an irrelevance. This reconceived ideal of what it meant to live heroically would go on to influence his subsequent attitude towards art, craft and design, society and government, cultural history and its preservation, as well as his later inclination to create popular myths in the form of prose fantasy. Far from being an incidental pastime, Morris's engagement with Old Norse literature was a crucial element in the development of his thought and the later passions on which much of his legacy rests.

William Morris and Eiríkur Magnússon Before 1868

Though the backgrounds of Morris and Eiríkur were very different, aspects of each man's character and youth were remarkably similar. Each of them had been excited by literature from a young age, each was motivated to pursue learning outside of formal education, and each made professional choices that may have been considered unconventional, or even eccentric, after initially planning to join the clergy. Morris was born in March 1834 into a wealthy middle-class family at Elm House, Walthamstow, then outside London in Essex. His father was a financier who made a 'small fortune' as a senior partner at a firm of bill brokers in the City (*LOT*, p. 1; *LWM*, I, pp. 1–3). One year older than Morris, Eiríkur was born in February 1833 in the parish of Berufjörður in the remote east of Iceland. The son of the Rev. Magnús Bergsson, who was descended from a line of ministers, in British terms Eiríkur came from a comparatively poor family, though it was middle-class by Icelandic standards (*SEM*, p. 1).[1]

Aspects of both Morris's and Eiríkur's early lives were idyllic. A 'great

---

[1] Also Stefán Einarsson, 'Eiríkur Magnússon – The Forgotten Pioneer', in *Studia Centenalia in honorem memoriae Benedikt S. Þórarinsson*, ed. Benedikt S. Benedikz (Reykjavík: Ísafoldarprentsmiðja, 1961), p. 35.

devourer of books' for as long as he could remember, Morris was an imaginative and sensitive child.[2] At Woodford Hall in Woodford, Essex, where the family moved when he was six, he enjoyed long days reading novels, fishing, hunting, gardening and riding his pony, all the while surrounded by gardens, orchards and parkland, with Epping Forest beyond (*LOT*, pp. 6–8). From the age of three, Eiríkur lived slightly further up the Icelandic coast from where he was born, in the small rural community of Stöðvarfjörður, about 245 miles (395km) from Reykjavík as the crow flies. Strong-minded and creative, he spent what he described as an *áhyggjulaus* ('carefree') childhood surrounded by spectacular mountain crags, deep narrow fjords and, from his earliest memory, poetry, songs and the psalms he heard at church (*SEM*, pp. 1–3).[3]

Iceland during Eiríkur's childhood was worlds apart from industrialised Great Britain. After a slow recovery from the eruption of the Laki volcanic fissure in 1783, which had led to the deaths of a quarter of the population,[4] in 1840 there were just under sixty thousand Icelanders in a country about half Britain's geographical size.[5] Local farming districts dwarfed scattered pockets of urban settlement,[6] with the population of Reykjavík in the same year fewer than nine hundred people.[7] Isolation was, in the words of Sigurður Gylfi Magnússon, 'the norm rather than the exception' in a landscape in which tracks rather than roads connected lone farmsteads, which became even more cut off from the outside world during the long dark winters.[8] Farming was the main occupation, with seasonal line-fishing in small rowing boats increasingly important in

---

[2] Letter to Andreas Scheu, dated 15 September 1883, in *The Collected Letters of William Morris*, ed. Norman Kelvin, 5 vols (Princeton: Princeton University Press, 1987), IIA, p. 228.

[3] Also Stefán Einarsson, 'Forgotten Pioneer', pp. 35–36.

[4] Jón R. Hjálmarsson, *A Short History of Iceland* (Reykjavík: Almenna bókafélagið, 1988), p. 94.

[5] Sven Tägil, *Ethnicity and Nation Building in the Nordic World* (London: Hurst, 1995), p. 37. By contrast, in 1841, the population of England and Wales was nearly sixteen million; see *The Encyclopædia Britannica*, ed. Hugh Chisholm, 11th edn, 29 vols (Cambridge: Cambridge University Press, 1910–11), IX, p. 418.

[6] Sigurður Gylfi Magnússon, *Wasteland with Words: A Social History of Iceland* (London: Reaktion, 2010), p. 18.

[7] Tägil, p. 37. By contrast, in 1841, well over two million people lived in Greater London, see *Encyclopædia Britannica*, XVI, p. 945.

[8] Sigurður Gylfi Magnússon, p. 21.

coastal communities like Stöðvarfjörður.[9] Hygiene was poor: adults rarely bathed, clothes might be washed in cooking pots filled with heated urine, lice were common and disease was often treated at home without a qualified doctor.[10] Elementary education was provided by the family under the guidance of the local minister and supplemented by the winter *kvöldvaka* ('evening wake'), during which the household gathered to hear sermons, sagas or poetry.[11] Minors had domestic responsibilities from a young age, which might include minding sheep day and night, and far from home.[12] In such an unforgiving environment, it was vital that every Icelandic child quickly learnt to survive the hazards of daily life.[13]

The relative simplicity of Morris's and Eiríkur's childhoods drew to a close in their teens. In the autumn of 1847, when Morris was thirteen, his father died unexpectedly (*LOT*, p. 26). A few months later he was sent to Marlborough College, Wiltshire, which had only recently opened and was poorly run, and his mother and siblings left Woodford Hall for the smaller Water House in Walthamstow (now the William Morris Gallery) (*LOT*, pp. 29, 33–34; *LWM*, I, pp. 15–19). As was expected of a minister, Eiríkur's father provided his son with both discipline and his elementary education until, aged sixteen in 1849, he won a place at the prestigious *Latínuskóli* ('Latin School') in Reykjavík: a significant achievement for a young Icelander (*SEM*, pp. 4–5). After confirmation into the Christian Church at the age of fourteen, most men of his generation expected to continue subsistence farming within their household or to become a servant elsewhere.[14] Graduating from the Latin School, however, offered each pupil the rare chance to train to be a member of the clergy or a public official, and, for a tiny minority, to win a place at university abroad.[15]

At Marlborough, Morris seems to have been regarded as a loner, even an oddball. With such a vivid imagination, he inhabited, in MacCarthy's words, 'that strange seam of the exotic that has always flourished even at the most philistine of English public schools' (*LOT*, p. 43), holding himself aloof from the mainstream, and apparently avoiding the worst

---

[9] Jón R. Hjálmarsson, p. 111; Guðni Thorlacius Jóhannesson, *The History of Iceland* (Oxford: Greenwood, 2013), p. 73.

[10] Sigurður Gylfi Magnússon, pp. 54–58, 60–61.

[11] Guðni Thorlacius Jóhannesson, p. 70; Sigurður Gylfi Magnússon, pp. 85–88.

[12] Sigurður Gylfi Magnússon, p. 115.

[13] Sigurður Gylfi Magnússon, p. 41.

[14] Sigurður Gylfi Magnússon, p. 118.

[15] Sigurður Gylfi Magnússon, pp. 35–37.

of the student riot of November 1851 that came to be known as 'the Rebellion' (*LOT*, pp. 46–48). Eiríkur, coincidentally, arrived at the Latin School just as it was experiencing a period of turmoil that erupted in a major uprising in January 1850, later known as *Pereatið* (an Icelandicised form of the Latin for 'down with him'), during which the headmaster was thrown out. Like Morris, Eiríkur seems to have remained on the periphery of the agitation, as well as, initially, academic life (*SEM*, pp. 5–7). At first Eiríkur preferred to pursue his own reading out of class, but by the end of his studies in 1856 he had buckled down, passing the School Leaving Certificate second in his year with good marks in Latin, Danish, German, Icelandic and Greek. When he was seventeen, he also began to read English, practising speaking with the Anglophone arrivals at the harbour, whose pronunciation he copied (*SEM*, p. 8).

On arrival at Exeter College, Oxford in January 1853, Morris immediately struck up a friendship with another first-year student, Edward Burne-Jones, which would last for the rest of his life (*LOT*, p. 53; *LWM*, I, pp. 34–35). The two spent time with a group of undergraduates from Birmingham that included Charles Faulkner who, with Burne-Jones and Morris, would later be amongst the partners of the furnishings and decorative arts company Morris, Marshall, Faulkner & Co. These young friends shared artistic, literary and political inclinations, initially referring to themselves as 'the Set' and then 'the Brotherhood' (*LOT*, pp. 59–63; *LWM*, I, pp. 35–37). Having always been drawn to the history, architecture and stories of the Middle Ages (Morris read the historical romances of Walter Scott as a small boy, visited Canterbury Cathedral with his father, and Avebury and Silbury Hill while at Marlborough [*LOT*, pp. 5–6, 18, 37–38]), Morris now discovered the medievalist mysticism of Thomas Carlyle's *Past and Present* (1843), the social and aesthetic discourse outlined in John Ruskin's *The Stones of Venice* (1851–53) (particularly in the chapter 'The Nature of Gothic') and the glories of Thomas Malory's *Le Morte d'Arthur* (*LOT*, pp. 69–71, 96–97; *LWM*, I, pp. 38–39, 81). At Oxford, he also began to write poetry (*LOT*, pp. 74–77; *LWM*, I, pp. 51–53).

Though Eiríkur was not from the poorest of backgrounds, the options available to him after graduating from the Latin School were limited. The most sensible choices were to attend the new *Prestaskóli* ('Theological College') in Reykjavík so as to follow in his father's footsteps (an option on which he was not wildly keen) or to study law at the University of Copenhagen to become a *sýslumaður* ('sheriff') back in Iceland (*SEM*,

p. 14).[16] The possibility of continuing to study languages or literature may have then seemed financially irresponsible, even impossible, for someone of Eiríkur's modest means. His decision at this time was likely affected by loyalty to his father, and his engagement in 1856 and marriage in 1857 to Sigríður Sæmundsen, a hat-maker's daughter from Reykjavík (*SEM*, pp. 13–14).[17] After teaching over the winter of 1856 and spring of 1857 in Ísafjörður in the north-west of Iceland, Eiríkur decided to attend the Theological College to become his father's *aðstoðarprestur* ('curate'), obtaining his degree in 1859, a year after Sigríður gave birth to the first of their two stillborn children (*SEM*, pp. 14–15).

Morris passed his 'Final Schools' at the University of Oxford at the end of 1855 when he was twenty-one. On coming of age, his share of an 1845 investment that his father had made in the copper (and later arsenic) mine Devon Great Consols made him very wealthy, affording him significant professional freedom (*LOT*, p. 65). At the beginning of 1856, having decided against a plan to join the clergy, he started an apprenticeship with the Oxford-based architect George Street (*LWM*, I, pp. 81–87), while using his considerable income to create *The Oxford & Cambridge Magazine* (a periodical that ran monthly for twelve issues and reflected the interests of 'the Brotherhood' [*LOT*, pp. 98–102]). Burne-Jones, for his part, apprenticed himself to the painter Dante Gabriel Rossetti who, though only a few years older than the new graduates, was already a renowned 'Pre-Raphaelite'. By the end of the year, Morris had already abandoned architecture to be a painter under Rossetti's guidance, joining the team that painted the Arthurian murals at the Oxford Union in the summer of 1857 (*LWM*, I, pp. 105–09). It was while painting these murals that he fell for the beautiful Jane (Janey) Burden, a local stablehand's daughter whom Rossetti and Burne-Jones had spotted in the audience at the theatre (*LOT*, p. 135). Morris and Burden were engaged in the spring of 1858, despite the difference in social class, and married a year later in a quiet ceremony in Oxford (*LOT*, pp. 139–40, 151–52).

In March 1858, Morris had his first collection of poetry published under the title *The Defence of Guenevere and Other Poems*. Based on Arthurian themes and medieval scenes by Jean Froissart, they were successful with neither the critics nor the public (*LWM*, I, pp. 129–35). Still intent on the life of an artist, he now planned a medievalist dream home: Red House in Upton (today part of Bexleyheath), Kent, whose exterior was completed

---

[16] Also Stefán Einarsson, 'Forgotten Pioneer', p. 36.
[17] Also Stefán Einarsson, 'Forgotten Pioneer', pp. 36–37.

in June 1860 (*LOT*, pp. 154–57; *LWM*, I, pp. 139–42). Decorated inside with murals, furniture and textiles that often depicted chivalric tableaux, the house soon became a seat of both tranquillity and endeavour: what MacCarthy calls a 'retreat' and where 'the knights ride out from' (*LOT*, p. 156). It was here that Morris's and Jane's two daughters were born: Jane (Jenny) Morris in January 1861 and Mary (May) Morris in March 1862 (*LOT*, pp. 185–87). It was also while living at Red House that, in April 1861, Morris founded Morris, Marshall, Faulkner & Co. with Rossetti, Burne-Jones, Faulkner, Ford Madox Brown, Philip Webb and Peter Paul Marshall (*LOT*, p. 166; *LWM*, I, pp. 148–52).

Meanwhile, in Reykjavík, Eiríkur had been working in local government administration since graduating from the Theological College in 1859 when a vacancy for a curate's post had arisen in the parish of Berufjörður, where he was born (*SEM*, pp. 20–21). It was just as he was about to take up this position that, in the spring of 1861, when Morris was founding 'the Firm', an event occurred that would change the course of his life: the English Quaker missionary Isaac Sharp arranged to have a revised Icelandic translation of the New Testament published in England on behalf of the British and Foreign Bible Society, and Eiríkur was offered the job of supervising the printing (*SEM*, p. 21).[18] He accepted and sailed for England with Sigríður at the end of June 1862 (*SEM*, p. 23). Having relinquished the modest but secure lifestyle of a rural Icelandic clergyman and his wife, the couple were now destined to spend a decade scraping by on Eiríkur's proof-reading, translation and teaching work abroad.

In the first few months of living in London, Eiríkur combined working on the proofs for the revision of the New Testament (published by Oxford University Press in 1863) with typical tourist trips: he was transfixed by the Crystal Palace and struck by the eeriness of the Tower of London (*SEM*, pp. 24–25). On the boat over, he had made friends with the Icelandophile George Ernest John Powell, with whom he spent his first Christmas away from home at Powell's grand eighteenth-century mansion, Nanteos at Rhydyfelin, near Aberystwyth. Eiríkur now began a period of collaboration with the Welshman that would lead to the two-volume selective translation of Jón Árnason's *Íslenzkar þjóðsögur og æfintýri* (1862–66) under the name *Icelandic Legends* (1864–66).[19]

---

[18] Also Stefán Einarsson, 'Forgotten Pioneer', p. 37.
[19] R. G. Thomas, 'George E. J. Powell, Eiríkr Magnússon and Jón Sigurðsson: A Chapter in Icelandic Literary History', *Saga-Book of the Viking Society for Northern Research*, 14 (1953), 123–24.

The following years – 1863, 1864 and 1865 – also brought a return visit to Iceland as Sharp's translator (*SEM*, p. 27), as well as trips to France, Germany and Denmark undertaken as part of certain never-to-materialise projects with Powell, which included a dictionary made redundant by the Clarendon Press's 1866 decision to finance what would become the ground-breaking 1874 *Icelandic–English Dictionary*, compiled by Richard Cleasby and Guðbrandur Vigfússon (*SEM*, pp. 32–39, 46–50, 54–58).[20]

By 1864, living at Red House had become a problem for Morris. The increasing success of 'the Firm', which was by now producing his wallpapers and was particularly in demand for its stained glass, meant that his time was occupied more and more in London, with the commute taking as long as four hours per day (*LOT*, pp. 182–83, 193). Exhaustion was exacerbated by a bout of rheumatic fever caught on the long, wet journey, and the decision was, therefore, taken to move in the autumn of 1865 to a flat above the workshops of 'the Firm' at 26 Queen Square, Bloomsbury (*LWM*, I, pp. 163–65). Morris, Marshall, Faulkner & Co. was going from strength to strength, receiving commissions in 1866 to decorate rooms in St James's Palace and the South Kensington Museum (today the Victoria and Albert Museum) (*LOT*, pp. 211–13). Morris was also developing as a writer. By 1867 drafts of a major poetical project, on which he had been working since the early 1860s, had filled six notebooks (Preface to *TEP*, I, pp. 9–10).

Eiríkur moved back to London in April 1866 where he was temporarily involved in a business venture importing Icelandic sheep to Newcastle (*SEM*, p. 68). His collaboration with Powell was now noticeably less productive. Having worked together on a translation of *Hávarðar saga Ísfirðings* from as early as 1863, Eiríkur had also begun to translate *Egils saga* but Powell seems to have been incapable of applying himself to sustained work and neither text was ever finalised.[21] Early in 1867, Eiríkur worked alone on his edition and translation of the fourteenth-century Icelandic religious poem 'Lilja' ('The Lily') by Eysteinn Ásgrímsson, which was published later in 1870. He spent the summer in Iceland, before returning to England where he unsuccessfully sought work from Oxford University Press, having supervised the printing of the entire

---

[20] Also Stefán Einarsson, 'Eiríkr Magnússon and his Saga-Translations', *Scandinavian Studies*, 13 (1933), pp. 20–21; Thomas, 'Chapter in Icelandic Literary History', pp. 124–25.

[21] Stefán Einarsson, 'Saga-Translations', pp. 21–22; Wawn, *Vikings*, pp. 361–62.

revised Icelandic Bible the year before. With few new projects on the horizon, by the end of 1867 Eiríkur was suffering growing professional frustration and financial insecurity.

The first part of Morris's major poetical project to be published appeared to considerable acclaim in June 1867 as *The Life and Death of Jason*, a retelling of the voyages of the Argonauts (*LWM*, I, pp. 183–85). The following year in April 1868 Parts I and II of Morris's 48,000-line poem *The Earthly Paradise* were published, initially in a single volume.[22] Set in the fourteenth century, the frame story tells of a group of Norwegian wanderers who set sail from Europe to flee the Black Death in pursuit of paradise, only to discover an Atlantis-like island inhabited by men who still worship the ancient Greek gods. Here, in Morris's homage to Boccaccio and Chaucer, the two cultures exchange tales, which then comprise the rest of the work. Containing stories that centre on characters as diverse as Atalanta and Ogier the Dane, the first volume of *The Earthly Paradise* was an enormous success with the critics and the public, making Morris a nationally, and then internationally, famous poet (Introduction to *TEP*, I, pp. 25–27).[23] Having probably already based some drafts of the tales that the Norsemen would tell on English translations or epitomes of Old Norse texts (see Author's Note, p. xi), it was just as he was preparing their stories for Part III of *The Earthly Paradise* that he was put in contact with Eiríkur by his friend and employee George Warington Taylor. So it was that, in July 1868, with Eiríkur down on his luck and living at 9 South Crescent, Bedford Square, just a few minutes' walk from the Morrises' Queen Square home, Morris asked Eiríkur if he would teach him to read the sagas in the language in which they were written, and Eiríkur readily agreed.[24]

---

[22] For the complicated publication history of *The Earthly Paradise*, see Introduction to *TEP*, I, pp. 33–40.

[23] Also Florence Saunders Boos, 'Victorian Response to *Earthly Paradise* Tales', *The Journal of the William Morris Society*, 5.4 (1983–84), 16–29 (pp. 17–21).

[24] For the precise timing of Morris and Eiríkur's first meeting, see Stefán Einarsson, 'Saga-Translations', p. 23; Introduction to *CW*, VII, p. xv; Preface to TSL, 6, p. xii; Anderson, p. 43. Morris mentions in a letter to Cormell Price, dated 12 October 1868, that Eiríkur had little money in the early stages of their acquaintance, Kelvin, I, pp. 66.

The 1868–76 'Old Norse Period'

Although Morris's passion for the literature of medieval Iceland was only truly ignited in the autumn of 1868 when Eiríkur began to teach him to read it in Old Norse, he had, in fact, shown a clear interest in English translations of Old Norse literature as early as his university days. At Oxford, Morris had read Benjamin Thorpe's *Northern Mythology* (1851–52), which contains English renderings of parts of the *Prose Edda* and various sagas such as *Völsunga saga*. In an undated account of Eiríkur's relationship with her father that Morris's daughter May used in her introduction to the seventh volume of his *Collected Works* (which was published in 1911), Eiríkur explains that on first meeting him in 1868 Morris already knew of the sagas of Icelanders, through George Webbe Dasent's pioneering *The Story of Burnt Njal* (1861) and *The Story of Gisli the Outlaw* (1866), as well as through Walter Scott's 'Abstract' of *Eyrbyggja saga*, which appeared alongside synopses of *Kormáks saga*, *Njáls saga* and *Laxdæla saga* in the 1847 edition of Thomas Percy's *Northern Antiquities* (1770). In addition, Morris was familiar with the *Poetic Edda* through Thorpe's *Edda Sæmundar hinns fróða* (1866) and A. S. Cottle's *Icelandic Poetry, or The Edda of Sæmund* (1797), and was acquainted with the history and geography of Iceland through Finnur Jónsson's *Historia Ecclesiastica Islandiæ* (1772–78) (Introduction to *CW*, VII, p. xvi). It is also probable that he knew Dasent's translation of the *Prose Edda* (1842), which is listed in the catalogue of his books auctioned after his death.[25] Likewise, Karl O. E. Anderson emphasises Morris's pre-1868 acquaintance with Samuel Laing's translation of *Heimskringla* (1844) and suggests that Thorpe's *Yule-Tide Stories* (1853), Annie Keary's *The Heroes of Asgard and the Giants of Jötunheim* (1857), as well as Powell and Eiríkur's *Icelandic Legends* (1864–66), and the novels of Walter Scott and Friedrich de la Mott Fouqué, generally shaped his early attraction to the north.[26]

This early attraction is clear in the sustained references to Scandinavian-related subject matter that appear in Morris's writing before 1868. His short story 'Lindenborg Pool', for example, written in 1856 for *The Oxford & Cambridge Magazine*, is based on a Danish tale in Thorpe's *Northern Mythology*, which also provides the Northern European names of several characters (Sigurd, Gunnar, Svanhild, Olaf, Eric, Svend, Valdemar, Siur and Cisella) that appear in other stories he wrote for the same publication.

---

[25] 'Catalogue (1898)', p. 26.
[26] Anderson, pp. 2–44.

The poems 'Rapunzel' and 'The Wind' from the *Defence of Guenevere* contain references to 'Norse torches' and 'Olaf, king and saint' (*CW*, I, pp. 65, 110).[27] Additionally, the Norwegian wanderers in the frame story of *The Earthly Paradise* emigrate from medieval Norway in search of a better life, much like the first generation of Icelandic settlers portrayed in many of the sagas of Icelanders. Given the consistency of these Scandinavian-inspired references, it appears as though the passion for Old Norse literature that emerged between 1868 and 1876 was, to an extent, latent in Morris throughout his twenties and early thirties, before it was vigorously awoken on meeting 'a real Icelander' and beginning to read the sagas in their original language (Introduction to *CW*, VII, p. xv).

The first phase of Morris's sessions with Eiríkur lasted from around September 1868 to when Eiríkur moved to become Under-Librarian at Cambridge University Library in autumn 1871, a job that Morris was instrumental in him getting.[28] The work they covered in this early phase was particularly concentrated, with Morris experiencing it almost viscerally. He would sometimes 'rise and pace his room, discoursing on the high art these poets possessed' (Preface to TSL, 6, p. xv) and insisted from the beginning on translating at sight rather than being instructed formally in grammar and syntax, telling Eiríkur, 'You be my grammar as we translate. I want the literature, I must have the story' (Preface to TSL, 6, p. xiii). Eiríkur was later unclear on how often the sessions took place before he moved to Cambridge. In 1905, he recalled running through 'the best of the sagas' 'at daily sittings, generally covering three hours' (Preface to TSL, 6, p. xiv), but in Eiríkur's account of her father that May used in Morris's *Collected Works*, Eiríkur remembered resuming 'lessons with him on the old system – three days a week' after the Morrises returned from their stay at Bad Ems in the summer of 1869 (Introduction to *CW*, VII, p. xx).

Whatever the precise frequency, in the initial stage of their working relationship Eiríkur would read through the day's text with his pupil, before presenting him with an English translation at the next lesson, which Morris would then alter with the Old Norse edition in front of him. With this amended translation (which was checked by Eiríkur and subsequently rechecked by Morris) becoming the printer's copy, the collaborators produced a remarkable number of saga translations in

[27] See also Anderson, pp. 9–11.
[28] See letters to Price, dated 12 October 1868, cited in footnote 24, above, and to Eiríkur, dated 1 July 1871, in Kelvin, I, p. 138.

quick succession. Their translation of *Gunnlaugs saga ormstungu*, enti-tled 'The Saga of Gunnlaug the Worm-Tongue and Rafn the Skald', was published in the *Fortnightly Review* in January 1869 and their translation of *Grettis saga* appeared in April 1869 as *The Story of Grettir the Strong*. Morris finished 'The Lovers of Gudrun' (based on his and Eiríkur's translation of the central narrative in *Laxdæla saga*) in the summer of 1869, and *The Story of the Volsungs and the Niblungs* (a combination of *Völsunga saga* and several poems from the *Poetic Edda*) appeared in late April or early May 1870. The last translation published during this initial phase of intense collaboration was *The Story of Frithiof the Bold* (*Friðþjófs saga hins frækna* in Old Norse), which was serialised in the March and April 1871 issues of *The Dark Blue*.

Eiríkur's recollection of his student telling him 'You be my grammar' should not lead to the presumption that Morris had a casual attitude towards translation, as some scholars have supposed.[29] The large number of reference books that he owned on Icelandic language, literature and history indicates that he approached the task assiduously.[30] Nor does Morris's initial attitude towards his lessons mean that he lacked the apti-tude to learn Old Norse. Indeed, by the time that Eiríkur left London for Cambridge, Morris's Old Norse and Modern Icelandic (he often did not distinguish between the two, referring to them both simply as 'Icelandic') had improved to the extent that on the 1871 trek across Iceland he regu-larly conversed with Icelanders in their native language (*CW*, VIII, pp. 26, 63, 68), and by February 1873 he was claiming that only Icelandic was spoken when he visited Eiríkur and his wife at 26 (later 31) Bateman Street, Cambridge.[31] It is clear, in fact, that Morris possessed considerable linguistic ability. In a letter that Eiríkur wrote to Powell soon after he began to teach Morris, he remarked that '[h]e has in the lapse of three months mastered the language [...] in a marvellous degree'.[32] Despite this, it remains difficult to assess precisely Morris's level of competence in Old Norse at any one time, although it certainly improved over the course of the twenty-seven years that he published saga translations.

In light of Morris's developing confidence in Old Norse, it is not

---

[29] See Peter Preston, '"The North Begins Inside": Morris and Trollope in Iceland', *The Journal of the William Morris Society*, 14.2 (2001), 8–28 (p. 25).

[30] See Whitla, pp. 56–57.

[31] See letter to Aglaia Ionides Coronio, dated 11 February 1873, in Kelvin, I, p. 179.

[32] Quoted in Stefán Einarsson, 'Saga-Translations', p. 24.

surprising that the translation method that he and Eiríkur used evolved over time. Letters that Morris is thought to have sent to Eiríkur in 1872, by which time the two men had begun the mammoth project of translating *Heimskringla*, show Morris clearly seeking his collaborator's help primarily in relation to the verses, which suggests that he had already attempted to translate his portion of the prose alone (the two of them having divided up the initial translation of *Heimskringla* between them [see this chapter, p. 14–15, below]).[33] A more equal dynamic in their working relationship certainly seems to have been established by the time that *Three Northern Love Stories* was published in 1875, which contained revisions of *The Story of Gunnlaug* and *The Story of Frithiof the Bold*, as well as *The Story of Viglund the Fair* (*Víglundar saga*), 'The Tale of Hogni and Hedinn' ('Sörla þáttr'), 'The Tale of Roi the Fool' ('Hróa þáttr heimska') and 'The Tale of Thorstein Staff-Smitten' ('Þorsteins þáttr stangarhöggs'). Though it may be that some of the newly published translations in this volume were first made in the early phase of their relationship before Eiríkur moved to Cambridge, Morris later recalled playing a more substantial role in the preparation of the second edition of their translation of *Gunnlaugs saga*: with the 1869 version, his contribution 'was necessarily confined to helping in the search for the fittest English equivalents to the Icelandic words and phrases, to turning the translations of the "vísur" into some sort of English verse, and to general revision in what might be called matters of taste', but with the *Three Northern Love Stories* version, he remarked that the translation 'went through a very careful revision, in which we both shared'.[34] The wine, meat and wallpaper that the letters of 23 May 1872 and 30 October 1872 show Morris to be in the process of sending to Eiríkur also point to the possibility that he was paying him in kind by this stage rather than money, further indicating a more evenly balanced working relationship.[35]

---

[33] See letters to Eiríkur, dated (only probably, in the case of the latter three) 23 May 1872, 4 October 1872, 30 October 1872 and 4 November 1872, in Kelvin, I, pp. 158–59, 164, 168–69. For a summary of the letters exchanged by two men that relate to their translations (including evidence that Morris translated the first draft of *Heiðarvíga saga* on his own), see Richard L. Harris, 'William Morris, Eiríkur Magnússon, and Iceland: A Survey of Correspondence', *Victorian Poetry*, 13 (1975), 119–30 (pp. 121–24).

[34] Letter to the editor of *The Athenaeum*, dated 12 May 1879, in Kelvin, I, pp. 513–14.

[35] See letters to Eiríkur, dated (only probably, in the case of the latter two) 23 May 1872, 30 October 1872 and 4 November, in Kelvin, I, pp. 158–59, 168.

Although it is not thought that the collaborators undertook any new translations from Old Norse after Morris published his last long poem *Sigurd the Volsung* in 1876, in the early 1890s he and Eiríkur returned to the sagas after a fifteen-year hiatus, during which time Morris had become an active public speaker, vigorously campaigning to preserve ancient buildings and reform the place of art in society, as well as pioneering the cause of socialism in Britain. In this later period, the two men revised translations that had either been started or completed in the 1868–76 period for publication in a series they called The Saga Library (1891–1905).[36] Despite the long interruption to their collaboration, when, in the early 1890s, they came to revise the sagas that they included in The Saga Library, their working relationship was as close to a joint partnership as it would ever become. With Eiríkur's primary task being to ensure that the semantic sense of the translation was accurate, and Morris's being to determine the style and versification, Volume 1 of The Saga Library (1891) provided the public with *The Story of Howard the Halt* (*Hávarðar saga Ísfirðings*), *The Story of the Banded Men* (*Bandamanna saga*) and *The Story of Hen Thorir* (*Hænsa-Þóris saga*); Volume 2 (1892) with *The Story of the Ere-Dwellers* (*Eyrbyggja saga*) and *The Story of the Heath-Slayings* (*Heiðarvíga saga*); and Volumes 3 to 5 (1893–95) with *The Stories of the Kings of Norway Called the Round World* (*Heimskringla*). Eiríkur's comments in Volume 6 of The Saga Library (published in 1905 by Eiríkur alone, nine years after Morris's death, and comprising indices for their version of *Heimskringla*) indicate that Morris had prepared the preliminary translation of Volume I of *Heimskringla* (Volume 3 of The Saga Library) and Eiríkur had then checked the draft, but that this process was reversed for Volumes II and III (Volumes 4 and 5 of The Saga Library) (Preface to TSL, 6, p. vii).[37]

---

[36] A note in a manuscript of the sagas contained in Volume 1 of The Saga Library in the Fitzwilliam Museum, Cambridge, indicates the early date of their initial translation. Georgiana Burne-Jones has written: 'The three Stories in this book were translated from the Icelandic by William Morris and Eiríkr Magnússon. They were written out, and all the Illuminated letters were designed and painted by William Morris, about the year 1873. He then gave the book to me, and I now give it to the Fitzwilliam Museum, Cambridge, in memory of him. Georgiana Burne-Jones. Sep: 18: 1909'. See back fly-leaf of 'The Story of Hen Thorir; The Story of the Banded Men; The Story of Haward the Halt', trans. William Morris and Eiríkr Magnússon (Fitzwilliam Museum, Cambridge, [n.d.]), Morris/Icelandic, William Morris Collection.

[37] For details of the order and allocation of work on The Saga Library as a whole, as well as the current locations of the extant manuscripts, see Philip Chase, 'William Morris and Germanic Language and Legend: A Communal Ideal' (unpublished Ph.D., Drew University, 2002), pp. 167–78.

This division of labour is confirmed by the extant manuscripts: the manuscript of *The Story of Harald Greycloak and Earl Hakon* in the Huntington Library, San Marino (which would form part of Volume I of their translation of *Heimskringla*) is in Morris's handwriting with corrections by Eiríkur, while the manuscript of *The Story of Olaf the Holy* in the Brotherton Library, Leeds (which would form the whole of Volume II of their translation of *Heimskringla*), is in Eiríkur's handwriting with corrections by Morris. It is likely that Eiríkur prepared the initial translation of the verses in all volumes. Of all the sagas that Morris and Eiríkur published, only two had already appeared in English versions. These were George Stephens's *Frithiof's saga, A Legend of Norway* (1839) and Laing's *The Heimskringla; or Chronicle of the Kings of Norway* (1844), although Stephens's work was translated from a Swedish poetic paraphrase of the saga and Laing's from a Dano-Norwegian translation of the Old Norse text.[38]

The translations that Morris and Eiríkur published do not represent the totality of their work together. From the evidence of extant fragments or complete manuscripts of unpublished sagas, as well as several calligraphic manuscripts that Morris made from their translations in the early 1870s,[39] it is clear that between 1868 and 1876 they also translated (either entirely or partially) *Egils saga, Kormáks saga, Vapnfirðinga saga, Halldórs þáttr Snorrasonar, Norna-Gests þáttr* and *Odds þáttr Ófreigssonar*.[40] In addition, it is apparent from references in Morris's literary writing, journals and letters that (with varying degrees of familiarity) he knew *Ragnars saga loðbrókar, Vatnsdœla saga, Finnboga saga ramma, Víga-Glums saga, Jómsvíkinga saga, Bjarnar saga Hítdœlakappa, Tristrams*

[38] Esaias Tegnér's *Frithiofs saga* was published in Stockholm in 1825 and Jacob Aall's *Norske Kongers sagaer* in Christiania (now Oslo) in 1838. The union of Denmark–Norway was dissolved in 1814, the same year that Norway's personal union with Sweden began.

[39] For the extant evidence of Morris's Norse-related calligraphic manuscripts, see Chase, pp. 164–65; Alfred Fairbank, 'A Note on the Manuscript Work of William Morris', in *SoK*, pp. 53–72; Whitla, pp. 44–54, 80–95; Alessandro Zironi, 'William Morris and the Poetic Edda', in *The Hyperborean Muse: Studies in the Transmission and Reception of Old Norse Literature*, ed. Judy Quinn and Adele Cipolla, Acta Scandinavica, 6 (Turnhout: Brepols, 2016), pp. 211–37 (pp. 217–19).

[40] Anderson believed that Morris translated partially or entirely at least twenty-one sagas or *þættir*, while Whitla puts the figure at thirty-three sagas or *þættir* with thirteen poems of the *Poetic Edda*. See Anderson, pp. 608–09; Whitla, p. 60.

saga and *Sturlunga saga*.[41] The partial catalogue of his library from around 1876, held in facsimile at the Society of Antiquaries, London, also confirms that, by the time he published *Sigurd*, Morris owned the best available scholarly editions of *Orkneyinga saga, Færeyinga saga, Njáls saga, Fagrskinna, Kristni saga, Fostbræðra saga, Karlamagnús saga, Alexanders saga, Konungs skuggsjá* and *Landnámabók*, as well as editions of both the *Gulaþing* and *Grágás* law codes, and the 1513 *editio princeps* of Saxo Grammaticus's *Gesta Danorum*.[42]

Along with providing the motivation for the two sonnets associated with *The Story of Grettir the Strong*, 'Gudrun' and *Sigurd* (which Eiríkur claimed to have personally persuaded Morris to write) (Preface to TSL, 6, p. xv), Morris's enthusiasm for Old Norse literature and Iceland also inspired the lyric poems 'Prologue in Verse' (that precedes *The Story of the Volsungs and the Niblungs*), 'To the Muse of the North', 'Gunnar's Howe Above the House at Lithend', 'Iceland First Seen' and the three fragments published by May Morris in 1936.[43] The extraordinary feat of Icelandic-related production in the 1868–76 period is made more remarkable by the fact that in the same interval he completed the other poems of Parts III and IV of the *Earthly Paradise*, the masque *Love is Enough* (1873), his translation of the *Aeneid* entitled *The Aeneids of Virgil* (1876), and ten Danish, Swedish and Modern Icelandic ballad translations for which he apparently received no help from anyone.[44] In addition, in 1874, Morris determined to restructure Morris, Marshall, Faulkner & Co., reorganising it under his sole ownership to become Morris & Co. the next year, while simultaneously starting to revive techniques in natural dyeing (*LOT*, pp. 341–44, 348–57). All of this was achieved despite the fact that in the late 1860s and early 1870s his marriage seems to have come under strain when Jane began an affair with Rossetti, which is generally thought to have lasted until 1875 (*LOT*, pp. 221–26, 364–65).

---

[41] See Anderson, pp. 215, 609; Preface to TSL, 6, p. xi; letters to Faulkner, dated 18 November 1872, and to Jón Sigurðsson, dated 18 November 1872 and 18 March 1873, in Kelvin, I, pp. 170, 181.

[42] Morris and Morris, 'Partial Catalogue (1876)', pp. 3–20.

[43] May Morris, *William Morris: Artist, Writer, Socialist*, 2 vols (Oxford: Blackwell, 1936), I, pp. 461–65.

[44] Anderson, pp. 147–75.

How the 1868–76 'Old Norse Period' Has Been Understood

Other than to undertake surveys of the sources of references to Old Norse texts in Morris's writing, perhaps the simplest scholarly response to his saga-inspired works since his death in 1896 has been to discuss their relative success in capturing the 'spirit' of medieval Icelandic literature. In Conrad Hjalmar Nordby's laudatory 1901 pamphlet he praises Morris's ability in *Sigurd* to adapt 'the saga story to our civilization and our art, holding to the best of the old and supplementing it by new that is ever in keeping with the old'.[45] In Nordby's view, if Morris modified the plot or ethos of his source, it was because he was helpfully rendering an alien culture accessible to his audience out of 'a desire to impress present-day readers with the story'.[46] Karl Litzenberg also considers Morris successful in his attempt to render the essence of the sagas in *Sigurd*, arguing that 'No other modern English writer has re-created the temper of Old Norse literature so completely and so adequately'.[47]

Conversely, perhaps the most vociferous detractor of Morris's translations from Old Norse, Dorothy M. Hoare, finds them 'too exact in their effort to follow the words and syntax', so that they consequently 'fail lamentably to give the particular feeling of the original'.[48] J. N. Swannell asserts, rather tentatively, that there is 'something, certainly something, of the starkness of saga narrative' in 'Gudrun',[49] but agrees with Hoare that Morris's tendency to moralise and admit aspects of romance-evoking gallantry into the poem is inappropriate in relation to the character of *Laxdæla saga*.[50] Hoare and Swannell disagree on whether Morris was aware that he was altering the character of his sources. Hoare is certain that he entirely misconceived 'the style and the matter with which he was dealing',[51] while Swannell is confident that, in 'Gudrun' at least, 'Morris

---

[45] Conrad Hjalmar Nordby, *The Influence of Old Norse Literature on English Literature*, Columbia University Germanic Studies, 3 (New York: Columbia University Press, 1901), p. 35.

[46] Nordby, p. 33.

[47] Karl Litzenberg, *The Victorians and the Vikings: A Bibliographical Essay on Anglo-Norse Literary Relations*, Contributions in Modern Philology, 3 (Ann Arbor: University of Michigan Press, 1947), p. 2.

[48] Dorothy M. Hoare, *The Works of Morris and Yeats in Relation to Early Saga Literature* (Cambridge: Cambridge University Press, 1937), p. 62.

[49] J. N. Swannell, 'William Morris as an Interpreter of Old Norse', *Saga Book of the Viking Society for Northern Research*, 15 (1957), 365–82 (p. 370).

[50] Swannell, *Norse Literature*, p. 13.

[51] Hoare, p. 54.

deliberately departs from what he knows to be the authentic Norse atmosphere'. In explanation for this departure, Swannell suggests that in *The Earthly Paradise* Morris had already 'perfected a particular style of story-telling in verse' and did not want, therefore, to divert from it.[52]

Closely linked to discussions of Morris's success in rendering the spirit of the sagas is the issue of the literal style that he gradually developed for his Icelandic translations. Hoare felt that, rather than mimicking the archaic structures of Old Norse in English, Morris should have found an idiom that reproduced for his contemporary audience the effect that the saga would have had on its original audience. For her, 'a good translator ought to reduce this difference to a minimum [and] be so imbued with the tone and atmosphere [...] that the miracle of capturing that in other words is almost achieved'.[53] This is the opposite view to that taken by E. Paul and Dorothy Durrenberger, who implicitly praise the jarring style of Morris's translations when they argue that: 'If one's objective [in translation] is to appreciate and understand cultural differences, then the differences must be preserved, perhaps even accentuated, rather than obliterated.'[54] Litzenberg felt that the style of Morris's translations gave them 'strength and life' despite being widely unpopular.[55] Anticipating Philip Chase's opinion that Morris's literal translations are better suited as cribs for a reader with access to the source edition than as texts in their own right,[56] Randolph Quirk condoned Morris's apparent decision not to 'convey an equivalent effect to that conveyed by the sagas to the medieval Icelanders', suggesting that in his style Morris was seeking a 'transmission of his own experience': by linking the reading of the translation to the reading of the Old Norse, Quirk proposes that Morris hoped his readers would share the 'acute pleasure which the forms and arrangements of the Icelandic' gave him.[57]

---

[52] Swannell, *Norse Literature*, p. 15.

[53] Hoare, p. 51.

[54] Introduction to *The Saga of Gunnlaugur Snake's Tongue with an Essay on the Structure and Translation of the Saga*, trans. E. Paul Durrenberger and Dorothy Durrenberger (Rutherford: Farleigh Dickinson University Press, 1992), p. 77.

[55] Karl Litzenberg, 'The Diction of William Morris: A Discussion of His Translations from the Old Norse with Particular Reference to His "Pseudo-English" Vocabulary', *Arkiv för nordisk filologi*, 53 (1937), 327–63 (p. 362).

[56] Chase, p. 233.

[57] Randolph Quirk, 'Dasent, Morris, and Problems of Translation', *Saga-Book of the Viking Society for Northern Research*, 14 (1955), 64–77 (p. 76).

By contrast, Swannell argues that the idiosyncratic style of the translations should be understood as a method of rendering a medieval
Teutonic language that was in Morris's eyes 'too noble and precious to
endure the contaminating touch of common speech'. Though, in Swannell's view, Morris was ultimately mistaken in this endeavour, since
the sagas 'are woven of the stuff of reality, and to wrap them in remote,
contrived language [...] is to rob them of that vivid actuality which is
their great virtue', he was earnestly attempting to find a register of English
appropriate to the dignity of a cognate Germanic language.[58] James Leigh
Barribeau pursues this idea that the style was an attempt to Teutonise the
idiom of the translations, arguing that, in line with a tradition that goes
back to Sir John Cheke in the sixteenth century, Morris was attempting
to return to an English unaffected by what he deemed the linguistic and
cultural devastation wrought by the Norman Conquest.[59] Chase also
argues that, in his style, Morris was attempting to find 'the closest thing
to a purely Germanic English', proposing that just as he 'wished for a
return to Germanic polity, he may have wished for a return to Germanic
language'.[60] In a similar vein, Marcus Waithe suggests that Morris coined
an exotic pre-Norman Conquest dialect for his translations because he
'wanted to make the invigorating strangeness of heroic society known to
his readership', but that he was simultaneously 'conscious of the risk that
his material would be sanitized in the process'.[61]

Since Morris's first biographer J. W. Mackail delicately linked his
obsession with Old Norse literature to his estrangement from Rossetti,
arguing that 'the beginning of Morris's Icelandic studies can be definitely
fixed [...] to what might be called the final extinction of Rossetti's influence over him as an artist' (*LWM*, I, p. 200), the most common scholarly explanation for the advent of the 1868–76 'Old Norse period' as a
whole has been that Morris immersed himself in Iceland and the sagas
to distract himself from his wife's infidelity. It is not known how sexually intimate her relationship with Rossetti became, though he certainly

[58] Swannell, *Norse Literature*, pp. 19–20.
[59] James Leigh Barribeau, 'The Vikings and England: The Ninth and the
Nineteenth Centuries' (unpublished Ph.D., Cornell, 1982), p. 232; James Leigh
Barribeau 'William Morris and Saga-Translation: "The Story of King Magnus,
Son of Erling"', in *The Vikings*, ed. R.T. Farrell (Ithaca: Cornell University Press,
1983), pp. 239–55 (pp. 251–52).
[60] Chase, p. 146.
[61] Marcus Waithe, *William Morris's Utopia of Strangers: Victorian
Medievalism and the Ideal of Hospitality* (Cambridge: D. S. Brewer, 2006), p. 90.

stayed with Jane without Morris being present (*LOT*, p. 316). Neither are Morris's feelings regarding his wife's potential adultery plain, but his letters clearly demonstrate a phase of depression between the Icelandic trips of 1871 and 1873 that coincides with the breakdown of his friend-ship with Rossetti.[62] It may be presumed that Morris wanted his family protected from scandal and that his decision in the summer of 1871 to lease Kelmscott Manor in Kelmscott, Oxfordshire, jointly with Rossetti (where Jane and he could spend time quietly) may have been a radical method of simultaneously tolerating and disguising the relationship.

Whatever the truth of the matter, a number of scholars, including John Purkis, Philip Henderson, Paul Thompson, Jack Lindsay, Roderick Marshall, Fiona MacCarthy, Clive Wilmer and Marcus Waithe, have each associated the unhappiness in his marriage with his new interest in the sagas and Iceland.[63] This association has usually taken one of two forms. Most frequently the significance of the saga translations has been played down and the trips to Iceland proposed as Morris's direct response to his marriage difficulties. The fact that he undertook the lease of Kelmscott Manor with Rossetti in the same summer that he first visited Iceland has led to the widely held belief that Morris left England either to allow his wife and her paramour time alone together, or to avoid them: Purkis claims that 'there was an arrangement to leave Janey and Rossetti at Kelmscott with himself out of the way';[64] Lindsay states that Morris went 'to escape the miseries of the settling-in';[65] while Marshall argues that 'Rossetti continued to upset Morris more than he expected. So he sought a new means of relief' by travelling to Iceland.[66] Only a minority of critics have disagreed with this view, with Frederick Kirchhoff highlighting the

---

[62] See letters to to Coronio, dated probably dated 25 November 1872 and 23 January 1873 in Kelvin, I, pp. 172–73, 176–77.

[63] John Purkis, *The Icelandic Jaunt: A Study of the Expeditions Made by Morris in 1871 and 1873* (Dublin: Dolmen Press, 1962), p. 6; Philip Henderson, *William Morris: His Life, Work and Friends* (Harmondsworth: Penguin, 1973), p. 149; Paul Thompson, *The Work of William Morris* (London: Heinemann, 1967), p. 26; Jack Lindsay, *William Morris: His Life and Work* (London: Constable, 1975), p. 217; Roderick Marshall, *William Morris and His Earthly Paradises* (Tisbury: Compton Press, 1979), pp. 168–78; *LOT*, pp. 279, 304, 310; Clive Wilmer, 'Maundering Medievalism: D. G. Rossetti and William Morris as Poets', *PN Review (Manchester)*, 29 (2003), 69–74 (p. 72); Waithe, p. 74.

[64] Purkis, p. 6.

[65] Lindsay, *Life and Work*, p. 175.

[66] Marshall, p. 186.

fact that Morris had planned the trip to Iceland before he found Kelmscott Manor.[67]

Those scholars who have linked the 1868–76 'Old Norse period' as a whole (rather than simply the journeys to Iceland) to Morris's crumbling marriage have tended to argue that his engagement with the sagas, and particularly those that concentrate on love triangles, provided a cathartic experience as his relationship with Jane failed. Marshall suggests that 'it may be that Morris gravitated to the barbarous and often horrible Icelandic tales as a means of neutralising murderous fantasies about Rossetti and Jane', while J. M. S. Tompkins maintains that in 'narrative and lyric' Morris expressed 'shame that he sometimes seemed to himself an easy cuckold'.[68] Stephen Coote and Andrew Wawn both imply that 'Gudrun' allowed Morris to articulate his personal suffering in the tortured love affairs of Bodli, Kiartan and Gudrun,[69] while Grace J. Calder proposes that 'Iceland and its literature continued to occupy him until the love affair began to ebb' (Introduction to *SoK*, p. 13). Kirchhoff, for his part, has contended that readings that relate the saga narratives directly to Morris's home life are fundamentally reductive.[70]

Tangentially related to the view that Morris turned to medieval Icelandic literature in order to avoid the pain of his marriage is the notion that he was more positively drawn to something that he found extraordinary in it. Since Mackail declared that Iceland had 'an importance in Morris's life which can hardly be over-estimated, and which, even to those who knew him well was not wholly intelligible' (*LWM*, I, p. 240), scholars have tended to allude to whatever drew him to the island and its sagas in effusive, almost mystical terms: May Morris declares that 'it was the Northern genius itself that something deeply rooted in him recognized as *familiar*';[71] Purkis that 'there was a definite quest, a desire to find something in the wilderness of Iceland';[72] and Peter Preston that 'that country again seemed to answer to his mood'.[73] Critics considering

---

[67] Frederick Kirchhoff, *William Morris: The Construction of a Male Self, 1856–1872* (Athens: Ohio University Press, 1990), p. 217.

[68] Marshall, p. 169; J. M. S. Tompkins, *William Morris: An Approach to the Poetry* (London: Cecil Woolf, 1988), p. 150.

[69] Stephen Coote, *William Morris: His Life and Work* (London: Garamond, 1990) p. 85; Wawn, *Vikings*, pp. 263–65.

[70] Kirchhoff, p. 196.

[71] May Morris, *Artist*, I, p. 447.

[72] Purkis, p. 7.

[73] Preston, p. 13.

what it was that drew him have generally emphasised the importance of Iceland the country over the literature, deeming the journeys of 1871 and 1873 to be, in the words of Pamela Bracken Wiens, the 'centrepiece of [his] middle life, the culmination of his immersion in Northern saga'.[74] The trips are widely agreed to have been therapeutic: Purkis refers to the 'personal revitalisation' that they provided Morris,[75] while Ruth Kinna suggests that they 'acted as restoratives'.[76]

Since E. P. Thompson argued that 'Morris drew his strength [...] from the energies and aspirations of a people in a barren northern island in the twelfth century',[77] it has been regularly asserted that what attracted Morris to Iceland was essentially a form of bravery. Paul Thompson suggests that Morris's acquaintance with real-life Icelanders helped him to discover a new resolve: the 'stoicism of these hard-worked people in bearing a life so much more difficult than his own, and the help which they found in the old stories' made Morris's 'own morbidity seem cowardly',[78] while Wawn argues that 'the solemnity and stoicism which he came to associate with Iceland afforded him real succour'.[79] Those critics who have considered what attracted Morris to the sagas themselves have also frequently concluded that he was drawn to the kind of bravery that he perceived in them. In May Morris's eyes, it was the fact that the heroes lived in 'an age in which intellect and stern courage rule side by side' that most appealed to her father.[80] Marshall suggests that Morris identified in particular with the 'courage and probity' of the outlaws of the sagas of Icelanders,[81] while Wilmer argues that the fortitude that Morris perceived in the sagas was 'a virtue he felt he gravely needed'.[82]

Aside from the discovery of courage, a secondary but nevertheless enduring explanation for what attracted Morris to Old Norse literature has been that he perceived a way of life in Iceland and the sagas

[74] Pamela Bracken Wiens, 'Fire and Ice: Clashing Visions of Iceland in the Travel Narratives of Morris and Burton', *The Journal of the William Morris Society*, 11.4 (1996), 12–18 (p. 14).

[75] Purkis, p. 15.

[76] Ruth Kinna, *William Morris: The Art of Socialism* (Cardiff: University of Wales Press, 2000), pp. 6–7.

[77] E. P. Thompson, *William Morris: Romantic to Revolutionary* (London: Lawrence & Wishart, 1955), p. 176.

[78] Paul Thompson, p. 33.

[79] Wawn, *Vikings*, p. 247.

[80] May Morris, *Artist*, I, p. 447.

[81] Marshall, p. 180.

[82] Wilmer, 'Maundering Medievalism', p. 73.

that moulded his social and political ideals. Mackail suggests that, for Morris, the 'philosophy or religion that lived under these half-humanized legends was something quite real and vital: and it substantially represented his own guiding belief' (*LWM*, I, p. 333). Litzenberg proposes that Morris's understanding of the Norse apocalypse *ragnarök* ('the doom/ destruction of the gods' or 'the twilight of the gods', depending on how the *rök* element is interpreted) came to inform his view of the socialist revolution,[83] a view that has more recently been reiterated by Heather O'Donoghue, who claims that Morris used *ragnarök* 'as a unifying (but imminent as well as immanent) signifier'.[84] Paul Thompson asserts that Morris 'came to see in the north a separate value of its own, differing from medieval feudal romanticism and chivalry',[85] while Lindsay emphasises 'the part played by the turn to Norse sagas and Iceland in driving Morris to look outwards to find a pattern of significance in the social and political hurly-burly'.[86]

Certain scholars have stressed Morris's tendency to contrast his primitivist view of medieval Iceland with that which he considered degraded in Victorian society. Kirchhoff believes that through his attraction to the old culture Morris faced the philistine reality of his own time: 'In seeking to link himself with the geographical setting of the sagas, he confronts his separation from the creative spirit of their poets. His feelings may rise in the Icelandic landscape, but they rise to an essentially modern perception of difference and distance.'[87] Preston suggests that the 'immediacy of Morris's apprehension of this heroic past made sharper and more depressing the contrast with the modern world, for he believed that since the days of the sagas life had shrunk and taken on a kind of insignificance.'[88] Waithe argues that 'Iceland came, for Morris, to symbolize an alternative way of life':[89] by contrasting a primitive stage of the past with the present in his translations and treks, he found 'a method of

[83] Karl Litzenberg, 'The Social Philosophy of William Morris and the Doom of the Gods', *Essays and Studies in English and Comparative Literature*, 24 (1933), 183–203; Litzenberg, *Victorians*, pp. 24–25.

[84] Heather O'Donoghue, *English Poetry and Old Norse Myth: A History* (Oxford: Oxford University Press, 2014), p. 173.

[85] Paul Thompson, p. 26.

[86] Lindsay, *Life and Work*, p. 215.

[87] Kirchhoff, p. 223.

[88] Preston, p. 9.

[89] Waithe, p. 116.

challenging the dominance of contemporary social forms.'[90] Gary L. Aho has trodden a lonely path by suggesting that critics may have exaggerated what Morris saw in Iceland and the sagas, arguing that 'in their attempts to push Morris's interests and achievements into coherent patterns', scholars 'have understood too much' about his passion for the country, especially in relation to how it informed his later views of a socialist constitution.[91]

William Morris and the Icelandic Sagas

Given the differing critical opinions on what attracted Morris to Old Norse literature and the nature of his subsequent treatment of it, a thorough study of the relationship between his rearticulation of the sagas and the source material on which he drew would appear worthwhile. This book consequently considers the significance for Morris of a literature that Swannell considered his 'greatest single inspiration', by comparing his translations and Norse-inspired poetry against a more detailed analysis of their Icelandic sources than has previously been conducted.[92] In particular, it considers whether he altered what he found in Old Norse literature to suit a developing ideal of heroism. In light of the importance of this literature to Morris, and the potential influence of his engagement with it on the growth of Old Norse studies in Britain, the lack of such a study until now is conspicuous. Its absence to date may reflect the fact that Victorianists who have approached this subject have rarely possessed the necessary knowledge of the sagas or Old Norse language to perform such an analysis, most often relying on the more accessible Icelandic journals for illumination because they were unable to compare Morris's translations with the original. In contrast, this book compares his translations and adaptations closely with their sources in Old Norse.

To facilitate tracing the development of Morris's treatment of medieval Icelandic literature, I have attempted to analyse his relevant works in loosely chronological order, beginning in Chapter 1 with the earlier of his saga-inspired long poems 'The Lovers of Gudrun' (published in 1869). In Chapter 2, I look mainly at translations begun in the late 1860s and early 1870s, and in Chapter 3, I look at translations begun in the same period but also at the Icelandic journeys that were undertaken in 1871

---

[90] Waithe, p. 75.

[91] Gary L. Aho, 'William Morris in Iceland', *Kairos*, 1 (1982), 102–33 (p. 102).

[92] Swannell, *Norse Literature*, p. 21.

and 1873. In Chapter 4, I consider Morris's translation of *Heimskringla*, which he and Eiríkur worked on predominantly in 1872 and 1873 before returning to it in the early 1890s,[93] as well as the general development of their translation style. In Chapter 5, I look at the later of the two saga-inspired long poems *Sigurd the Volsung* (published in 1876) and, in Chapter 6, I consider the extent to which Morris's work after 1876, particularly his social campaigning and 'late' romances, was influenced by the 1868–76 'Old Norse period'.

Despite the fact that Morris returned to publishing translations from Old Norse in the 1890s, I have decided to concentrate on the 1868–76 period because it was then that the vast majority of translation work was first performed and Morris's interest in the sagas was at its height. Even though the publication of The Saga Library demonstrates an enduring commitment to Icelandic literature, it should be understood as part of the wider project of publishing (or republishing) his earlier work that Morris undertook towards the end of his life, rather than as evidence of a phase of renewed interest in Old Norse. I have, therefore, generally referred to the saga translations published in the 1890s only when they confirm evidence of a tendency that is already under way in the 1868–76 period (for example, in relation to Morris's growing insistence on a literal style).

In concentrating on what the translations from Old Norse tell us about Morris, I do not mean to minimise Eiríkur's considerable involvement throughout the entire project. However, from the beginning of their collaboration, it was Morris, as the famous poet, native English speaker and wealthy patron, who had the final word on what form the publications would eventually take, especially when it came to the verses. In 1892, for instance, he considered it an unwelcome development that Eiríkur had attempted to versify his translation of the stanzas before sending them to Morris to finalise: 'having read them the metre and style won't get out of one's head, and prevent me from writing things in *my way*' [my italics].[94] Since, as Litzenberg put it, 'the Icelander provided grammatical structure and word-meanings upon which the Englishman built his final versions',[95] I have felt justified in concluding that the

---

[93] For the timing of the translation of *Heimskringla*, see Anderson, pp. 180–84; Chase, pp. 165–66.

[94] Letter to Eiríkur Magnússon, possibly dated 24 August 1892, in Kelvin, III, p. 435.

[95] Litzenberg, 'Diction', p. 331.

published translations, as well as Morris's other Norse-inspired writing, largely represent his own distinct vision. Quite what that vision was, and how it developed, is the subject of this book.

1

'The Lovers of Gudrun' and the Crisis of the Grail Quest

IT HAS BEEN suggested that 'The Lovers of Gudrun', the 'medieval'
poem that Morris composed for the November section of Part III of
The Earthly Paradise (1868–70), marks some kind of departure in his
poetry. Based on the love triangle between the foster-brothers Kjartan
Ólafsson and Bolli Þorleiksson, and the heroine Guðrún Ósvífrsdóttir in
Laxdœla saga, one of the most famous of the sagas of Icelanders, 'Gudrun'
contains an emotional starkness that has been described as 'low-keyed
realism'.[1] Though it is arguable whether there is much in the poem that is
low-key, it is undeniable that the vivid emotionality of 'Gudrun' encom-
passes a quality of strength and humanity that distinguishes it from the
dreamier tales that come before it. Tompkins felt that at the time that
'Gudrun' was written Morris and his critics 'seem to have hoped that a
change was impending, a return, or advance, to more overtly human
themes',[2] while Linda Julian has argued that Morris 'sensed his own
artistic development' in the poem, which led 'to a different style'.[3]

It is certainly true that 'Gudrun' is distinct from the poems that
precede it in *The Earthly Paradise*, most obviously because of its more
severe tone and considerable length. Having begun the period of intense
translating activity with Eiríkur Magnússon only a few months earlier,
Morris drafted 'Gudrun' at the height of his initial engagement with Old
Norse literature in the spring and summer of 1869, before it was published
in Part III of *The Earthly Paradise* that November. Since E. P. Thompson
associated *The Earthly Paradise* as a whole with despondency, calling it

---

[1] Charlotte H. Oberg, *A Pagan Prophet: William Morris* (Charlottesville:
University Press of Virginia, 1978), p. 52.
[2] Tompkins, pp. 171–72.
[3] Linda Julian, '*Laxdaela Saga* and "The Lovers of Gudrun": Morris'
Poetic Vision', *Victorian Poetry*, 34 (1996), 355–71 (p. 355).

'the poetry of despair',[4] scholars have often understood the new-found starkness of 'Gudrun' to relate to a crisis of confidence in Morris's middle years, most frequently tied to unhappiness in his marriage due to Jane Morris's apparent affair with Rossetti. Oscar Mauer suggests that Morris 'was adapting the saga material in a direction that reflected his own trouble',[5] and Florence Saunders Boos that 'one could readily adduce a number of parallels with [the tale and] Morris's and Rossetti's painfully complex but nonviolent rivalry' (*TEP*, ii, p. 284).

Leaving aside the fact that the correspondence that immediately follows his completion of the draft of 'Gudrun', some time before the first week of August 1869, betrays nothing but kindly cordiality between husband and wife – 'Ah hah! the letter you sent me wasn't sent for nothing. Janey got a pain in her back from laughing at it'[6] – arguments that relate the poem's departure in tone directly to Morris's private unhappiness risk associating the growth of his priorities as a writer too narrowly to his home life. In making this point, I neither intend to underplay Jane's affair with Rossetti nor the possibility that it caused Morris pain. However, as I see it, critics have tended to propose the infidelity as a wide-ranging explanation for various themes in Morris's writing across a considerable period of time, despite the fact that the textual evidence for its nature and timing is far from explicit. Even though Jane's and Rossetti's intimate friendship may have begun in the late 1860s, it seems pertinent to note, for example, that Morris wrote 'Gudrun' a full two years before he and Rossetti decided to lease Kelmscott Manor together, and over three years before Morris's correspondence show their friendship to have deteriorated significantly (see Introduction, pp. 19–20).

Arguments that read biographical analogies into the plots of Morris's work (such as those that assume he was essentially writing about himself when he re-created the love triangle from *Laxdæla saga* in 'Gudrun') make him seem incapable of sustaining an engagement with ontological questions that look beyond his immediate situation. However, if one looks closely at 'Gudrun', it becomes clear that the new tone of the poem is in fact the result of a significant development in Morris's ideological outlook away from what might be described as a Carlylean paradigm that celebrated the attempt to transcend the mundane, towards an attitude

---

[4] E. P. Thompson, p. 132.

[5] Oscar Mauer, 'William Morris and *Laxdæla Saga*', *Texas Studies in Literature and Language*, 5 (1963), 422–37 (p. 436).

[6] Letter to Philip Webb, probably dated 15 August 1869, in Kelvin, i, p. 88.

that aimed to make the best of earthly conditions with no opportunity for escape. The former perspective had shown itself in Morris's sustained engagement with Arthurian romance, especially with the transcendent quest for the Holy Grail, as well as perhaps in his aspiration to create a 'palace of Art' at Red House.[7] Though the latter stance may already have been evolving gradually throughout the 1860s as Morris returned to live in London and began work on *The Earthly Paradise*, it was radically galvanised in late 1868 when he started to study Old Norse literature, in which he perceived a worldly tenacity that stimulated his new ideal of the heroic.

Much of Morris's work prior to 'Gudrun' had drawn on the medieval romance quest, in which, in Helen Cooper's words, a knight errant 'sets out from the court into the unknown and returns, bringing with him whatever he has learned'.[8] Several of the romances that Morris wrote for *The Oxford & Cambridge Magazine* (1856) exhibit this three-stage 'essentially linear' quest structure.[9] The hero begins in some state of ignorance or delusion and subsequently travels through a disorienting dimension, before he re-emerges with his appreciation of reality transformed. Thus, in 'A Dream', a knight passes through a legendary cave where he is condemned to search for his lover over several lifetimes until they are finally reunited. In 'Lindenborg Pool', the dreamer is invited into a supernatural castle, which he eventually flees, only to hear behind him 'a roar as if the world were coming in two' as the edifice mutates into a 'deep black lake' (*CW*, I, p. 253). Similarly, in 'The Hollow Land: A Tale', the hero gradually discerns a netherworld in which he suffers a series of ordeals before apparently experiencing deliverance. Though the quest that Morris's early protagonists pursue is often equivocal, the suggestion of allegory, in Gillian Beer's words, 'constantly creeping around its fringes',[10] means that these stories invariably imply a process of psychological or spiritual growth; what Cooper describes as: 'the dusty and sweaty journey from inexperience into knowledge, even from the fallen world to a triumphant ending in the immortality of heaven'.[11]

---

[7] Letter to Edward Burne-Jones, probably dated November 1864, in Kelvin, I, p. 38.

[8] Helen Cooper, *The Romance in Time: Transforming Motifs from Geoffrey of Monmouth to the Death of Shakespeare* (Oxford: Oxford University Press, 2004), p. 55.

[9] Helen Cooper, p. 46.

[10] Gillian Beer, *The Romance* (London: Methuen, 1970), p. 19.

[11] Helen Cooper, p. 46.

Indeed, the pre-'Gudrun' Morris appears to have been especially drawn to the quest's potential for mystical allegory. Even in short poems from the collection *The Defence of Guenevere and Other Poems* (1858) that offer only glimpses into the journeyings of his knights, such as 'Sir Galahad: A Christmas Mystery' and 'The Chapel in Lyoness', the hero rides in pursuit of the transcendent state, the fully realised nature. Galahad is exhorted to 'go on, | Until at last you come to ME' (*CW*, I, p. 28) while Sir Ozana exclaims 'Christ help! I have but little wit: | My life went wrong' (*CW*, I, p. 33). In such lines the reader witnesses fleetingly the spiritual search for the self that R. R. Bezzola called 'le chevalier à la recherche de lui-même'.[12]

Even as late as the summer of 1867 when Morris was completing the frame-narrative of *The Earthly Paradise*, he had his wanderers embark on a quest 'whose compulsion they cannot resist',[13] sailing in search of a land of eternal youth in which they seemingly hope to transcend their fallen state. Often employing Galahad-like figures, as well as allusions to the Fisher King, the spear of Longinus, the wasteland and the dolorous stroke, the quest of discovery that the younger Morris seems compelled to write and rewrite is akin to a quest for the *sancgreal* or Holy Grail, which, as he knew it in Malory's rendering, culminates in the especially esoteric revelation of Christ: 'my true children whiche ben com oute of dedely lyf in to spyrytual lyf I wyl now no lenger hyde me frome yow, but ye shal see now a parte of my secretes and of my hydde thynges'.[14]

In the romances that he wrote for *The Oxford & Cambridge Magazine*, Morris is noticeably preoccupied with the Malorian progression from the deadly to the spiritual life, routinely using motifs associated with the grail, which in these stories leads to a form of clear seeing or enlightenment. Only a short time after Florian has entered the titular wasteland in 'The Hollow Land', he falls into an expanse of water, through which he dimly perceives a boatman holding 'a long slender spear, barbed like a fish-hook' that is suddenly plunged into his shoulder. Awakening from the stroke in a state of dispossession, he re-enters his father's hall (resembling a grail castle) with 'as little clothes, as little wealth, less memory

[12] R. R. Bezzola, *Le sens de l'aventure et de l'amour (Chrétien de Troyes)* (Paris: La Jeune Parque, 1947), p. 83; quoted in Helen Cooper, p. 49.

[13] Jessie Kocmanová, *The Poetic Maturing of William Morris: From the Earthly Paradise to the Pilgrims of Hope* (Prague: Státni Pedagogické Nakladatelství, 1964), p. 22.

[14] Thomas Malory, *Le Morte Darthur*, ed. Robert Southey, 2 vols (London: Longman, Hurst, Rees, Orme and Brown, 1817), II, p. 310.

and thought' than when he 'came into the world fifty years before' (*CW*, I, pp. 282–83). Here he re-encounters the Fisher King (effectively now the grail keeper) and they set about studying divine judgements and the behaviour of people in the hope that both their nature and acuity will be transformed in the process:

> And as the years went on and we grew old and grey we painted purple pictures and green ones instead of scarlet and yellow so that the walls looked altered; and always we painted God's judgements. And we would sit in the sunset and watch them, with the golden light changing them, as we yet hoped God would change both us and our works. Often too we would sit outside the walls and look at the trees and sky, and the ways of the few men and women we saw. (*CW*, I, p. 287)

Within the inner recesses of the castle, Florian accesses the grail of authentic knowledge. Initially guilty of gross egotism and pride, killing Queen Swanhilda in ignoble circumstances, he eventually relinquishes these base responses to realise humility and sensitivity to humanity. Finally recognising the now befriended fisherman as his original enemy Harald, he travels back through the Hollow Land, passing into 'a great space of flowers' and appearing to transcend earthly life altogether (*CW*, I, p. 290).

In 'A Dream' the narrator (whose father was prevented from undertaking the quest of the red cavern by some kind of dolorous stroke to the shoulder) recounts the tale of Lawrence, a knight who undertakes the quest into the cave and, in doing so, gains entry to a strange region not unlike the Hollow Land (*CW*, I, p. 159). Imprisoned in an ivory house (again reminiscent of a grail castle), from where, over an unearthly time he journeys in continual pursuit of his love, Ella – 'the old man came last night to the ivory house and told me it would be a hundred years, ay, more, before the happy end' (*CW*, I, p. 170) – Lawrence endures a series of excruciating incarnations before finally surrendering corporeal existence altogether: 'And as they gazed, the bells of the church began to ring […] And there beneath the eyes of those four men the lovers slowly faded away into a heap of snow-white ashes' (*CW*, I, p. 174).

Beginning the tale in possession of a self-important conceit of love, after pompously entering the cavern to prove his manliness, Lawrence is required (possibly by the old man of the ivory tower who, again, seems like a grail keeper) to undergo a process of gruelling dispossession before he realises the disposition of selfless devotion. In both of these quests, the hero begins as fundamentally deceived by his worldly perception and unknowingly commits some kind of hubristic sin in his ignorance, before commencing the succession of trials that will result in the attainment of the equivalent of the mystical grail.

Despite its discernibility, the grail quest is, however, noticeably distorted in Morris's early romances, often becoming so destabilised by the uncanny that it is difficult to determine what is intended allegorically by the end of each tale. As the narrator of the 'The Hollow Land' looking back on his own story, for example, Florian appears to have already lost the transcendent state that his tale describes him acquiring (*CW*, I, p. 254). It is also unclear as to whether the physical disintegration that Lawrence and Ella experience at the climax of their tale is an indication of triumph or loss (*CW*, I, pp. 174–75).

Considering Morris to be fundamentally ambivalent about whether to engage with or escape from contemporary society, Amanda Hodgson has argued that these kinds of contortions in the early tales 'deliberately undercut the beliefs and conventions of the Middle Ages and present them as inadequate standards by which to live'.[15] For her, Morris seems 'always to be straining after a resolution which he cannot allow himself to achieve', so that in the 'narrative disjunctions, the idiosyncrasies of syntax, the impression of confusion and disorientation' he is essentially rejecting romance's 'most important implication', namely the possibility of 'lasting harmony as a counterbalance to its depiction of struggle and evil'.[16]

Though it is indisputable that Morris sometimes confounds the quest structure in the early stories by consigning his characters to what can seem like an endless cycle of displacement, it does not necessarily follow that in the mid-1850s he was sceptical of the adequacy of the chivalric virtues embodied in romance, nor that he deemed the endeavour to attain enduring harmony to be futile. A century later, Northrop Frye argued against Morris's use of romance being regarded as 'an "escape" from his social attitude',[17] later emphasising the genre's capacity as a narrative of revolution in which it is 'much more frequently the individual, the hero or heroine, who has the vision of liberation, and the society they are involved

---

[15] Amanda Hodgson, *The Romances of William Morris* (Cambridge: Cambridge University Press, 1987), p. 36.

[16] Hodgson, p. 45.

[17] Northrop Frye, *Anatomy of Criticism: Four Essays* (Princeton: Princeton University Press, 1957), p. 305.

with that wants to remain in a blind and gigantic darkness'.[18] Rather than implying a rejection of the virtuous ideals embodied in romance, it seems more likely that the quality of uncanny distortion in Morris's grail quests – the pregnant, immanent mystery that lurks beneath – is, in fact, integral to his expression of it: the more fraught the process of becoming conscious, the more valuable the perseverance in the attempt to transcend the earthly.

In addition, it seems probable that the especially disorienting quality in *The Oxford & Cambridge Magazine* stories is influenced by Morris's reading of Carlyle, whose 'denunciation of capitalist society as a sham' and 'emphasis on re-establishing genuine human relationships', were, in the judgement of Nicholas Salmon, such an early influence on him. While Salmon asserts that Morris and Burne-Jones 'had first read *Past and Present* while students at Oxford' and that 'it is probable that they went on to read all Carlyle's major works',[19] it is certain that his thought played a central part in *The Oxford & Cambridge Magazine*, which devoted five essays to him across its twelve issues.[20]

Carlyle, impressed by the limited understanding of transcendental idealism that he had gleaned from a partial reading of Kant's *Kritik der reinen Vernunft* ('Critique of Pure Reason'), in works such as *Sartor Resartus* (1833–34), *On Heroes* (1841) and *Past and Present* (1843) had argued fervently that the material world is an illusion that conceals behind it the true spiritual reality.[21] In his view, corporeal phenomena were merely 'Apparitions' or 'Souls rendered visible' that arose from the concealed, godly dimension.[22] Frequently employing pictorial images to portray the illusory display of phenomena, Carlyle compares the

---

[18] Northrop Frye, *The Secular Scripture: A Study of the Structure of Romance* (Cambridge, MA: Harvard University Press, 1976), p. 139.

[19] Nicholas Salmon, '"The Down-Trodden Radical": William Morris's Pre-Socialist Ideology', *The Journal of the William Morris Society*, 13.3 (1999), 26–43 (p. 27).

[20] See the issues for April, pp. 193–211, May, pp. 292–311, June, pp. 336–52, November, pp. 697–712 and December, pp. 743–70.

[21] For an account of Carlyle's understanding of Kant, see Rosemary Ashton, *The German Idea: Four English Writers and the Reception of German Thought, 1800–1860* (Cambridge: Cambridge University Press, 1980), pp. 92–95.

[22] Thomas Carlyle, *Sartor Resartus: The Life and Opinions of Herr Teufelsdröckh in Three Books*, ed. Rodger L. Tarr and Mark Engel, The Norman and Charlotte Strouse Edition of the Writings of Thomas Carlyle (Berkeley: University of California Press, 2000), p. 17. Morris owned the first edition published in 1838 by Saunders and Otley. See 'Catalogue (1898)', p. 22.

onlooker's experience of the sham world of the here-and-now to a spectator gazing at a phantasmagoria, dream-grotto or canvas:

> We sit as in a boundless Phantasmagoria and Dream-grotto; boundless, for the faintest star, the remotest century, lies not even nearer the verge thereof; sounds and many-coloured visions flit round our sense [...] But the same WHERE, with its brother WHEN, are from the first the master-colours of our Dream-grotto; say rather, the Canvass (the warp and woof thereof) whereon all our Dreams and Life-visions are painted.[23]

In conceiving of mundane appearance as merely a spectacular display of sounds and visions, Carlyle lamented the fact that in contemporary society most people were caught up in erroneous experience, only becoming aware of immanent reality in those rare moments when '[t]he world, with its loud trafficking, retires into the distance; and, [...] the sight reaches forth into the void Deep, and you are alone with the Universe, and silently commune with it.'[24] Arguing that in the Middle Ages men lived in continual communion with authentic existence, Carlyle encouraged his readership to throw off the sham in pursuit of the lost but genuine way of life: 'To this and the other noisy, very great-looking Simulacrum [...] he can say, composedly stepping aside: Thou are not *true*; thou art not extant, only semblant; go thy way!'[25]

The uncanny quality in Morris's early grail quests appears to be linked to Carlyle's post-Kantian worldview in a number of ways. In general, Morris's disruption of the known world reflects a broad preoccupation with the illusory nature of the materiality that recalls Carlyle. More specifically, the Carlylean dream-grotto that holds the '[c]anvass [...] whereon all our Dreams and Life-visions are painted' resonates with the hall in Morris's grail castle in which Florian and the Fisher King observe mankind and paint God's judgements. In *Sartor Resartus*, the imagined room in which the dreams are painted is a kind of inner sanctum in which emanations from the mysterious, hidden reality are processed. Similarly, in 'The Hollow Land' and 'A Dream' the equivalent room in Morris's grail castle is located in a deeply enclosed, private space, in which Florian and

---

[23] Carlyle, *Sartor Resartus* (2000), p. 42.

[24] Carlyle, *Sartor Resartus* (2000), p. 41.

[25] Thomas Carlyle, *On Heroes, Hero-Worship & the Heroic in History*, ed. Michael K. Goldberg, Joel J. Brattin and Mark Engel, The Norman and Charlotte Strouse Edition of the Writings of Thomas Carlyle (Berkeley: University of California Press, 1993), p. 151.

Lawrence learn to distinguish truth from fallacy. By creating the impression of a hidden potential for seeing the world more accurately, the young Morris appears to be emulating Carlyle's worldview, which is structured around the unreliability of ordinary human perception and the necessity of awakening to the truth of existence that lies behind it.

A further characteristic of these early stories that appears to be shaped by Carlyle is the way in which the protagonists sometimes become aware of the proximity of the hidden reality through a kind of telescoping of sensory experience much like that described in *Sartor Resartus*. In 'The Hollow Land', as Florian approaches the latent entrance to the wasteland, he notices tiny geographical details that imbue the strange landscape with a mesmeric, tranquil quality evocative of heightened awareness during trauma or perhaps the thinness of the mountain air: 'And we still neared the pass, and began to see distinctly the ferns that grew on the rocks, and the fair country between the rift in them spreading out there blue-shadowed' (*CW*, I, p. 270). The possibility of a strange, lurking realm of truth is made overt when a mysteriously sagacious knight confronts him with words that might have been written by Carlyle himself: 'how would you feel inclined if you thought that everything about you were glamour, this earth here, the rocks, the sun, the sky? [...] Brave men, brothers, ought to be the masters of *simulacra*' (*CW*, I, p. 272). Finally confronted with the sham, the world appears to retire into the distance as Florian now perceives ultimate existence behind it:

> So I looked towards the pass, and when I looked I no longer doubted any of those wild tales of glamour concerning Goliah's Land: for though the rocks were the same, and though the conies still stood gazing at the doors of their dwellings, though the hawks still cried shrilly, though the fern still shook in the wind, yet beyond, O such a land! not to be described by any because of its great beauty; lying a great Hollow Land. (*CW*, I, pp. 273–74)

At this moment Carlyle's notion of transcendent reality and the wasteland motif of the grail quest meet one another in Morris's vision of the Hollow Land.

Whereas Carlyle's conception of the hidden reality and divinity within it is categorically benevolent, Morris's otherworld is darker and more forbidding, possibly intimating the particular arduousness of awakening in what was for him the aberrant industrialised culture of nineteenth-century Britain. Despite this, both writers portray the pursuit for the transcendent life as fundamentally heroic. The endurance of Lawrence's quest, for instance, has earned him fame amongst the people long before he completes it: 'have we not heard of thee even before thou camest hither?' (*CW*, I, p. 171). Morris continues to portray as funda-mentally admirable the nightmarish displacement of his heroes in their quest for transcendence, despite the fact that the lack of any explanation for his hidden realities means that they verge on what Tzvetan Todorov considered to be the purely fantastic.[26] In light of this, Morris's use of disjunction and dislocation may not indicate a rejection of the medi-eval, as Hodgson proposes (see this chapter, p. 32, above), but rather an embrace of the romance type that Helen Cooper calls the 'ethical quest', in which it is the aspiration to pursue the object (which may be either endlessly ahead of the hero, unknown to him or impossible to achieve) that becomes paramount. In such an ethical quest, the hero is primarily celebrated for the strength of his intent to seek the chivalric virtues, which are difficult to attain but 'all the more necessary to strive for on account of that difficulty'.[27] Although Morris regularly emphasises the value of the undertaking more than its completion, the very possibility in his early romances of the otherworldly dimension implies that he still considers the grail – that is, the Carlylean transcendence of the protago-nist's specious earthly condition – to be worthy of pursuit.

By the time Morris began to write 'The Lovers of Gudrun' in the spring of 1869, he appears to have become sceptical of both the existence of, and value in, pursuing any transcendent dimension. His attraction to *Laxdæla saga* seems to have lain primarily in the fact that, in his view, it portrayed endurance of the earthly as everything and its transcendence as an irrel-evant impossibility. While, in his earlier grail-inspired stories, Morris implied that through extraordinary tribulation a state of transcendent insight might be realised, 'Gudrun' might be argued to mark the point in Morris's writing when the Carlylean possibility of passing beyond the mundane is explicitly relinquished. Where his Arthurian-inspired

---

[26] See Tzvetan Todorov, *The Fantastic: A Structural Approach to a Literary Genre*, trans. Richard Howard (Cleveland: Case Western Reserve University Press, 1973), p. 44. Rosemary Jackson describes Todorov's definition of the fantastic as developing from 'the marvellous (which predominates in a climate of belief in supernaturalism and magic) through the purely fantastic (in which no explanation can be found) to the uncanny (which explains all strangeness as generated by unconscious forces)'. For Todorov, she explains, the purely fantastic 'opens on a region which has no name and no rational explanation for its existence. It suggests events beyond interpretation.' See Rosemary Jackson, *Fantasy: The Literature of Subversion* (London: Methuen, 1981), pp. 14–15.

[27] Helen Cooper, p. 41.

characters enjoy the potential for deliverance from suffering, however unreliable, the poem's Norse protagonists are offered no such means of liberation.

Nevertheless, despite this shift in outlook, on a fundamental level Morris continued to employ a quest-like structure in 'Gudrun'. Though he considered the central story of Laxdœla saga 'magnificent', he did not appreciate the way that the plot develops through suggestive apposition and comparison. Far from seeing the 'subtle repetitions, parallels and echoes in gradually changing circumstances' that Keneva Kunz suggests create a 'symphonic structure',[28] Morris deemed the saga to have 'no pretensions to artistic unity' and its construction 'disjointed' and 'in some important places very bald'.[29] For his rendering of the story in 'Gudrun', he therefore dispensed with its contrapuntal form altogether and co-opted the central story into three linear stages that progressed from the delusion of contentment, through the bewilderment of stark disillusionment, to a state of suffering that he presented as the ineluctable consequence of clear seeing in a world in which there was now no means of escape.

Morris's freshly forged saga-based romance structure might be described as a kind of 'anti-quest' in that the grail object that holds the potential to convey the hero beyond this world is now non-existent, rather than simply impossible to achieve. Once the protagonists of 'Gudrun' cross the Rubicon of awakening, no Carlylean otherworld is intimated. Reality appears to be simply an empty, indifferent version of the space in which they previously dwelt in mistaken pleasure. In 'Gudrun' the initial stage of Morris's newly bleak quest structure takes the form of a golden time, in which the protagonists are guilty of ignorance of the fallacious nature of their happiness. In creating this dream-like period, Morris greatly augments the degree of idealised detail portrayed in Laxdœla saga. While the saga's Kjartan and Guðrún are initially described in superlative terms – Kjartan is famously 'allra manna vænstr þeira er fædst hafa á Íslandi' (LAX, p. 110)[30] and Guðrún 'kvenna vænst, er upp-óxu á Íslandi, bædi at ásiánu ok vitsmunum' (LAX, p. 122)[31] – the circumstances in which

---

[28] Introduction to The Saga of the People of Laxardal, in The Sagas of Icelanders: A Selection, trans. Keneva Kunz (London: Penguin, 2001), pp. 270–421 (p. 274).
[29] Letter to William Bell Scott, dated 15 February 1870, in Kelvin, I, p. 109.
[30] 'Of all men the finest to have been born in Iceland.'
[31] 'The finest of the women who were growing up in Iceland both in appearance and intelligence.'

they grow up are not idyllic. In 'Gudrun', however, the Laxdalers initially live in delightful domestic tranquillity. Kiartan's father, Olaf the Peacock, dwells amongst 'the great men of a noble day' on a 'knoll amidst a vale' '[n]igh where Laxriver meets the western sea' (*TEP*, ii, p. 287, ll. 3–5). The maids at the farm of his neighbour, Oswif, spend their time spinning '[w]ithin the bower', while Oswif goes 'in the firth a-fishing', and his wife passes 'through the meads | About some homely work' (*TEP*, ii, p. 289, ll. 56–57). Their daughter Gudrun, grown '[t]o perfect womanhood' (*TEP*, ii, p. 289, l. 33) by the time the story begins, is not merely superlative but flawless: 'Yet scarce she might grow fairer than that day; | Gold were the locks wherewith the wind did play' (*TEP*, ii, p. 290, ll. 73–74). Moreover, Kiartan is rendered practically superhuman: 'so fair of face and limb | That all folk wondered much, beholding him, | How such a man could be' (*TEP*, ii, p. 310, ll. 769–71).

Morris also heightens the poem's initial golden period by significantly increasing the degree of passion that Kiartan, Gudrun and Bodli experience at the beginning of their love affair. In *Laxdæla saga*, the love between Guðrún and Kjartan is established laconically after they meet each other by chance at the baths: 'þótti Kiartani gott at tala vid Gudrúnu, þvíat hún var bædi vitr ok væn ok málsniöll; þat var allra manna mál, at med þeim Kiartani ok Gudrúnu þætti vera mest jafnrædi þeirra manna er þá óxu upp' (*LAX*, p. 160).[32] The saga's laconic style means that this small statement of affection is equivalent to an indication of considerable fondness. By contrast, in 'Gudrun', Morris introduces a transformative love-at-first-sight scene that dramatically establishes the halcyon period of the affair:

> But, turning round,
> Kiartan upon the other hand she found,
> Gazing upon her with wild hungry eyes
> And parted lips; then did strange joy surprise
> Her listless heart, and changed her old world was;
> Ere she had time to think, all woe did pass
> Away from her, and all her life grew sweet,
> And scarce she felt the ground beneath her feet,
> Or knew who stood around. (*TEP*, ii, pp. 311–12, ll. 833–41)

---

[32] 'Kjartan found it good to talk to Guðrún because she was wise and beautiful and eloquent. It was the talk of everyone that of those people who were growing up then Kjartan and Guðrún were the best matched.'

Morris portrays Kiartan's initial desire for Gudrun as a kind of primal magnetism. His parted lips and hungry eyes seem ready to devour her, while his gaze, like some fantastic antidote, instantly transforms the heartache of her previous two marriages. The momentous effect of Gudrun's sudden love for Kiartan is created through the uncanny description of the transformation of her external environment, rather than her internal emotions. Rapturous pleasure follows: Oswif smiles '[t]o see her sorrow in such wise beguiled' (*TEP*, ii, p. 312, l. 870), while Olaf laughs 'for joy' (*TEP*, ii, p. 312, l. 871); Kiartan finds 'leisure for himself to weave | Tales of the joyful way that from that eve | Should lead to perfect bliss' (*TEP*, ii, p. 313, ll. 881–83), and Gudrun is born 'anew to love and life' (*TEP*, ii, p. 313, l. 906).

In addition, the degree to which Bodli is shown to experience love is greatly increased in this phase of Morris's adaptation. In *Laxdæla saga*, only the fraternal love between Kjartan and Bolli is stressed before the cousins leave for Norway, so that while it may be assumed that Bolli meets Guðrún too, it is only possible to guess at his interaction with her: 'þeir Kiartan ok Bolli unnust mest; fór Kiartan hvergi þess er ei fylgdi Bolli hönum. Kiartan fór opt til Sælíngsdals-laugar; jafnan bar svá til, at Gudrún var at laugu' (*LAX*, p. 160).[33] In 'Gudrun', however, the special intimacy of Bodli's friendship with Kiartan means that he spontaneously feels the joy of love when Kiartan does, though ominously, for the time being, his love lacks an object (*TEP*, ii, p. 315, ll. 969–72). The passionate intensity of Kiartan's and Gudrun's early love affair is, thus, bolstered by a kind of heady, adolescent camaraderie that includes Bodli:

> Things have been more strange,
> Than that we three should sit above the oars,
> The while on even keel 'twixt the low shores
> Our long-ship breasts the Thames flood, or the Seine. (*TEP*, ii,
>   p. 316, ll. 998–1001)

This sense of early friendship between all three young people is entirely lacking in the saga, in which we are simply told that Bolli often accompanies Kjartan wherever he goes.

Almost from the very beginning of 'Gudrun', however, Morris undercuts the initial phase of idealised happiness with intimations that it is

---

[33] 'Kjartan and Bolli loved each other most; Kjartan never went anywhere where Bolli did not follow him. Kjartan often went to the Sælíngsdalr-baths. Each time it happened that Guðrún was at the baths.'

a sham and that his narrative will ultimately concern itself with the destruction of the idyll:

> Now most fair
> Seemed Olaf's lot in life, and scarcely worse
> Was Oswif's, and what shadow of a curse
> Might hang o'er either house, was thought of now
> As men think of a cloud the mountain's brow
> Hides from their eyes an hour before the rain. (*TEP*, II, p. 289,
> ll. 42–47)

The potential curse that lurks like a cloud behind the mountain head suggests the naivety of Morris's characters to the true precariousness of their predicament. The pleasantness of Olaf and Oswif's lives is only possible because of their partial, unenlightened perspective, but the poem's real interest will lie in '[h]ow the sky blackened, and the storm swept down' (*TEP*, II, p. 289, l. 52). In addition, Morris augments Gudrun's early vulnerability in his interpretation of the passage in *Laxdaela saga* in which Gestr Oddleifsson interprets Guðrún's dreams. In the saga, the dream prophecy serves mainly to augur the inevitability of the four marriages that will structure the rest of Guðrún's life. Though Guðrún shows signs of feeling daunted by Gestr's predictions, flushing blood red on hearing them and exclaiming somewhat imperturbably 'en mikit er til at hyggja, ef þetta alt skal eptir gánga' (*LAX*, p. 130),[34] in 'Gudrun' the burden of prophecy overtly afflicts Morris's heroine psychologically with a premonition of the bogus world that recalls Carlyle's phantasmagoria:

> the may
> From her fair face had drawn her hands away,
> And sat there with fixed eyes, and face grown pale,
> As one who sees the corner of the veil,
> That hideth strange things, lifted for a while. (*TEP*, II,
> pp. 296–97, ll. 311–15)

In suddenly becoming aware of a creeping reality behind what she imagined her life might be, Gudrun is confronted with the fabric of existence in a manner that is never true of her saga counterpart, for whom questions of ontology are absolutely alien.

Building on these premonitions of the precariousness of reality, from the beginning of Kiartan and Gudrun's love affair Morris strews

---

[34] 'There is a great deal to think on if all this happens.'

the narrative with auguries that their world is more sinister and mysterious than it appears. Whereas in *Laxdæla saga*, Kjartan's father provides
uneasy presentiments about the budding relationship – 'ei veit ek [...] hví
mér er jafnan sva hug-þungt, er þú ferr til Lauga ok talar vid Gudrúnu'
(*LAX*, p. 160)[35] – in 'Gudrun', Morris introduces a haunted aspect to the
joy that the lovers initially experience, which makes it appear ominously
unsustainable. While Kiartan sometimes feels the need to speak in jest in
order 'to free | His heart from longings grown too sweet to bear' (*TEP*, II,
p. 317, ll. 1038–39), Gudrun is tortured with 'pangs of perplexèd pain' as
she thinks 'again | On Guest and his forecasting of her dream' (*TEP*, II,
p. 315, ll. 933–35). Bodli feels a 'shadow of a shade' rise within that makes
him 'deem the world less nobly made' (*TEP*, II, p. 317, ll. 1032–34), and
later falls into musings 'So dreamlike, that he might not tell his thought |
When he again to common life was brought' (*TEP*, II, p. 317, ll. 1054–56).

In the second phase of the three-stage structure of 'Gudrun', the
initial golden time is irreparably punctured by an experience of overwhelming disillusionment when Bodli pursues his love for Gudrun, and
the marriage between Kiartan and her becomes impossible. When his
protagonists recognise the change in circumstances, each experiences
a transformation of their environment into an austere realm of disorientation and isolation. While in the early quest narratives this realm is
represented objectively as some kind of discrete wasteland, in 'Gudrun'
the characters simply endure a major alteration in their experience of
the reality in which they already find themselves. Though in several
instances Morris employs a Carlylean technique of sensory telescoping
to portray the moment when each character's world is altered, crucially,
once the protagonists see past the sham of their contentment there is
nothing but an existence of barren suffering in their current dimension.
No otherworld exists: they have simply misconceived their own until
now. No sooner, for instance, has Bodli told Gudrun that Kiartan is likely
to remain with Ingibiorg in Norway than he experiences the uncanny
alteration of the world around him:

> when he turned,
> Blind with the fire that in his worn heart burned,
> Empty the hill-side was of anyone,
> And as a man who some great crime hath done

[35] 'I do not know why I am always so heavy-spirited when you go to
Laugar to speak to Guðrún.'

> He gat into his saddle, and scarce knew
> Whither he went. (*TEP*, ii, p. 343, ll. 1960–65)

The emptiness of the hillside suggests a transformation of Bodli's surroundings, as if his sensory appreciation of the environment has adjusted to his new status as a great criminal. Through obstructing Gudrun's relationship with Kiartan, a world is revealed to him in which he is blind, lost and utterly alone. Whereas the Bolli of the Old Norse text, after mendaciously implying that Kjartan is unlikely to return home (*LAX*, pp. 182–86), shows only dispassionate determination to win Guðrún, the ambiguous sin of Morris's Bodli quickly turns him into a figure of desolation:

> dry-eyed Bodli stood,
> Pale as a corpse, and in such haggard mood,
> Such helpless, hopeless misery, as one
> Who first in hell meets her he hath undone. (*TEP*, ii, p. 345, ll.
> 2026–29)

Kiartan experiences a similarly abrupt transformation of his environment the moment he discovers that Bodli has married Gudrun, becoming sightless and confused: 'O blind, O blind, blind! | Where is the world I used to deem so kind, | So loving unto me?' (*TEP*, ii, p. 354, ll. 2534–63). The shock leads to a telescoping of his perception as his experience of the world around him alters:

> And now she called his name; he turned about,
> And far away he heard the shipmen's shout
> And beat of the sea, and from the down there came
> The bleat of ewes; and all these, and his name,
> And the sights too, the green down 'neath the sun,
> The white strand and the far-off hill-sides dun,
> And white birds wheeling, well-known things, did seem
> But pictures now or figures in a dream,
> With all their meaning lost. Yet withal
> On his vexed spirit did the new thought fall
> How weak and helpless and alone he was.
> Then gently to his sister did he pass,
> And spake: Now is the world clean changed for me
> In this last minute, yet indeed I see
> That still will it go on for all my pain. (*TEP*, ii, pp. 354–55, ll.
> 2376–90)

Here, Kiartan's idyllic rural surroundings are suddenly hollow and dreamlike. The concentrated sounds of the shipmen's shout, the beat of the sea and bleat of the ewes, coupled with visual snatches of the down, sun, strand and birds combine to create an impression of disorientation that recalls Florian's initial inkling of the Hollow Land. Once familiar objects now seem like 'pictures' or 'figures in a dream', having lost their former significance. Even Bodli has become a bogus apparition: 'shall I learn to hate thee, friend, though thou | Art changed into a shadow and a lie?' (*TEP*, II, p. 354, ll. 2364–65). Yet, Kiartan perceives no benevolent Carlylean realm beyond the world of appearance with which he can commune, only the cold blankness of the known one. In perceiving the lack of a transcendent reality after the world is 'clean changed', he still experiences a form of meaning but it is now connected to enduring the dissonant solitude of his post-idyllic life, rather than to any possibility of a new experience of serenity. This is an indifferent reality that remains unresponsive to his pain. With any benign presence entirely absent, it offers no chance of transcendence.

For Gudrun too, the discovery that Bodli has misled her leads to the transformation of her surroundings. The Guðrún of the saga suffers quietly and inwardly when she discovers that Kjartan has in fact returned from Norway, telling Bolli with understated displeasure that 'henni þótti ei hafa sér alt satt til sagt um útkvamu Kiartans' (*LAX*, pp. 192–94).[36] It is left to the narrator to suggest that 'ætludu flestir menn, at henni væri enn mikil eptir-siá at um Kiartan, þó at hún hyldi yfir' (*LAX*, p. 194).[37] However, Morris's Gudrun expresses openly the turmoil that she has experienced:

> My curse upon thee! Knowst thou how alone
> Thy deed hath made me? Dreamest thou what pain
> Burns in me now when he has come again?
> Now, when the longed-for sun has risen at last
> To light an empty world whence all has passed
> Of joy and hope? (*TEP*, II, p. 363, ll. 2689–94)

The discovery that she might have successfully waited for Kiartan trans-forms Gudrun's world into one of suffering and emptiness. Wracked with

---

[36] 'It seemed to her that he had not been entirely truthful in what he said about Kjartan's returning to Iceland.'

[37] 'Most men thought that she was still grieving for Kjartan, though she covered it up.'

pain, like Bodli and Kiartan, she is suddenly entirely alone in an existence that lacks any chance of consolation or deliverance. There is a certainty in the impossibility of progress, amelioration or recovery in this reality that it so alien to the wasteland of Morris's earlier quest narratives.

Once his protagonists have been irrevocably disillusioned, in the third phase of his three-stage structure Morris provides no equivalent of a Holy Grail. Instead, he augments the degree of his characters' torment to such an extent that their response to the fact that it is inescapable appears to become his primary subject. Bodli's suffering is portrayed through repeated allusions to imprisonment and stasis that have little foundation in *Laxdæla saga*. Where the saga gives no indication of Bolli's emotional life when Kjartan returns to Iceland, merely indicating that Guðrún and he disagree on whether or not he misled her,[38] at this point Morris's poem explicitly stresses the fact that Bodli's ordeal will continue without remedy:

> upon Bodli the last gate of hell
> Seemed shut at last, and no more like a star,
> Far off perchance, yet bright however far,
> Shone hope of better days; yet he lived on. (*TEP*, II, p. 364, ll.
> 2735–37)

Like Florian or Lawrence, Bodli now exists in a position of purgatorial confinement "twixt good and ill, 'twixt love and struggling hate, | The coming hours of restless pain to wait' (*TEP*, II, p. 364, ll. 2736–37). Unlike them, however, there is nowhere else for him to go, and no chance to make amends. Kiartan too experiences the aftermath of Bodli's marriage to Gudrun in terms of isolation and disjunction. Whereas the saga's Kjartan merely behaves *fáliga* ('coldly') (*LAX*, p. 194) on first visiting Laugar after his return from Norway, Morris's hero stands with his foster-brother 'Each knowing somewhat of the other's mood | Yet scarce the master-key thereto', while his heart grows hard '[w]ith his despair' (*TEP*, II, p. 366, ll. 2818–22). Like Bodli, Kiartan sees no escape from his predicament. We are told that his pain 'stung | Bitterer at whiles, now that he knew his life, | And hardened him to meet the lingering strife' (*TEP*, II, p. 371, ll. 3006–07). The suggestion is that he now sees this more painful existence as his reality, and one that must be endured.

Morris also greatly augments Gudrun's suffering once she has experienced disillusionment. Rejecting the aspect of the saga's Guðrún that he

---

[38] For this scene in the Old Norse text, see *LAX*, pp. 193–94.

considered to be 'the stock "stirring woman" of the north',[39] he softened her strength and resolve to make his heroine more tortured and defenceless. While, for example, the saga's Guðrún responds courageously when Bolli tells her that Kjartan may not return from Norway 'því at eins er Kiartani fullbodit, ef hann fær góda konu' (*LAX*, p. 182),[40] only briefly flushing red to betray her true feelings, her counterpart in Morris's poem reacts to the tidings with agonised vulnerability, her passion rising to her throat 'As a grey dove, within the meshes caught, | Flutters a little, then lies still again' (*TEP*, ii, p. 344, ll. 2019–20). Where the audience of the saga sees only odd glimpses into Guðrún's private emotional state, Morris portrays the arc of his heroine's emotional distress overtly. When married to Bodli, she is subject to 'changes wild' (*TEP*, ii, p. 358, l. 2507), isolated by her despair as 'a cast-away | Upon the lonely rocks of life' (*TEP*, ii, p. 374, ll. 3113–14) in a kind of limbo existence '[b]etwixt two nameless miseries torn apart' (*TEP*, ii, p. 392, l. 3783). Eventually, the pain of the loss consumes her altogether. The 'black spot in her heart' overwhelms her 'till from the foiled desire | Cast back upon her heart, there sprang a fire | Of very hate' (*TEP*, ii, p. 396, ll. 3922–30) and in the end she is transformed into a Gothic spectre:

> There in the porch a tall black figure stood,
> Whose stern pale face, 'neath its o'erhanging hood,
> In the porch shadow was all cold and grey,
> Though on her feet the dying sunlight lay.
> They trembled then at what might come to pass,
> For that grey face the face of Gudrun was,
> And they had heard her raving through the day (*TEP*, ii, p. 411,
>   ll. 4471–78).

Once Gudrun has lost Kiartan, Morris portrays her as an ensnared victim, both of a preternatural physical transformation and of the loss of her senses.

Julian has argued that Morris's dominant concern in adapting *Laxdæla saga* lay in 'the characters' reactions to the doomed friendship'.[41] Jettisoning what might be considered to be the saga's central theme (the predicament of the imperative to attain and retain honour played out in an intricate examination of the impulses that constitute feud), it is

---

[39] Letter to Bell Scott, dated 15 February 1870, in Kelvin, i, p. 110.
[40] 'Because Kjartan can only be fully matched with a good wife.'
[41] Julian, p. 358.

true that Morris appropriated the principal moment of discord (Bolli's apparent betrayal of Kjartan in pursuing Guðrún) as his catalyst for disillusionment, thereby allowing him to explore his protagonists' emotional responses to it. What Mauer calls 'a man of moods',[42] Bodli is distraught and guilt-ridden, unlike his saga counterpart who, if anything, is remarkable for his insipidity. Tormented by an inner struggle, Bodli is 'denied even the briefest enjoyment of happiness' due to 'suffering that can find no vent in action'.[43] In Julian's eyes, 'Morris intensifies the interpretation of Bodli as victim',[44] so that he can do nothing but accept his pain passively until at last he finds 'a glory in his shame, | A pride to take the whole world's bitter blame' (*TEP*, ii, p. 400, ll. 4084–85). The poem's anti-hero is chiefly a figure of paralysis and inertia. Guilty of a misplaced love for Gudrun, his one action is his crime of pursuing her. While Morris makes Bodli perhaps the most accessibly human of his protagonists (a factor that has caused some critics to compare the character with Morris himself),[45] he is basically unheroic; a casualty of circumstance who is vanquished by the reality of pain. Morris appears at once to sympathise with his fallibility but simultaneously to reprove his lack of stoicism.

Gudrun too is rendered a casualty of circumstance. A fragile victim of her first two marriages (unlike her saga counterpart who, even as she grows resentful and unhappy, remains tough and defiant), Morris's 'Gudrun of the white hands, the beautiful weary face' simply cannot manage the grief she feels.[46] Once she realises that she will not marry Kiartan she is gradually afflicted by base emotions until she is so consumed with hate that she is scared of what she will become should he not die (*TEP*, ii, p. 398, ll. 4000–01). Morris appears to be fundamentally interested in her lack of equanimity. Rejecting the strength and severity of the saga's heroine, he replaces her with a woman who is essentially at the mercy of her feelings. By contrast, Kiartan, though in many ways the least detailed character of the three, is a figure of emotional fortitude. Responding to the disaster of disillusionment with quick insight, he immediately associates the preceding period of joy with mistaken naivety: 'Now then at last thou knowest of the earth, | And why the elders look askance on mirth'

[42] Mauer, p. 432.
[43] Mauer, p. 433.
[44] Julian, p. 360.
[45] See Tompkins, p. 175; Florence Saunders Boos, 'Morris' Radical Revisions of the "Laxdaela Saga"', *Victorian Poetry*, 21 (1983), 415–20 (p. 419).
[46] Tompkins, p. 173.

(*TEP*, II, p. 354, ll. 2372–73). More so than his saga counterpart (who is ultimately compelled to defend his honour against assault), Kiartan is a paragon of magnanimity:

> In the past days, when fair and orderly
> The world before our footsteps seemed to lie,
> Now in this welter wherein we are set,
> Lonely and bare of all, deem we not yet
> That for each these ill days we have made;
> Rather the more let those good words be weighed
> We spake, when truth and love within us burned,
> Before the lesson of our life was learned.
> What say'st thou? are the days to come forgiven?
> Shall folk remember less that we have striven,
> Than that we loved, when all the tale is told? (*TEP*, II, 384–5, ll.
> 3504–14)

Kiartan sees clearly that he has passed from a time of mutual contentment to one of solitary strife. Instead of allowing this to destroy him, however, he chooses to suffer the reality of pain while holding dear the love of the former time. As Tompkins argues, Kiartan is 'a new character in Morris's work', a man who 'rallies under a blow, and makes the best of things, without illusions [...] in spite of his unforgotten love and loss'.[47] Perhaps the clearest sign that Kiartan belongs to a new breed of worldly hero in Morris's writing lies in the manner of his death when, in a physical detail entirely absent in the saga, '[i]nto his shieldless side the sword [i]s thrust' (*TEP*, II, p. 407, l. 4351): he becomes the first of the poet's Fisher King martyrs to receive the dolorous stroke in an entirely earthly realm.

Boos has emphasised the degree to which Morris dispensed with *Laxdæla saga* in composing 'Gudrun', rewriting 'a feud-narrative of property negotiations and family rivalries into an exemplum of doomed friendship and heterosexual love'.[48] In doing so, he made his poem curiously bleaker than the saga. Though his assertion that the flaws in the saga's structure meant that the 'story had never been properly told'[49] suggests that Morris saw himself as the quasi-mystical restorer of the true saga that existed beyond the text that has been handed down (akin

---

[47] Tompkins, p. 175.
[48] Boos, 'Radical Revisions', p. 415.
[49] Letter to Bell Scott, dated 15 February 1870, see this chapter, footnote 39, above.

to *Laxdæla saga*'s platonic ideal), he in fact entirely transformed it. At its core, *Laxdæla saga* weighs the forces of hostility and conciliation within an ethical system that demands honour to be upheld at any cost. Even though the complexities of this dilemma lead inevitably to feud, there is always the sense that something vital is at stake in the saga. The audience's emotional involvement with its protagonists makes compelling the ethical dilemmas that *Laxdæla saga* portrays and the deliberation of conflicting moral virtues, therefore, seems important (even if human nature makes finding a solution to them unlikely). In 'Gudrun', by contrast, Morris presents no real weighing of values. Once the sham reality has been revealed, only a kind of nihilism remains: the reader must simply witness the attempts of the protagonists to bear the pain of living in a world that is fundamentally indifferent to them. There is a peculiar bleakness in the lack of any prospect of solace, as well as the apparent futility of ethical deliberation in the world of the poem.

In transforming the feud narrative of *Laxdæla saga* while retaining the disasters that it produces, Morris rendered key parts of his plot nonsensical. Whereas the saga's Bolli, for instance, appears to betray Kjartan by stealing Guðrún in order to gain the public standing that the marriage will provide him, the crime of the poem's Bodli is far from clear. When he tells Gudrun 'Thou mayst live long, yet never see the day | That bringeth Kiartan back unto this land' (*TEP*, II, p. 342, ll. 1927–28), not only does Bodli appear to be telling her the truth, but he is immediately contrite, explaining: 'Yet they lie | Who say I did the thing, who say that I, | E'en in my inmost heart, have wished for it' (*TEP*, II, p. 342, ll. 1932–34). He, thus, seems guilty only of loving Gudrun and not entirely suppressing it. Without any real necessity to uphold honour to motivate the plot, 'Gudrun' becomes what Hoare calls 'a series of situations strung on the same chain',[50] and Morris is left to assemble what Jessie Kocmanová describes as 'moods and emotions adequate to motivate the tragic events'.[51]

Rather than reflecting the saga's technique of providing laconic external indicators of emotion that cause the audience to project strong presumptions of internal experience onto the characters, Morris articulates his protagonists' feelings with almost gratuitous displays of emotion. It is true that the emotional texture of the poem might be accounted for, at least in part, by the aestheticised design of *The Earthly Paradise* as a whole.

---

[50] Hoare, p. 67.
[51] Kocmanová, p. 86.

In writing 'Gudrun', Morris was not attempting to translate *Laxdæla saga* in the same sense as the Old Norse translations that preceded it but rather to augment his much longer and more varied poetic collection of tales whose polyphonic structure, in the words of Boos, blends 'representative voices of a single poetic consciousness [that] seeks to express something of the "remembered" range of human suffering in communal narrative form'.[52] The increased emotion of 'Gudrun' might, therefore, be understood to echo the emotionality of other tales in *The Earthly Paradise*, which, as Carole G. Silver intimates, is at its base a fugue-like work whose stories 'parallel or reverse each other as they interweave the themes of love, fate, and death in multiple patterns'.[53]

Yet, it is equally true that, even within this textual design, Morris believed 'Gudrun' to be fundamentally faithful to the authentic saga behind the extant version of *Laxdæla saga*. His Kiartan and Bodli, he asserted confidently, were 'pretty much the men that were in the old storytellers mind'.[54] Why, then, did he create characters who are capable of displaying such overt emotions when this element is simply not portrayed in the extant saga? Certain scholars have presumed that Morris brought these concealed emotions into the open for the purposes of clarity. Julian echoes May Morris's justification of her father's depiction of sentiment when she suggests that, since he 'was attuned to the emotional turmoil lying beneath the conventional restraint of the sagas', he 'attempted to make accessible to his modern audience what might have been clear to the medieval Icelanders'.[55] In this Romantic view, Morris *the Poet* intuits the saga accurately and acts as an intermediary between the intentions of the author and the needs of his audience. By contrast, Tompkins argues that the emotionality of 'Gudrun' lies in the fact that 'Morris identified with his characters and imposed his own scale of emotion on them',[56] implying a more insensitive, blinkered understanding of the source text. On balance, the fact that Morris did not see a significant disparity between his poem and what he imagined to be the original story behind the extant saga would suggest that Tompkins's view is closer to the truth.

[52] Florence Saunders Boos, *The Design of William Morris' The Earthly Paradise*, Studies in British Literature, 6 (Lewiston: Mellen, 1990), p. 368.

[53] Carole G. Silver, 'The Earthly Paradise: Lost', *Victorian Poetry*, 13 (1975), 27–42 (p. 32).

[54] Letter to Bell Scott, dated 15 February 1870, see this chapter, footnote 39, above.

[55] Julian, p. 363.

[56] Tompkins, p. 173.

While Morris may not have identified personally with the saga characters in terms of seeing himself in them, it was their implicit emotional
reactions to their gruelling circumstances that particularly appealed to
him. He, therefore, amplified their responses, so that his theme became
something like the adoption of the wisest possible attitude to enduring
the torture of authentic earthly existence.

Those critics who have linked the uncommon emotional starkness
of 'Gudrun' to a period of disillusionment in Morris's life have often
compared the protagonists to him, Jane Morris and Rossetti. Such associations soon fall down, however, when one attempts to match fictional
character to living person. If anything, Morris's sympathies in 'Gudrun' lie
with the seducer (Bodli) rather than the cuckold (Kiartan), casting doubt
on the possibility that he was attempting to portray his own situation
indirectly via the Norse love triangle. It should also be remembered that
in stories such as 'Gertha's Lovers', written for *The Oxford & Cambridge
Magazine* (1856), Morris had chosen to write about a love triangle before
he and Jane had even met one another. Kocmanová, strongly rejecting
E. P. Thompson's contention that *The Earthly Paradise* was written in an
atmosphere of despair, which she counters was rather a positive, outward-
looking enterprise composed in 'an atmosphere of collective interest',[57]
argues that the new tone of 'Gudrun' was primarily due to the fact that at
this time Morris 'was gradually shedding all adhesion to Christian or religious ideology of any kind'.[58] Deeming his 'choice of the North' decisive
'not only for his poetic method [...] but for his entire world outlook', she
considers the nascent ideology of 'Gudrun' to mark the 'moment in [his]
poetry which crystallises his turn from romance to reality', inextricably
'bound up not only with his developing view of society, but also with his
progressive working-out of an atheist philosophy'.[59] For Kocmanová, the
shift away from the grail quest is, thus, connected to the disappearance
of Morris's belief in a deity: 'He could scarcely have introduced the Grail
legends without treating Christian themes in which he was no longer
interested.'[60] As his 'conception of the heroic developed', in Kocmanová's view, he 'cast out the medieval conception of the individual quest for

[57]   Kocmanová, pp. 11–12.
[58]   Kocmanová, p. 61.
[59]   Kocmanová, p. 80.
[60]   Kocmanová, p. 21.

happiness or fulfilment, and adopted as his heroes those [...] who voiced the heroic aspirations of the people'.[61]

It is difficult to pinpoint exactly when Morris lost his faith in God. Though Kocmanová looks to the late 1860s, scholars such as Fiona MacCarthy and Helen Timo have suggested that he was already an atheist by the time he wrote for *The Oxford & Cambridge Magazine*.[62] Lack of evidence makes it pointless to push for a conclusion to this speculation. Where Kocmanová is certainly right, however, is that 'Gudrun' marks a development in Morris's outlook towards a new worldview; one based on the here and now in a world from which God is most definitely absent. It is not inevitable that the difficulties in Morris's marriage were integral to this development. In his early twenties in the mid-1850s, he began to explore the possibility of surmounting earthly struggle with quests of Arthurian transcendence. However, at some point in the 1860s, the promise of mystical liberation that underlay Carlyle's belief in 'an Eternal living God, who owns and rules the world' finally disappointed him.[63] Inspired in the second half of 1868 by beginning to work with Eiríkur Magnússon, only a few months later in the spring of 1869 Morris drew on the apparent verisimilitude of the protagonists' resolve to structure 'Gudrun' as a three-stage romance-like narrative that possessed no potential for the unearthly. In the place of Carlylean transcendence lay the beginnings of a humbler (though, in Morris's view, perhaps more heroic) ideology in which the hero aspires to confront difficulty as tenaciously and honestly as possible, making the most of the worldly circumstances in which he finds himself. This was not yet a transformation, as Kocmanová has it, between a quest for individual fulfilment and one for the good of the community (which would come later in the 'late' romances, see Chapter 6, pp. 166–67), but rather between a quest for the unearthly and the earthly.[64] Now drawn to probing the hero's response to a universe in which, as Robert Wahl observes, the human spirit has been

---

[61] Kocmanová, p. 10.

[62] *LOT*, pp. 83–85; Helen Timo, 'A Church without God: William Morris's "A Night in a Cathedral"', *The Journal of the William Morris Society*, 4.2 (1980), 24–31 (pp. 24–30).

[63] Vernon Lushington, 'Carlyle: Chapt. 1 – His "I Believe"', *The Oxford & Cambridge Magazine, Conducted by Members of the Two Universities*, April 1856, 193–211 (p. 194).

[64] Kocmanová, p. 10.

'thrown back on its own resources with no God to aid it',[65] Morris wrote 'Gudrun' at a time when he was effectively in search of a consolation for the loss of the grail of transcendence. He found that consolation in a new ideal of heroism that the Icelandic sagas helped him to cultivate.

---

[65] Robert Wahl, 'The Mood of Energy and the Mood of Idleness: A Note on "The Earthly Paradise"', *English Studies in Africa*, 2 (1959), 90–97 (p. 96).

2

The Sagas of Icelanders and the
Transmutation of Shame

S CHOLARS WHO HAVE considered the importance of the Icelandic
sagas to Morris have frequently acknowledged that his engagement
with Old Norse literature was connected to a personal sense of what
it meant to be heroic. MacCarthy has asserted that he 'looked on himself
as a quasi-saga hero', personally identifying with the 'defiant spirit and
unflinching sense of duty of the warriors he read about' (*LOT*, p. 291),
while Calder has suggested that 'Morris seems to have felt the need of
learning to accept the painful realities of life in the courageous spirit
of the men and women of the sagas' (Introduction to *SoK*, p. 11). Even
Eiríkur Magnússon stressed the affinity between the outlook of the saga
heroes and his collaborator: 'he found on every page an echo of his own
buoyant, somewhat masterful mind' (Preface to TSL, 6, p. xiv).

Though it is evident that Morris found the heroes of Old Norse literature inspiring, what has been less clearly recognised is the extent to which
the portrayal of heroism in the sagas differs from what Morris thought
he saw in them. In the previous chapter, I showed how, in 'Gudrun',
he altered the impulse for feud depicted in *Laxdæla saga*, resulting in
the motivations and virtues of his characters becoming fundamentally
different from those of their saga counterparts. Yet, even in his translations, which he attempted to render as literally as possible, Morris
distorted the portrayal of the Icelandic heroes by attenuating conduct
that might appear ruthless, coarse or brutal. This chapter examines this
distortion, considering in particular how Morris transformed the perfor-
mance of masculinity in his translations, and especially how he altered
the representation of *níð*: a form of institutionalised shaming that is regularly portrayed in the sagas but also existed in medieval Iceland itself.
It considers what kind of hero Morris wanted to depict, and concludes
that his desire to liberate the ethos of the sagas for his own time made
it necessary for him to universalise the conception of honour that they

portray in order to bring Icelandic morality and his own developing ideal of heroism closer together. While contemporary legislation no doubt restricted his freedom to depict the obscene, to some extent, Morris's devotion to the saga heroes and desire that his audience might appreciate their virtues blinded him to what is inhumane in them. His devotion caused him to perceive a greater affinity than really existed between the sagas' definition of heroic manliness and his own.

Competition between men and the maintenance of masculinity is fundamental to the world portrayed in the sagas of Icelanders. Indeed, the compulsion for male characters to maintain their manliness (which constitutes a crucial component of high social standing) frequently propels the feuds that make many of their plots so distinctive. As Preben Meulengracht Sørensen has stated: 'In the world of the sagas nothing hits a man harder than the allegation that he is no man.'[1] Carol Clover has demonstrated that a primary cause of the struggle for manliness in these narratives lies in the volatility of the maleness that they portray. Instead of being simply based on a biological binary of gender, Clover suggests that maleness in the saga world is based on a character's ability to be deemed *hvatr* ('bold, active, vigorous' in relation to people, and 'male' in relation to an animal) as opposed to *blauðr* ('soft, weak' in relation to people, and 'female' in relation to an animal).[2] Since these categories are based on factors that are largely variable (strength, vitality and conduct, for example) manliness can be won and lost: 'The frantic machismo of Norse males [...] would seem on the face of it to suggest a society in which being born male precisely did *not* confer automatic superiority, a society in which distinction had to be acquired, and constantly reacquired, by wresting it away from others.'[3]

In highlighting the frenetic contest inherent in the male characters' pursuit of masculinity, Clover calls attention to their vulnerability. If the status system is akin to a kind of market economy in which distinction is a finite commodity, one man must lose what another gains. The social standing of the most prominent characters is, thus, incessantly under threat, running on a 'fault line' between 'able-bodied men (and

---

[1] Preben Meulengracht Sørensen, *The Unmanly Man: Concepts of Sexual Defamation in Early Northern Society*, The Viking Collection, 1 (Odense: Odense University Press, 1983), p. 11.

[2] Carol J. Clover, 'Regardless of Sex: Men, Women, and Power in Early Northern Europe', *Speculum*, 68 (1993), 363–87 (pp. 363–65).

[3] Clover, p. 380.

the exceptional woman) on the one hand and, on the other, a kind of rainbow coalition of everyone else (most women, children, slaves, and old, disabled and otherwise disenfranchised men)'.[4]

Central to the competition for masculinity in the sagas of Icelanders is the social institution known as *níð*. Essentially meaning 'libel' or 'slander', *níð* comprises a number of formalised practices that publicly malign their victim in a manner that, if not adequately avenged, is wholly devastating to his social standing. As well as appearing in the sagas, provision is made for these practices in the collection of laws that survive from early Iceland known as *Grágás*, which Morris owned in the 1829 Copenhagen edition that includes a parallel Latin translation.[5] The law treats the consequences of defamatory language in considerable detail, including mockery, exaggeration and *níð*-verse, in which the victim was insulted in especially composed slander poetry. It also details the customs of erecting *tré-níð* ('timber' or 'wood' níð) and a *níðstöng* ('níð-pole'): the former being a carved wooden depiction of the victim in an obscene sexual or otherwise slanderous position; and the latter involving the erection of a pole displaying a mare's head that had the effect of ridiculing the intended target (*GRÁ*, II, pp. 147–52).

Closely associated with *níð* in both *Grágás* and the sagas themselves are three defamatory words for which the law stated the victim had the right to kill if slandered with them: 'ef maþr kallar mann ragan eþr stroþinn eþr sorþinn, oc scal sva sökia, sem önnor fullrettis orþ, enda a maþr vigt i gegn þeim orþum þrimr' (*GRÁ*, II, p. 147).[6] Of the three words, *stroðinn* and *sorðinn* are the least ambiguous. In his dictionary of 1874 Guðbrandur Vigfússon explains that they are the past participles of the verbs *streða* and *serða* (*streða* is a metathesised from of *serða*), which he defines rather coyly as meaning: '*struprare*, with the notion of Sodomitic practices'.[7] Since the words imply that the man has been the passive partner in homosexual sex, in the twenty-first century they can only

[4] Ibid.

[5] Morris and Morris, 'Partial Catalogue (1876)', p. 20; 'Catalogue (1898)', p. 48.

[6] 'If a man calls a man *ragr* or *stroðinn* or *sorðinn*, then these shall also be prosecuted like other words for which full atonement is due, in such cases a man may kill for these three words.'

[7] Richard Cleasby and Gudbrand Vigfusson, *An Icelandic–English Dictionary* (Oxford: Clarendon Press, 1874), p. 523. The 1876 partial catalogue of Morris's library makes it clear that he owned the 1874 dictionary by the time the catalogue was created. See Morris and Morris, 'Partial Catalogue (1876)', p. 20.

effectively be translated into English as 'fucked'. The other word *ragr* is harder to translate. Guðbrandur initially suggests 'craven' and 'cowardly', but goes on to clarify that it is equivalent to saying 'that a man is a woman (blauðr)', which is 'the gravest abuse in the language'.[8] Meulengracht Sørensen asserts that the adjective signifies 'a quality or tendency' in a man who was 'willing or inclined' to be *stroðinn*,[9] while Folke Ström goes as far as stating that a *ragr* man was 'a coward and a homosexual'.[10] Ultimately, the word came to comprise a complex of highly offensive taboos connected to unmanliness that blurred the boundary between physical and moral degeneracy.[11]

In addition to these words, an act of violence that brought together the slander of *níð* and the intimation that a man was *ragr* in early Iceland and the sagas was the *klámhögg* ('shame-blow'):

> Þat metz sem hin meiri sar, ef maþr scerr tungo or höfþi manni, eþr stingr augo or höfþi, eþr scerr af mann nef, eþr eyro, eþr brytr tenn or höfþi manni. En þa er scorit, er skeddr beini eþr briosci. Sva er oc ef maþr geldir mann eþr höggr klamhögg um þio þver. (*GRÁ*, II, pp. 11–12)[12]

As William Ian Miller has clarified, 'the shame-stroke was the intentional stabbing or cutting of a man's buttocks and the shame of the stroke was clearly the shame of being sodomized'.[13] While the shame-blow across the buttocks is portrayed explicitly in the sagas, other acts of aggression that violate the physical modesty of a character, or otherwise constrain them in such a way that they are humiliated, also appear to convey an extreme degree of shame.[14] In chapter 53 of *Njáls saga*, for example, Gunnarr of Hlíðarendi ultimately kills Otkell Skarfsson for grazing his face with a spur and, in chapter 47 of *Laxdæla saga*, Ósvífr's sons find Kjartan's confining them indoors – so that they cannot use the privy

---

[8] Cleasby and Vigfusson, p. 481.

[9] Meulengracht Sørensen, p. 18.

[10] Folke Ström, *Níð, Ergi and Old Norse Moral Attitudes*, The Dorothea Coke Memorial Lecture in Northern Studies (London: Viking Society for Northern Research, 1974), p. 4.

[11] Meulengracht Sørensen, pp. 18–20.

[12] 'It counts as a major wound if a man cuts the tongue out of the head of a man or pokes the eyes out of the head, or cuts off a man's nose, or ears, or knocks the teeth out of a man's head. Also, when a cut catches bone or gristle. So is it too when a man gelds a man or strikes a shame-blow across the buttocks.'

[13] William Ian Miller, *Bloodtaking and Peacemaking: Feud, Law, and Society in Saga Iceland* (Chicago: University of Chicago Press, 1990), p. 63.

[14] See Meulengracht Sørensen, pp. 67–70.

– more humiliating than if one of them had been killed (see this chapter, p. 66, below).

While it is impossible to know how closely Morris knew any particular passage of *Grágás*, instances of *níð* and its associated practices are so central to many of the sagas he translated that it is probable that he and Eiríkur discussed the phenomenon during the course of their work together. The practice of composing *níð*-verse is explained explicitly in chapter 33 of *Saga Óláfs Tryggvasonar*, which Morris translated as chapter 36 of *The Story of Olaf Tryggvison*, and a graphic depiction of *tré-níð* appears in *Bjarnar saga Hítdœlakappa*, which Morris remembered so well that he amazed Eiríkur by narrating the whole saga from memory one evening on the Iceland trip of 1871 (Preface to TSL, 6, pp. x–xi). Additionally, Morris could have used the parallel Latin translation in his edition of *Grágás* to help him with the Old Norse if he read it without Eiríkur, and he was well-enough acquainted with the legal system of the medieval Icelanders to claim in the introduction to The Saga Library that 'their ancient laws, of which they have full record, were nearly the same as those under which the freemen of Kent and Wessex lived' (Preface to TSL, 1, pp. v–vi). In the same introduction he lists *Grágás* amongst 'other important works that do not come within the scope of the Saga Library' (Preface to TSL, 1, p. xii).

In his translations, Morris generally treats episodes comprising *níð* in one of two ways. Often (especially when the implication of the act of shaming is obscene) he blurs the detail of the event, so that it becomes unclear exactly what is happening. On other occasions he explicitly ennobles the behaviour associated with the intention to humiliate, so that his characters engage in less brutal conduct. In the passage in chapter 12 of his translation of *Kormáks saga,* for example, in which Kormákr's rival Bersi fights a duel against Kormákr's uncle Steinarr Önundarson, Morris blurs the humiliation associated with the *klámhögg* ('shame-blow') that Steinarr deals Bersi:

> Kormákr brá upp skildinum, í því hjó Steinarr til Bersa ok kom á skjaldar röndina, ok ljóp af skildinum ok á þjóhnappa Bersa, ok rendi ofan eptir lærunum í knèsbætur, svâ at sverðit stóð í beini ok fèll Bersi. (*KOR*, p. 120)[15]

---

[15] 'Kormákr lifted the shield up, and at this Steinarr struck at Bersi and hit the rim of his shield, and slid off the shield onto Bersi's buttocks and ran down over his thighs to the hollows of his knees, so that the sword stuck in the bone and Bersi fell.'

Morris translates this passage as:

> Kormak threw up the shield, and even therewithal, Steinar smote Bersi on
> the boss of the shield, and the sword glanced there from on to Bersi's loins,
> and cut down along the thigh into the back of the knee so that it smote into
> the bone; and therewith Bersi fell. (*SoK*, p. 103)

Morris's decision to translate the word *þjóknappar* (literally 'thigh-knobs'
but meaning 'buttocks') as 'loins' veils the specific anatomical detail that
makes the injury so shameful to Bersi. In the Old Norse text, Steinarr's
response to the blow 'nú er goldit fèit fyrir Kormak' (*KOR*, p. 120)[16]
demonstrates that he considers the humiliation of the injury adequate
compensation for Bersi's previous dishonouring of Kormákr, with the
implication being that Bersi is effectively repaying his opponents with
a transaction of shame. In Morris's translation, however, he distorts the
clarity of this shame transaction by obscuring the body part in question,
so that Steinar's retort of 'So is Kormak's money paid!' (*SoK*, p. 103) makes
less obvious sense. The choice of 'loins' suggests a certain propriety,
creating a somewhat elevated tone: in *Paradise Lost*, for instance, the
narrator explains that the angel Raphael's wings 'round | Skirted his loins
and thighs with downy gold | And colours dipt in Heav'n' [v. 281–83]).
The lack of anatomical clarity in Morris's translation, coupled with the
more dignified vocabulary, mask the base motivation of the characters in
the Old Norse text, rendering them more humane. Morris appears here
to want to avoid a conception of masculinity that is capable of brutality.

The entire subsequent episode in Morris's translation of *Kormáks saga*,
in which Bersi's wife Steingerðr becomes so disgusted with him that she
declares herself divorced, is now blurred by the fact that the detail of the
body part and the associated ridicule of the blow have been distorted:

> Við þessa atburði lagði Steingerðr leiðindi á við Bersa, ok vill skilja við
> hann; ok er hún er búin til brottfarar, gengr hún at Bersa ok mælti: fyrst
> vartu kallaðr Eyglu-Bersi, þá Hólmgaungu-Bersi, en nú máttu at sönnu
> heita Rassa-Bersi. (*KOR*, pp. 132–34)[17]

Morris translates this passage as:

---

[16] 'Now the money is paid for Kormákr.'
[17] 'Because of these events Steingerðr began to hate Bersi and wanted to
divorce him; and when she was ready to leave, she went to Bersi and said: "first
you were known as Bleary-eyed Bersi, then as Dueller-Bersi, but now you may
truthfully be called Arse-Bersi".'

> But because of these matters grew Steingerd to loath Bersi, and will depart from him: and when she was ready for going she came to Bersi, and said to him: 'First wert thou called Bersi Blackbrow; and then Holmgang Bersi; but now forsooth, mightest though well be called even Buttocks Bersi. (*SoK*, p. 105)

In the Old Norse text, it is clear that Steingerðr's disdain for Bersi relates directly to the derision caused by the unmanly nature of the injury. In his translation, however, Morris muddies the strength of the two most significant words in this passage, with the result that it is not clear exactly what Steingerd is determining to do or her reasons for it. By translating *skilja við* (here 'divorce' but literally to 'separate' or 'divide from') as 'depart from', and the insult *Raza-Bersi* ('Arse-Bersi') as 'Buttocks Bersi', Morris makes less distinct Steingerðr's decision to end her marriage because the injury has caused her husband to become such a laughing stock. While it is arguable that in translating *skilja við* as 'depart from' he was simply following his usual practice of opting for a literal choice (even though it is clear here that Steingerðr means to divorce Bersi), in the case of 'Buttocks Bersi' he may have purposefully avoided translating literally. It seems improbable that, with his hound-like scent for cognate words (see Chapter 4, pp. 119–20), Morris did not recognise *rass* as a metathesised form of Old Norse *ars* (a cognate of Modern English 'arse'), which, in late nineteenth-century Britain, was both an anatomical term for the posterior of an animal[18] and a vulgar word for a man's bottom, used in colloquial phrases such as 'hang an arse', meaning *hesitate* or *hold back*.[19] While it is probable that Morris liked the invigorating alliteration that the choice of 'Buttocks Bersi' provided his translation, it is also possible that he wished to lessen the degree of crudeness that *Arse-Bersi* would have evoked and, in doing so, preserve some of the character's dignity. Morris's propensity to cloud the significance of the shame-blow overall disturbs the moral foundation of the saga. By curbing the propensity for ferocity in the men of the sagas of Icelanders, Morris fundamentally interferes with the shaming ethos that is vital to the motivation of their plots, without introducing a fully coherent alternative ethos.

A similar distortion of the shame culture occurs in Morris's translation

---

[18] See Noah Webster, *A Complete Dictionary of the English Language*, rev. C. A. Goodrich and N. Porter, (London: Bell and Daldy, 1865), p. 77; *Chambers's English Dictionary*, ed. James Donald (London: Chambers, 1872) p. 45.

[19] See 'hang, v.', *OED Online*, Oxford University Press, March 2017 [accessed 25 April 2017].

of 'Þorsteins þáttr stangarhöggs' ('The Tale of Thorstein Staff-Smitten'), in which he blurs the particular associations that relate to a man being *ragr*. Early in the *þáttr* the hero Þorsteinn is involved in a horse-fight in which he is struck on the eyebrow by his opponent's horse-staff, causing the skin to hang down over his eye. To avoid an escalation of violence, he eschews vengeance by bandaging his forehead and pretending the blow was an accident. The community considers his forbearance dishonourable and he is branded with the humiliating nickname that gives the tale its title: 'Þeir Þorvaldr ok Þórhallr höfðu þetta fyrir kalsi, ok kölluðu hann Þorstein stangarhögg' (ÞOR, p. 49).[20] As Miller has indicated, the incendiary derision of *stangarhögg* (literally 'blow-with-a-pole') derives from its similarity to the *klámhögg* ('shame-blow').[21] The fact that Þorsteinn's father Þórarinn labels his son *ragr* when he learns of the incident demonstrates that he considers the violation to the eyebrow as shameful as a blow across the buttocks: 'Eigi mundi mik þess vara, at ek mynda ragan son eiga' (ÞOR, p. 49),[22] which Morris translates as: 'I should not have thought it, that I could have a faint-heart for a son' (*CW*, x, p. 152).

The English insult that Morris chooses is not loaded with the same degree of deviancy as the word *ragr*. To be labelled faint-hearted in late nineteenth-century Britain implied physical cowardice and even some degree of effeminacy. A contemporary dictionary definition of the term reads 'Wanting in courage; depressed by fear; easily discouraged or frightened; cowardly; timorous; dejected'.[23] However, being a faint-heart did not suggest the quality of sexual degeneracy implied by the Old Norse word that was inherent in other English words available to Morris, such as 'nancy' or 'molly'.[24] While it is difficult to compare degrees of shamefulness between medieval Iceland and Victorian Britain, at the time that Morris was translating, two men engaging in sexual intercourse was

---

[20] 'Both Þorvaldr and Þórhallr made a mockery of this and called him Þorsteinn "Staff-Struck".'

[21] Miller, p. 63.

[22] 'I never thought I would have a son who was *ragr*.'

[23] Webster, p. 491. Contemporary synonyms meaning 'Excess of fear' include 'Cowardice, pusillanimity, cowardliness, timidity, fearfulness, spiritlessness, faint-heartedness, softness, effeminacy', as well as 'Poltroonery, baseness, dastardness, dastardy, Dutch courage, the white feather, a faint heart', Peter Mark Roget, *Thesaurus of English Words and Phrases*, 1st edn (London: Longman, Brown, Green and Longmans, 1852), pp. 211–12.

[24] See 'molly, n.1', '†Miss Molly, n.', 'nancy, n. and adj.', 'Miss Nancy, n.', *OED Online*, Oxford University Press, March 2017 [accessed 25 April 2017].

not only commonly deemed unspeakably disgraceful, it was illegal. Sex between men had only ceased to carry the death penalty in England and Wales in 1836, and from 1861 onwards carried a sentence of hard labour of between ten years and life.[25] If Morris was looking for a term that conveyed the grievous implications of being labelled *ragr* in medieval Iceland, one that could critically threaten a man's public standing and even justify him in killing his accuser, it seems that those words available to him that implied homosexuality (or simply having engaged in sexual degeneracy with another man) were closer than those that suggested only physical timidity. That he chose to use words that conveyed timidity alone means that where honour is quite literally a matter of life and death in the sagas of Icelanders, for Morris's translated heroes it became more of an issue of personal mettle.

Later in his translation of 'Þorsteins þáttr stangarhöggs', Morris further mitigates the horror of what it would have meant for a medieval Icelandic father to have a son who was *ragr* at the moment that Þórarinn instructs Þorsteinn to fight his enemy Bjarni:

> tak nú vápn þín, ok ver þik sem sköruligast, því at þar mundi verit hafa minnar æfi; at eigi munda ek bograt hafa fyrir slíkum, sem Bjarni er; er Bjarni þó hinn mesti kappi, þykkir mèr ok betra at missa þín, enn eiga ragan son. (ÞOR, p. 53)[26]

Morris translates this passage as:

> so take thy weapons and do thy manliest. Time has been when I would not have budged before such as Biarni: yet is he the greatest of champions. Now would I rather lose thee than have a coward son. (*CW*, x, p. 156)

Morris's choice of 'budged' for *bograt* (which has the sense of 'bowed' or 'bent over' in Old Norse) entirely avoids the intimation that Þorsteinn avoiding the fight would be equivalent to assuming the passive role in homosexual sex. While the choice of 'coward' here to translate *ragr* might imply a stronger degree of public condemnation than 'faint-heart' (and indeed it was the choice of Gwyn Jones in his 1961 translation, and of

---

[25] Jeffrey Weeks, *Coming Out: Homosexual Politics in Britain, from the Nineteenth Century to the Present* (London: Quartet, 1977), pp. 13–14.

[26] 'Now take your weapons and defend yourself at your bravest, because there was a time when I would not have bent over in front of the likes of Bjarni; even though Bjarni is a great champion, it seems better to me to lose you than to have a *ragr* son.'

Anthony Maxwell in his 1997 translation),[27] the fact that Morris does not explicitly invoke any sexual connotations in Thorstein's father's words again brings the conception of cowardice in Morris's tale closer to feebleness than perversion.[28] Unmanliness in the world of Morris's translations seems to be synonymous with deficient fortitude, rather than moral indecency.

By consistently blurring the coarseness of the humiliations associated with the shame culture, but simultaneously retaining the strong emotional responses to it, Morris renders his characters high-flown and affected. This impression is exacerbated by his tendency to choose literal translations at the most local level, without seeming to consider the fact that a more idiomatic rendering of the phrase as a whole might portray the nuance of the characters' motivation more clearly (see, for example, the difference between Steingerd *divorcing* or *departing from* Bersi in this chapter, on p. 59, above). Morris's versions of the sagas of Icelanders are deprived of the impact of their sources because their plots cease to be impelled by coherent ethical motivation. Where the narratives of the Old Norse texts are overtly propelled by the avoidance of shame and maintenance of public standing that Clover describes, Morris's more dignified translations no longer have this frantic struggle for masculinity at their centre. Even though, as I show later in this chapter, on pp. 73–75, below, it was necessary for Morris to blur obscene material in order to avoid prosecution. Nevertheless, his apparently wider desire to prevent his heroes from appearing to be governed by boorish or primitive impulses resulted in him undermining the clarity of the ethical struggle that impels the medieval Icelandic narratives.

Morris's inclination to portray his saga heroes as more dignified than they might appear in the Old Norse texts is also evident in the moments in his translations and poems when he actively ennobles depictions of *níð* and its associated insults, rather than simply blurring them. In this process of ennoblement, it is possible to discern his preferred view of

[27] 'Thorstein Staff-struck', in *Eirik the Red and Other Icelandic Sagas*, trans. Gwyn Jones (Oxford: Oxford University Press, 1961), pp. 78–88 (p. 84); 'The Tale of Thorstein Staff-struck', trans. Anthony Maxwell, in *The Sagas of Icelanders: A Selection* (London: Penguin, 2001), pp. 677–84 (p. 681).

[28] A contemporary dictionary definition of 'coward' reads 'A person who lacks courage to meet danger; a timid or pusillanimous man; a poltroon', Webster, p. 306. Contemporary synonyms for the word include 'poltroon', 'dastard', 'recreant', 'shy-cock', 'dunghill-cock', 'milksop', 'white liver' and 'nidget', (none of which connote sexual deviancy), Roget, p. 212.

masculinity. In his translation of *Gunnlaugs saga*, for example, the nuance of the passage in which Gunnlaug stumbles onto a group of men mocking his ability to fight his rival Raven implies that their contempt is for the weakness of the rivals' blows, rather than any intrinsic effeminacy in not adequately attacking one another:

> ok á völlum fyri þeim var mannhríngr, ok í hrínginum innan voru ii menn með vapnum, ok skylmdust; var þar annarr nefndr Hrafn, en annarr Gunnlaugr. Þeir mæltu, er hjá stóðu, at Íslendingar hyggi smátt, ok væri seinir til at muna orð sín. Gunnlaugr fann, at hèr fylgði mikit háð, ok hèr var mikit spott at dregit, ok gekk Gunnlaugr í brott þegjandi. (*GUN*, p. 265)²⁹

Morris translates this passage as:

> on the meads before them they saw a ring of men, and in that ring there were two men with weapons fencing; but one was named Raven, the other Gunnlaug, while they who stood by said the Icelanders smote light, and were slow to remember their words. Gunnlaug saw the great mocking hereunder, and much jeering was brought into play; and withal he went away silent. (*CW*, x, p. 41)

Though Morris's translation follows the Old Norse text reasonably closely, the sense of 'smote light' evokes enfeebled Arthurian gallantry, rather than aggressive Icelandic derision. The choice of 'meads', 'fencing' and the fact that the jeering is 'brought into play' suggests something more like a romanticised tournament than the fierce display of communal scorn associated with *níð*. Morris's translation censures the lack of physical determination in his heroes but stops short of ridiculing their fundamental nature. Again, in his rendering, personal fortitude is emphasised as masculine over the enjoyment of high reputation in the eyes of the community.

This more courtly quality in Morris's presentation of *níð* is particularly apparent in the almost 240-line section of 'The Lovers of Gudrun' entitled 'Kiartan fetches the Price of the Coif'. In this passage he adapts

---

²⁹ 'And in the fields in front of them was a ring of men and inside the ring were two men with weapons fencing each other; one of them there was named Hrafn, and the other Gunnlaugr. The people standing by said that the Icelanders were striking blows lightly and were slow to remember their vows. Gunnlaugr sensed that there was great scoffing here and he was being made a mockery, and he went away silently.'

the brief episode in *Laxdæla saga* in which Kjartan shames the Laugar men by laying siege to the household so that they are forced to defecate indoors for three days:

> Eptir jól um vetrinn safnar Kiartan at sér mönnum, urdu þeir saman LX manna; ecki sagdi Kiartan födur sínum hversu af-stódst um ferd þessa; spurdi Olafr ok lítt at. Kiartan hafdi med sér tiöld ok vistir; rídr Kiartan nú leid sína þar til er hann kemr til Lauga. Hann bidr menn stíga af baki ok mælti, at sumir skyldu geyma hesta þeirra, en suma bidr hann reisa tiöld. I þann tíma var þat mikil tízka, at úti var salerni ok ei allskamt frá bænum, ok sva var at Laugum. Kjartan lét þar taka dyrr allar á húsum ok bannadi öllum mönnum útgöngu, ok dreitti þau inni III nætr. (*LAX*, p. 208)[30]

In his version of this episode, Morris transforms the crude expedition of physical humiliation into what Kocmanová describes as 'a chivalric piece out of Froissart',[31] in which Kiartan and his retinue take livestock from the Bathstead men as payment for the theft of the 'coif' (a word that itself evokes Middle English or Old French literary genres). Morris makes the paraphernalia of Kiartan's men vaguely knightly. They go to Bathstead clad in gallant 'war-array' (*TEP*, II, p. 389, l. 3679) and Kiartan in 'the best war-gear' (*TEP*, II, p. 389, l. 3685). The tents mentioned in the saga (which are presumably simply practical make-shift shelters to provide somewhere to sleep for the three days of the siege) become more like marquees at a tourney. The 'laugh and song' that the glowering Bathstead men hear 'mingled with the clank | Of mead-horns' (*TEP*, II, p. 392, ll. 3787–89) presumably comes from inside the 'gay-striped tent | Just raised upon the slope-side 'gainst the hall' (*TEP*, II, p. 391, ll. 3725–56), as the cattle-raiders enjoy a courtly feast.

To a large degree, the romanticism of this episode can be explained by the aestheticised story-world conception of *The Earthly Paradise*, in which, as I mentioned in Chapter 1, the myriad threads of tales and

---

[30] 'After Yule that winter Kjartan gathered men together until there were sixty of them. Kjartan did not tell his father anything about the journey and Óláfr asked little about it. Kjartan took with him tents and provisions. Kjartan now rode the way there until he came to Laugar. He told his men to dismount and said that some should watch the horses and asked others to put up the tents. At that time, it was mainly the custom that the privy was outside and not far from the farmhouse, and so it was at Laugar. Kjartan had all the doors of the house guarded and prevented anyone from leaving, and they were forced to relieve themselves indoors for three nights.'

[31] Kocmanová, p. 90.

frame-narratives are interwoven into an opulent transcultural tapestry (see Chapter 1, pp. 48–49). The rich allure of the raiders' array reflects the sensuous texture of the tales that immediately precede 'Gudrun': 'The Man Who Never Laughed Again' and 'The Story of Rhodope'. Nevertheless, it remains true that the transformation of the *níð* element in 'Gudrun' is consistent with Morris's wider tendency to transmute shaming behaviour in his saga translations. Despite the fact that, as I also discussed in Chapter 1, 'Gudrun' is not a translation in the same sense as those made with Eiríkur Magnússon, Morris believed that he was faithfully portraying the character of Kiartan as he stood in the original saga (see Chapter 1, p. 49). This raises the question of whether Morris, in his decision to portray Kjartan in the more magnanimous act of taking cattle, essentially misunderstood – or otherwise chose to discount – Kjartan's potential for brutality.

In Morris's more civilised rendering, the saga's transaction of shame becomes a transaction of material value, introducing a courteous atmosphere of fair exchange:

> Come ye not forth
> Until I bid you, if of any worth
> Ye hold your lives; and meantime for the sake
> Of what I had and have not, I will take
> My due from mead and byre. (*TEP*, ii, p. 391, ll. 3760–64)

Morris transforms the ethos of the saga from one in which shame is paid for with an equivalent retributive and public act of shaming to one in which the theft of the coif has a price that is intrinsic to the crime itself (and can, thus, be repaid justly according to its inherent moral value). The humiliation associated with the incident becomes more abstract in 'Gudrun', and Kiartan's moral outlook is romanticised so that his cattle raid becomes something more like an expedition of decorous justice than of competitive hostility: 'From Yule till now I gave you, a long day, | To pay the debt that needs was ye must pay' (*TEP*, ii, p. 394, ll. 3849–52). The closest Kiartan comes to gratuitously punitive behaviour is to suggest to the Bathstead men that in taking twice the worth of the coif in cattle he has left them a wedding present of shame for Bodli and Gudrun's marriage:

> This is my bridal gift, think well of it;
> In your own fields it waxed, while ye did sit
> Plotting across the meadhorns. (*TEP*, ii, pp. 394, 3854–56)

Despite this, the hint here that Kiartan is partly motivated by regret at Gudrun and Bodli's marriage softens his aggression. Unlike his saga counterpart, Kiartan may not simply be retaliating for the theft of the headdress but responding to the pain of a lost love.

In *Laxdæla saga*, it is evident from the response of Guðrún and her brothers that Kjartan's action at this point in the narrative is profoundly degrading. The saga states that 'Þeim Lauga-mönnum [...] þótti þetta miklu meiri svívirðíng ok verri, enn þótt Kiartan hefdi drepit mann eda II fyrir þeim',[32] and indeed the incident leads to open hostility between the households: 'Gerist nú fullkominn fiandskapr milli Lauga-manna ok Hiardhyltínga' (*LAX*, p. 210).[33] In Morris's poem, however, the victims of Kiartan's raid experience only a dreamy impression of humiliation. The household men shrink back at Kiartan's demand for them to remain indoors '[c]owed into sullen rage' (*TEP*, ii, p. 392, ll. 3767), Oswif sits apart 'with wrinkled brow' (*TEP*, ii, p. 392, l. 3785), and Gudrun is so outraged that she demands that Bodli face Kiartan: 'And thou, wilt thou not go? | Knowst thou the name of him who shames us so?' (*TEP*, ii, p. 393, ll. 3806–07). Without the explicit physical abasement inherent in Kjartan's publicly forcing them to defecate indoors, the humiliation in Morris's poem amounts to a rather intellectual form of shaming that poses little imminent danger. Morris's definition of dishonour becomes a vaguer, conceptual idea of impotence in the face of theft, rather than a very real loss of standing through a public act of emasculation.

The Morrisian cattle raid appears more like an act of justice in a 'guilt culture', in which social order is maintained through feelings of remorse that arise from actions that an individual believes to be wrong. In contrast, the saga's siege looks like an act of vengeance in a 'shame culture', in which social order is maintained through the threat of ostracism due to loss of honour in the community.[34] In carrying out the raid Kiartan shows that, for Morris, manly heroes possess a quality of conscientiousness and fairness that is simply irrelevant to the heroes of the Old Norse text, who act according to values dictated by public consensus rather than private conscience.

---

[32] 'To the men of Laugur it seemed a far greater shame, and worse disgrace than if Kjartan had killed one or two of them.'

[33] 'Now full enmity grew up between the men of Laugar and Hjarðarholt.'

[34] The distinction between shame and guilt cultures was first made by E. R. Dodds in chapter 2 of *The Greeks and the Irrational* (Berkeley: University of California Press, 1951), pp. 28–63.

Morris's tendency to replace a model of manliness that permits base physical humiliation with a more chivalrous attitude is perhaps most evident in his heroes' treatment of women. In his translation of *Kormáks saga*, for example, he makes the sexually insulting *níð*-verse directed at Steingerðr significantly more courteous:

> Vilda ek hitt at veri
> vald-eir gömul jalda
> stærilát í stóði,
> Steingerðr, en ek reyni;
> væra ek þráða þrúði
> þeirri stöðvar geira
> gunnörðigra garða
> gaupelz á bak hlaupinn. (*KOR*, p. 194)[35]

Morris translates this verse as:

> Would that the stiffnecked Steingerd
> Were midst a stud of horses,
> An old mare mocked of man-folk
> For me to try at leisure:
> Then lightly would I leap
> On the back of wrist-fires' lady,
> The gem decked, for whose gaining
> The spear-field groweth steady. (*SoK*, p. 120)

It is necessary for the maintenance of the plot that this verse is reasonably insulting because it is designed to trick Steingerd into disliking Kormak. By making Steingerd into a mare for riding rather than mating, and Kormak into a horseman rather than a stallion, Morris transmutes the most explicit implication of the verse while allowing a vestige of sexual slander to remain. The last two kennings of the Old Norse stanza, in particular, lose any potential for sexual obscenity. Morris translates *gaupelz* ('of the fiery hole/cupped palms, > *vulva/vagina*') as 'of wrist-fires' (presumably imagined as a kenning for 'gold') and unites *garða*

---

[35] Prose word order of stanza: *Vilda ek hitt, at veri vald-eir, Steingerðr, gömul, stærilát jalda í stóði, en ek reyni; væra ek hlaupinn á bak þráða Þrúði þeirri er stöðvar geira gunnörðigra gaupelz garða.* 'I would have liked the powerful goddess [> woman], Steingerðr, to be an old proud mare in a stud and I a stallion; I would have leapt on the back of that valkyrie of threads [> woman], whose fiery hole's wall/enclosed space [> vulva/vagina] halts/soothes the battle-erect spears [> penises].'

and *geira* (suggesting 'yard/enclosure of spears') in his creation of 'spear-field' (which would appear to be intended as a kenning for battle).³⁶ In Morris's more ambiguous verse, the battle grows steady when the warrior has gained the golden lady, who may be imagined as a mare that he is riding in the fray. Although it is plausible that 'try at leisure', 'leap | On the back' and 'gaining' might be interpreted sexually, the verse may equally be read as an entirely gallant portrayal of an idealised woman aiding the battle exploits of a knightly hero. While Morris does not seem to intend to suppress the insulting imagery altogether here, his verse contains none of the brutal crudeness of the Old Norse stanza. Not only does he appear to want the men of the sagas to be resolute in their fortitude, fair and magnanimous, he wants them to be gracious towards women.

Indeed, Morris's reluctance to portray his heroes as engaged in unrefined sexualised slander extends to his translation of all sexual activity that might portray them in a degrading light, whether or not the conduct is associated with *níð*. In his translation of *Grettis saga*, Morris transforms Grettir Ásmundarson into a man of courtesy, more intent on playing innocent games with his amours than having sexual liaisons. In chapter 17, the crew of a ship are outraged when Grettir shirks his duties to pursue a liaison with the captain's wife: 'þykkir þèr betra, sögðu þeir, at klappa um kviðinn á konu Bárðar stýrimanns, enn at gjöra skyldu þína á skipti' (*GRE*, p. 32),³⁷ which Morris translates as '"Thou art more fain," said they, "of playing with Bard the mate's wife than doing thy duty on board ship"' (*CW*, vii, p. 34). Though Morris's choice of *playing with* may be interpreted sexually, it sounds reasonably innocent in contrast to the unequivocally crude euphemism *klappa um kviðinn* ('stroke the belly'), as though the two passengers might be embarked on some kind of harmless, and more dignified, amusement together. In his translation of *Gunnlaugs saga*, Morris goes as far as removing altogether the reference to the sexual relationship between Helga and her husband Hrafn: 'Nýtti Hrafn síðan ekki af samvistum við Helgu, þá er þau Gunnlaugr höfðu fundizt' (*GUN*, p. 254) ('Hrafn never enjoyed togetherness/intimacy/sexual intercourse with Helga after Gunnlaugr and she had met again') becomes 'but Raven

---

³⁶ The syntax of this verse is not clear or easily understood and there have been various interpretations. See footnotes to the stanza in *Vatnsdœla saga; Hallfreðar saga; Kormáks saga; Hrómundar þáttr halta; Hrafns þáttr Guðrúnarsonar*, ed. Einar Ól. Sveinsson, Íslenzk fornrit, 8 (Reykjavík: Hið íslenzka fornritafélag, 1939), pp. 277–78.

³⁷ 'It seems better to you, they said, to stroke the belly of Skipper Bárði's wife, than to do your duties onboard.'

had nought of Helga's *fellowship* after her meeting with Gunnlaug' (*CW*, x, p. 36) [my italics].

In his translation of a later episode towards the end of *Grettis saga*, Morris attenuates a highly sexualised passage that in the Old Norse text contains explicit references to the small size of Grettir's penis. Grettir has lived as an outlaw on the island of Drangey for two years when he swims across the strait to the farm at Reykir to get fire. Arriving in the middle of the night, he falls asleep and is discovered the next morning in a state of undress:

> en er á leið morguninn, stóðu heimamenn upp, ok kvámu konur tvær í stofu fyrst; þat var griðkona ok dóttir bónda. Grettir var við svefn, ok höfðu fötin svarfazt af hánum ofan á gólfit. Þær sáu, hvar maðr lá, ok kenndu hann. Þá mælti griðkona: svá vil ek heil, systir, hèr er kominn Grettir Ásmundarson, ok þykkir mèr raunar skammrifjamikill vera, og liggr berr; en þat þykki mèr fádœmi, hversu lítt hann er vaxinn niðr, ok ferr þetta eigi eptir gildleika hans öðrum. (*GRE*, pp. 170–71)[38]

Morris translates this passage as:

> Now as the morning wore the home folk arose, and two women came unto the chamber, a handmaid and the goodman's daughter. Grettir was asleep, and the bedclothes had been cast off him on to the floor; so they saw that a man lay there, and knew him.
>
> Then said the handmaiden: 'So may I thrive, sister! here is Grettir Asmundson lying bare, and I call him right well ribbed about the chest, but few might think he would be so small of growth below; and so then that does not go along with other kinds of bigness.' (*CW*, VII, p. 184)

The extraordinary proportions of the rest of Grettir's body have been repeatedly confirmed in the saga, so in the Old Norse text it is a moment of wry enjoyment when it is discovered that Grettir is poorly endowed. At first, Morris follows the Old Norse relatively closely, in which the servant girl does not explicitly use a word that denotes Grettir's genitalia. The phrase *hversu lítt hann er vaxinn niðr* (literally 'how little he is grown

---

[38] 'As the morning passed the household got up and two women came into the room first; who were a maidservant and the farmer's daughter. Grettir was asleep, and his clothes had fallen off him onto the floor. The two of them saw where a man lay, and recognised him. Then the maidservant said: Bless me, sister, here is Grettir Ásmundarson and seems to me really broad in his chest and is lying naked; but it seems extraordinary to me how small he is grown below and this does not match the rest of his size.'

below') becomes Morris's 'so small of growth below', which partially registers the taboo body part but only by innuendo. However, Morris's convoluted choice of syntax in translating *ok ferr þetta eigi eptir gildleika hans öðrum* ('and this does not follow his size otherwise') as 'so then that does not go along with other kinds of bigness' renders the joke about the size of Grettir's penis less distinct. While this may simply be the result of a tendency to translate literally, he may also have wanted to avoid the humour here becoming too lewd, perhaps not only to protect the serving girl from appearing licentious but also to protect Grettir from being reduced to an object of undignified mockery.

In his translation of the two verses that follow, Morris transforms the graphic defence that the saga hero gives of his genitalia – before he overpowers the girl sexually – into a more considerate reflection on the importance of a resolute spirit over physical strength, as well as the sustenance that a weakened man may receive from the arms of an idealised woman. In the first of these verses in *Grettis saga*, Grettir exclaims:

> Váskeytt er far flaska;
> fár kann sverð í hári
> eskiruðr fur öðrum
> örveðrs sjá gjörva.
> Veðja ek hins, at hreðjar
> hafi-t þeir, enn vèr meiri,
> þó at eldraugar eigi
> atgeira sin meiri. (*GRE*, p. 170)[39]

Morris translates this verse as:

> Stay a little, foolish one!
> When the shield-shower is all done,
> With the conquered carles and lords,
> Men bide not to measure swords:
> Many a man had there been glad,

---

[39] Prose word order of stanza: *Váskeytt er far flaska; fár örveðrs eskiruðr kann gjörva sjá sverð í hári fur öðrum; veðja ek hins, at þeir hafi-t meiri hreðjar en vèr, þó atgeira eldraugar eigi meiri sin.* 'The conduct/motion of the gaping/rushing one [> serving girl] is fickle/shifty. Few of those desirous of the arrow-gale [arrow-gale > battle, those desirous of battle > warriors] succeed in seeing the hair-sword(s) [> penis(es)] of others. I bet they do not have bigger balls than me, though the trees of the sword-shower [> warriors] have a bigger one *OR* their halberds of the shower-tree [shower-tree > warrior, halberds of the warrior > penises] are bigger than this one *OR* he has a/they have bigger halberd(s) of the shower-tree [> penis(es)].'

Lesser war-gear to have had,
With a heart more void of fear;
Such I am not, sweet and dear. (*CW*, VII, p. 185)

Whereas the Old Norse verse works simply as a humorous, linguistically dexterous riposte to the girl's derisory comments (Grettir effectively retorts that even if he has a smaller penis than other men, he is confident that his testicles are bigger), Morris's translation takes a moral stance that deems smaller corporeal size or slighter weaker physical aptitude ('Lesser war-gear') preferable to an uncourageous disposition ('a heart more [full] of fear'). Overall, it suggests that once a difficulty is overcome ('the shield-shower is all done') it becomes irrelevant who was previously best equipped to deal with it ('Men bide not to measure swords'), thereby privileging action and determination over a browbeaten temperament. By introducing this attitude, Morris transforms the character of the verse entirely from that of a bawdy rejoinder to counteract the offence to Grettir's masculinity to a moral affirmation of the nature of fortitude. Though he does not excise the possibility of penile imagery in his stanza (those aware of the character of the original might understand 'swords' and 'lesser-war gear' as phallic allusions), any latent sexual imagery is concealed enough that they are undetectable to readers ignorant of the verse in Old Norse (especially given that *The Story of Grettir the Strong* marked the first time that English readers had been introduced to the saga). Morris treads a careful line between censoring the poem altogether and thereby robbing Grettir of his prowess, and portraying a conception of masculinity in which the hero is guilty of sexual incivility.

In his translation of Grettir's next verse, however, Morris excises any possibility of phallic allusion:

> Sverðlítinn kvað sæta,
> saumskorða, mik orðinn;
> Hrist gjörir hreifa kvista
> hœlin satt at mæla.
> All-lengi má ungum
> (eyleggjar, bíð þú, Freyja)
> lágr í læra skógi,
> lautu faxi mèr vaxa. (*GRE*, p. 171)[40]

---

[40] Prose word order of stanza: *Sæta, saumskorða kvað mik orðinn sverðlítinn; hœlin hreifa kvista Hrist gjörir satt at mæla. All-lengi má lágr faxi vaxa mér ungum í læra skógi; eyleggjar Freyja, bíð þú lautu.* 'Solitary seamstress, you say that I am grown small in sword; the gossiping Valkyrie of the twig

Morris translates this verse as:

> Sweet amender of the seam,
> Weak and worn thou dost me deem:
> O light-handed dear delight,
> Certes thou must say aright.
> Weak I am, and certainly
> Long in white arms must I lie:
> Has thou heart to leave me then,
> Fair-limbed gladdener of great men? (*CW*, VII, p. 185)

While in the Old Norse verse Grettir responds to the girl with boorish machismo, suggesting that though his penis is small when flaccid it grows much larger when erect (before apparently proceeding to rape her), in Morris's translation the allusion to the inadequate size of Grettir's penis is transformed into a generalised malaise of weakness and fatigue in the hero. Morris translates *saumskorða kvað mik orðinn sverðlítinn* (literally 'the seamstress calls me become/grown little-in-sword') as 'Weak and worn out thou dost me deem', thereby transforming the allusion to the propensity of Grettir's penis to grow much bigger when he is aroused into the suggestion that his weakened strength may grow much stronger by lying '[l]ong' in her 'white arms'. In Morris's translation the inference to impending sexual aggression in *eyleggjar Freyja, bíð þú lautu* ('Woman, get ready for action') becomes a gentle appeal for the girl to stay and embrace him, since only she can restore his spirit. As an epitome of masculinity for Morris, Grettir is portrayed in this verse as romantically respectful.

In light of Grettir's increased sensitivity in his translation, it is perhaps unsurprising that Morris goes on to moderate the rape at the end of this scene, so that what has occurred becomes less clear. In the Old Norse text, before speaking the second verse, Grettir sweeps the girl up onto the *pallr* (the 'dais' or 'platform' at the end of an Icelandic hall) and subsequently overcomes her: 'Griðka œpti hástöfum, en svá skildu þau, at hón frýði eigi á Gretti, um þat er lauk'(*GRE*, p. 171),[41] which Morris translates as 'The handmaid shrieked out, but in such wise did they part that she laid

---

[possibly penis] of the hand > finger [Valkryie of the finger > girl] speaks truly; the low-maned one [> (small?) penis] in the forest of the thighs [> pubic hair] of the youth may grow very long for me; Goddess of the island-forearm/island-stone/gemstone [> woman], get ready for action.'

[41] 'The housemaid cried out but by the end she no longer taunted Grettir once they had separated.'

no blame on Grettir when all was over' (*CW*, VII, p. 185). The insinuation in *Grettis saga* that Grettir's sexual prowess is such that the girl ultimately ceases to resist his seduction (thus offsetting the issue of his small penis) is transformed in Morris's translation. Though Grettir sweeps the hand-maid onto a 'bed', the activity that is implied by 'when all was over' is indistinct. The courtesy of Morris's hero in the previous verse, coupled with his apparent virtuousness in the fact that after the mysterious deed the girl lays 'no blame' on him (instead of ceasing to taunt him), suggests that, for Morris, masculinity is embodied in the chaste and decorous activity of a chivalrous suitor, rather than the carnal or violent conquest of a womaniser.[42]

At the simplest level, it was necessary for Morris to attenuate obscene material such as Grettir raping the servant girl, or acts of humiliation that allude to homosexual sex because of its potential to break the law. In 1857, appalled by a trial that highlighted the literary iniquities on sale in Holy-well Street (a lane of dingy pornographic bookshops standing on the east side of present-day Aldwych), the Lord Chief Justice Lord Campbell had initiated legislation that, as Lynda Nead has explained, was intended to target 'the products of cheap, mass culture, made possible by new printing technologies and circulating in the city streets in greater numbers and at lower prices than ever before'.[43] Although Campbell never meant for the Obscene Publications Act 1857 to apply to 'high culture' or 'the private consumption of art',[44] it nevertheless had far-reaching consequences on the publication of literature. After the notorious obscenity case *R. v. Hicklin* in April 1868, in which the definition of obscene material was defined for the first time as that which possessed a tendency 'to deprave

[42] Having made this point, it is notable that, characteristically, Morris's loyalty to the saga and its hero caused him to refine the degree of crudeness here, rather than cut the passage altogether (see this chapter, pp. 75–76, below). By contrast, in his 1914 translation, George Ainslie Hight entirely omits the two obscene verses along with the section of prose that describes the sexual attack, see George Ainslie Hight, *The Saga of Grettir the Strong* (London: Dent, 1914), p. 195.

[43] Lynda Nead, 'Bodies of Judgement: Art, Obscenity and the Connoisseur', in *Law and the Image: The Authority of Art and the Aesthetics of Law*, ed. Costas Douzinas and Lynda Nead (Chicago: University of Chicago Press, 1999), pp. 203–25 (p. 210). For the history of Holywell Street leading up to this judgement, see Lynda Nead, *Victorian Babylon: People, Streets and Images in Nineteenth-Century London* (New Haven: Yale University Press, 2000), pp. 161–203.

[44] Nead, 'Bodies of Judgement', pp. 210–11.

and corrupt those whose minds are open to such immoral influences,[45] in the words of M. J. D. Roberts, the Act was 'successfully (though [...] unsystematically) exploited to control or suppress the publication of a variety of works of serious literary and scientific aspiration.'[46]

Since published material was now to be judged on its potential effect on the most vulnerable in society, rather than on whether it had been intended to corrupt in the first place, the law began to be applied more freely to what Geoffrey Robertson describes as 'purple passages in great literature, as well as to respectably written passages in scientific or philosophical criticism of accepted truths.'[47] Renowned English works, often published in expensive editions, were left intact for their discerning middle- and upper-class audience: Hamlet's 'country matters' pun [*Hamlet*, III.2.100] and Malvolio's 'these be her very C's, her U's, and her T's' [*Twelfth Night*, II.5.80], for instance, are untouched in five editions of *The Complete Works of Shakespeare* published between 1864 and 1880.[48] However, as Roberts highlights, translations of obscene foreign material, which might 'safely be allowed a gentleman in the original language in a private library but not an only recently literate mass audience in its own language', were arbitrarily suppressed and their publishers prosecuted. Cheap translations of Boccaccio and Rabelais were blocked from publication in the mid-1870s and, in the late 1880s, the English publisher of the novels of Zola was sentenced to a prison term.[49] Indeed, the atmosphere within the literary industry in the years immediately following the Hicklin case was such that in 1875 a contributor to the *Athenaeum* remarked that

---

[45] Colette Colligan, *The Traffic in Obscenity from Byron to Beardsley: Sexuality and Exoticism in Nineteenth-Century Print Culture* (Basingstoke: Palgrave Macmillan, 2006), p. 176; Geoffrey Robertson, *Obscenity: An Account of Censorship Laws and Their Enforcement in England and Wales* (London: Weidenfeld and Nicolson, 1979), p. 30.

[46] M. J. D. Roberts, 'Morals, Art, and the Law: The Passing of the Obscene Publications Act, 1857', *Victorian Studies*, 28 (1985), 609–29 (p. 628).

[47] Robertson, p. 30.

[48] *Complete Works of W. Shakespeare*, ed. Samuel Johnson, George Steevens and Isaac Reed (Edinburgh: Nimmo, 1864), pp. 194, 548; *The Plays and Poems of William Shakespeare*, ed. Thomas Keightley (London: Bell and Daldy, 1865), pp. 218, 599; *The Complete Works of Shakspere: With a Memoir* (London: Dicks, 1868), pp. 17, 585; *The Works of William Shakespeare, Complete. With Life and Glossary* (London: Ward, Lock and Tyler, 1877), pp. 63, 874; *The Complete Works of Shakespeare*, ed. William Horwood (London: Murdoch, 1880), pp. 64, 356.

[49] Roberts, 'Morals, Art, and the Law', p. 268.

'so timid are Englishmen where there is a question of being charged with encouraging vice, that I can fancy the effect upon an average bookseller [...] is like that which would once have been produced by the call of a functionary of the Inquisition upon a Spanish Jew'.[50]

As Morris first began to publish his saga translations in the immediate aftermath of *R. v. Hicklin*, for them to reach an audience he would either have had to create a society for limited private circulation such as The Kama Shastra Society of London and Benares, which first published *The Kama Sutra of Vatsyayana* in 1883,[51] or translate the text to a standard that satisfied his publisher that they would not face what Colette Colligan has called the 'very real threat' of prosecution for obscenity.[52] In refraining from forming a private society, Morris ensured that translations he came to consider to be the shared cultural heritage of the English could be generally disseminated to a popular audience. He, therefore, had to ensure that the translations would fall within the restraints of the Obscene Publications Act.

However, if Morris's only motive in attenuating coarseness and shaming behaviour had been to escape prosecution, he might have followed the example of Dasent who had generally cut obscene allusions altogether, or else altered them to such an extent that they could be read without indecency. In *The Story of Burnt Njal* (1861), for example, Dasent had removed almost entirely the notorious moment in *Njáls saga* when Unnr Marðardóttir informs her father that her husband Hrútr's penis is too big for them to have sex, rather politely translating 'hon svarar. þegar hann kemr við mik þá er horund hans sva mikit at hann má ekki eptirlęti hafa við mik. en þó hofum við bęði breytni til þess á alla vega at við męttim nióta3. en þat verðr ekki'[53] as 'she told him how she and Hrut could not live together, because he was spell-bound, and that she wished

---

[50] Quoted in M. J. D. Roberts, 'Making Victorian Morals? The Society for the Suppression of Vice and Its Critics, 1802–1886', *Historical Studies*, 21 (1984), 157–73 (p. 173); Gowan Dawson, *Darwin, Literature and Victorian Respectability* (Cambridge: Cambridge University Press, 2007), p. 135.

[51] Ben Grant, 'Translating/"The" Kama Sutra', *Third World Quarterly*, 26 (2005), 509–16 (pp. 509–10).

[52] Colligan, p. 71.

[53] 'She replied, as soon as he gets against me his penis is so big that he can have no enjoyment from me, though we have both tried lots of ways that we might enjoy each other, but nothing comes of it.' The Old Norse is quoted from Olaus Olavius, *Sagan af Niáli Þórgeirssyni*, p. 13. See also Wawn, *Vikings*, p. 155.

to leave him'.[54] Later in the same translation, Dasent had rendered Skar-pheðinn's response to Flosi's asking why he should require effeminate clothing, 'Því þá ef þú ert brúðr Svínfellsáss sem sagt er hveria ina níundu nótt at hann geri þik at konu'[55] as 'Because [...] thou art the sweetheart of the Swinefell's goblin, if, as men say, he does indeed turn thee into a woman every ninth night',[56] thereby creating the possibility that the charge is to have been magically transformed into a woman, rather than to have been used sexually like a woman.

In comparison to Dasent, Morris seems to be doing something subtly different with coarseness and obscenity in his translations. While Dasent actually ceases to follow the Old Norse text on occasion (something Morris never does) to produce a censored paraphrase, or otherwise replaces the obscene image with something more decent, he does not blur or otherwise obfuscate it in the same way as Morris, nor romanticise or ennoble the conduct of his characters to the same degree. In the instances in Morris's translations above, such as the obscene verses in *Kormáks saga* and *Grettis saga*, Morris appears to be treading a careful line between defending his translation from suppression under the Obscene Publications Act, retaining some degree of what is in the Old Norse text, and protecting the saga heroes from appearing brutish. He does not want to censor the material entirely but nor does he wish it to appear obscene or base.

Even in instances that would surely not have been considered obscene, Morris does not want the heroes of the sagas to be deemed ignoble by his audience. In his rendering of *Eyrbyggja saga*, for example, he avoids the crudeness of a poetic reference to defecation when he translates the instruction 'eigi skyldi þar álfrek ganga'[57] as 'none should go there for their needs' (TSL, 2, p. 9). In removing the literary allusion to faeces of *álfrek* (literally 'that which drives elves away'), Morris avoids crudeness at the expense of a particularly colourful kenning. Similarly, in his translation of *Gunnlaugs saga*, his rendering blurs an overt reference to the exposure

---

[54] *The Story of Burnt Njal; or, Life in Iceland at the End of the Tenth Century*, trans. George Webbe Dasent, 2 vols (Edinburgh: Edmonston and Douglas, 1861), I, p. 25.

[55] 'Because if you are the bride of the Svínfell's spirit as it is said he makes you into a woman every ninth night.' The Old Norse is quoted from Olaus Olavius, *Sagan Af Niáli Þórgeirssyni*, p. 190.

[56] *Story of Burnt Njal*, II, p. 155.

[57] 'Nobody should go for their elf-repellers there.' The Old Norse is quoted from *Eyrbyggja saga*, ed. Guðbrandr Vigfússon (Leipzig: Vogel, 1864), p. 7.

of babies that seems unlikely to have been considered obscene. Morris translates the instruction '[þú] skal þat barn út bera, ef þú fæðir meybarn, en upp fæða, ef sveinn er' (*GUN*, p. 198)[58] as 'thy child shall be cast forth if thou bear a woman; but nourished if it be a man' (*CW*, x, p. 10), with the choice of *cast forth* for *bera út* (literally 'carry' or 'bear outside' but idiomatically 'to expose') suggesting something more like banishment from the household rather than death from exposure.[59] While this last example may be due more to Morris's penchant for literal translation and disdain for explanatory footnotes than anxiety that the saga characters should be seen to act cruelly, the effect of his translation is to obscure to some extent the unequivocal severity of the Old Norse passage.

Though it may well have led to prosecution if he had translated sexually insulting verses as they stand in the Old Norse editions, it might have been possible to portray a genuine quality of humiliation or cruelty in his renderings without necessarily including obscenity. The verse aimed at insulting Steingerd, for example, might have captured a more overtly hostile tone without appearing indecent. Likewise, even if he felt it was impossible to translate *ragr* with words that would have alluded to sexual deviancy, or to describe Grettir's sexuality and anatomy graphically, it would surely have been possible to capture more accurately the physical effeminacy for which Gunnlaugr and Hrafn are ridiculed in the mock fight, or even the primitiveness of being prevented from leaving the house to use the privy in *Laxdæla saga*. Even the physical humiliation of the shame-stroke in *Kormáks saga* might have been more straightforwardly linked to Steingerd's disgust, without explicit reference being made to the latent sexual aberration that it implied.

It was not only obscenity that Morris avoided in his translations of the sagas of Icelanders but inhumanity. What Clover describes as the 'frantic machismo of Norse males' (see this chapter, p. 54, above) means that, on occasion, the saga heroes are harsh and vindictive, even vicious. Even if, in some of the instances of *níð* that he translated, Morris had been able to include a quality of visceral malignity without risking 'depraving' or 'corrupting' those whose minds the law deemed 'open to such immoral influences', the fact is that he did not want to. Translating the desperation

---

[58] 'You must expose that child if you give birth to a girl but bring it up if it is a boy.'

[59] One of the senses of the verb *expose* in late nineteenth-century British English was explicitly to withdraw parental care and leave a child to perish, see Webster, p. 483.

in the fight for masculinity as it stands in the sagas would have involved representing heroes whose instincts and actions are reasonably frequently self-serving, grasping and downright cruel.

In the eyes of a scholar such as Vilhjálmur Arnason, Morris's view of manliness would fall squarely within what he terms a 'romantic' response to the sagas of Icelanders. Typically concentrating on the 'individual qualities and attitudes' of the protagonists rather than the moral lesson revealed by the text as a whole, Vilhjálmur argues that romantic readings of the sagas tend to infer a nostalgic admiration for the strength of honour in the hero, who is often deemed a 'tragic figure' bound to take vengeance by dutiful 'values and virtues of Nordic heathen origin'.[60] Such readers are inclined to universalise the morality of the sagas, regarding it, as Kristján Kristjánsson puts it, as an 'atemporal, universal moral outlook relevant to modern concerns'.[61] Once the sagas' values have been universalised, they can then be 'liberated from their original traditions' and 'made viable in the contemporary world'.[62]

Arguing against the atemporality of saga morality, Svavar Hrafn Svavarsson has employed Bernard Williams's distinction between thick and thin moral concepts to demonstrate the parochial, incommensurable and sociologically entrenched moral outlook of medieval Iceland, where 'questions of value [were] questions of fact'.[63] Distinguishing between 'traditional [...] homogeneous societies' (which he associates with 'shame cultures') that are dominated by thick moral concepts and not given to ethical reflection, and 'moral communities that have evolved an ethical theory' by contemplating thin moral concepts (which he associates with 'guilt cultures'), Svavar Hrafn argues that saga morality is 'very thick' and, thus, firmly embedded within an intrinsically unreflective, insular, shame culture.[64] In his view, the first step for anyone wishing to liberate saga morality for the modern world must necessarily be to downplay this thick embeddedness (what he calls 'the chasm between the shame

[60] Vilhjálmur Árnason, 'An Ethos in Transformation: Conflicting Values in the Sagas', ed. Vésteinn Ólason, *Gripla*, 20 (2009), 217–40 (p. 220).

[61] Vilhjálmur Árnason, 'Ethos', p. 221; Kristján Kristjánsson, 'Liberating Moral Traditions: Saga Morality and Aristotle's Megalopsychia', *Ethical Theory & Moral Practice*, 1 (1998), 397–422 (p. 407).

[62] Vilhjálmur Árnason, 'Ethos', p. 221.

[63] Svavar Hrafn Svavarsson, 'Honour and Shame: Comparing Medieval Iceland and Ancient Greece', ed. Vésteinn Ólason, *Gripla*, 20 (2009), 241–56 (p. 250).

[64] Svavar Hrafn Svavarsson, pp. 250–51.

cultures of old and modern guilt cultures'),[65] thereby endowing honour 'with a timeless quality' and 'depriving it of its contingency'.[66]

In Morris's transmutation of the shame culture in his translations of the sagas of Icelanders his primary impetus appears to have been exactly this: to deprive honour of its contingency. In sublimating the qualities of masculinity that he perceived in the sagas for the society in which he lived, it seems that Morris was inclined to rehabilitate these values to make them universally embraceable. By adjusting his sources so that, for example, Kiartan now politely acquires cattle in response to the theft of the coif rather than humiliating the culprits, and Thorstein Staff-Smitten's father calls him an ungallant faint-heart rather than a sexually degenerate nancy, Morris transforms what Vilhjálmur calls 'the objective ethical order' of the sagas' shame culture (in which characters 'accept what they have to do and do it without moral reflection') into something more like a privately motivated guilt culture, in which the individual's sense of honour is ultimately dictated by an ideal of decency residing in his conscience.[67] The more decent world that Morris creates possesses little of the life-and-death necessity of saga culture, in which the personal annihilation inherent in social ostracism is a very real threat. Morris's characters seem unlikely to be destroyed for failing to live up to what they should be as men, because honour in their world has been altered from something based entirely on public reputation to something emanating from goodness of heart and commitment to conscientious conduct.

Though Morris must have been conscious of the requirements that his publisher needed to meet in relation to obscenity, it appears unlikely that he was aware of his tendency to elevate the virtues of the saga heroes to timeless moral concepts. Indeed, from his comments on the sagas of Icelanders at the beginning of The Saga Library it seems that he believed that the saga authors had already universalised their works for all time:

> the literary style which they have received does not encumber or falsify them, but serves them as a vehicle of expression, so that they have become capable of being understood outside the narrow limits of the family or district where the events told of happened, or were imagined to have happened. The literature in which they are enshrined has taken them out of the category of mere parish records, and made them valuable to the world at large. (Preface to TSL, 1, p. x)

[65] Svavar Hrafn Svavarsson, p. 248.
[66] Svavar Hrafn Svavarsson, p. 253.
[67] Vilhjálmur Árnason, 'Morality and Social Structure in the Icelandic Sagas', *The Journal of English and Germanic Philology*, 90 (1990), 157-174 (p. 163).

For Morris, the sagas of Icelanders were essentially honest accounts of human life enshrined in a literary language that had rendered them relevant to all mankind forever. By focusing so wholeheartedly on what he venerated in the heroes and, to an extent, inventing the context that they exist in, he misled himself into believing that the ethos of Old Norse literature was closer than it actually was to the one portrayed in his translations and poems.

His fondness for the heroes caused Morris to find affinity with their virtues when, in fact, they were integral to a largely alien sociologically entrenched shame culture in which acts of humiliation were a fundamental element in the struggle for honour. Just as shaming reflected the wider culture contemporary to the sagas, so Morris's attraction to a more dignified code of heroism reflected a wider cultural development in his own time. As Martin J. Wiener has argued, in nineteenth-century England: 'The newer expectation for men, to manifest peaceableness and self-restraint in more and more areas of life [...] was extended [...] in two directions: from gentlemen to all men, and from public male-on-male violence to "private" violence against subordinates, dependants and the entire female gender.'[68]

In reality it seems that Morris was either blind to (or simply not interested in) key aspects of saga morality, rejecting its ferocity as too coarse. Though he found the certitude of thick moral concepts appealing because they bound the saga heroes by a duty to act spontaneously and (by their own standards) virtuously, it was actually thin moral concepts such as *fairness* and *goodness* that he spent a lifetime pursuing. Morris mistakenly thought that the saga heroes exemplified these values when, in fact, they are foreign to the moral universe of the sagas. Instinctively compelled perhaps to protect what he regarded as the most valuable element of the sagas – their existence within world literature as testaments to heroic living – he was inclined to jettison the most hostile aspects of the shame culture that inspired them. In doing so, he brought the medieval Icelandic definition of masculinity closer to his own developing ideal of heroism, emphasising qualities such as fortitude, magnanimity, civility and humaneness, and thereby rendering the heroes more acceptable to both their new nineteenth-century British audience and himself.

---

[68] Martin J. Wiener, *Men of Blood: Violence, Manliness, and Criminal Justice in Victorian England* (Cambridge: Cambridge University Press, 2006), p. 6.

3

Grettir the Strong and the Courage of Incapacity

I F MORRIS REJECTED crudeness and ferocity in the saga heroes, he embraced their courageousness. Reflecting in the autumn of 1883 on what had attracted him to the sagas some fifteen years before, he declared that it was 'the delightful freshness and independence of thought of them, the air of freedom which breathes through them, their worship of courage'.[1] Four years later, in his 1887 lecture 'The Early Literature of the North – Iceland', he lauded the medieval Icelanders as a people 'whose religion was practically courage',[2] and later, more emphatically, whose 'real religion was the worship of Courage' (note the substantiating capitalised 'C').[3] These explanations of the bravery that he had discovered in Old Norse works have strongly influenced scholarly accounts of what drew him to Iceland and its literature. E. P. Thompson argues that there 'can be few more striking examples of the regenerative resources of culture than this renewal of courage and of faith in humanity which was blown from Iceland to William Morris',[4] while Robert Page Arnot maintains that Morris was 'powerfully affected by this literature, in which the quality of courage is so highly developed as to make much of contemporary medieval literature appear like bravado'.[5] More recently Waithe has proposed that Morris 'admired the passionate reserve of the typical saga-hero, and may even have found comfort in the sagas' stoical view at

---

[1] Letter to Scheu, dated 15 September 1883, in Kelvin, IIA, p. 229.
[2] From 'The Early Literature of the North – Iceland', in *The Unpublished Lectures of William Morris*, ed. Eugene D. LeMire (Detroit: Wayne State University Press, 1969), pp. 179–98 (p. 185).
[3] From 'The Early Literature of the North – Iceland', in LeMire, p. 190.
[4] E. P. Thompson, p. 176.
[5] Robert Page Arnot, *William Morris: The Man and the Myth* (London: Lawrence and Wishart, 1964), p. 21.

a time when his marriage was failing',[6] while Richard Frith has asserted that Morris 'strove to embody the same qualities of courage and stoicism in his own works – lived as well as written'.[7]

Notwithstanding their influence on scholars, in these retrospective accounts Morris presents a simplified definition of the model of courage that he perceived in the sagas shortly after meeting Eiríkur Magnússon. While there is no doubt that the sagas proved a salient inspiration for him, and that the Icelandic treks he undertook in 1871 and 1873 provided an enigmatic psychic test that helped steel his resolve to forge a more robust path at a difficult time in his personal life, it should be remembered that the man reminiscing in the mid-1880s was in a very different position from the one who began lessons with Eiríkur in the late 1860s. By 1887, he was a successful factory owner, firmly steering the reins of the flourishing Morris & Co., Rossetti was dead, and Morris's passion for socialism at its peak.[8] Considered in this light, the ease with which Morris fondly invokes the courage of the Icelanders in these instances seems to reflect a slight glibness that perhaps arises from his more buoyant personal confidence, as well as the zealous assurance that his writing acquired during the socialist years.

A consequence of this simplified account of the courage that had first attracted him to medieval Icelandic literature has been that scholars have tended to paraphrase a narrative (and often only in passing) that 'Morris discovered courage in Iceland' in an imprecise manner that risks confusing the definition of courageous manliness that he perceived in the sagas with a differing and widespread Victorian construction of Norse masculinity, primarily based on indomitability. Since Percy began his Preface to *Five Pieces of Runic Poetry* (1763) by noting that the ancient inhabitants of Scandinavia were 'generally known under no other character than that of a hardy unpolished race, who subdued all the southern nations by dint of

---

[6] Waithe, p. 74.

[7] Richard Frith, '"Honorable and Notable Adventures": Courtly and Chivalric Idealism in Morris's Froissartian Poems', *The Journal of the William Morris Society*, 17.3 (2007), 13–29 (p. 15).

[8] In 1884, Jane Morris met Wilfrid Scawen Blunt with whom she embarked on an affair that lasted from 1887 (at the latest) to 1894. This relationship does not appear to have unsettled her marriage to the same degree as that with Rossetti. See Debra N. Mancoff, *Jane Morris: The Pre-Raphaelite Model of Beauty* (San Francisco: Pomegranate, 2000), p. 98.

courage and of numbers',[9] variations on the image of the unconquerable Viking had steadily emerged out of the Romantic Movement until, in the words of Ingrid Hanson, they became 'commonplace in Victorian discussions of the literature as well as the character of Northern Europe'.[10] Whether one considers the 'indomitable energy and courage' that Laing associates with the 'Sea-Kings of Norway' in the remarks preceding his *Heimskringla* (1844),[11] the valour of the 'Northern conquerors' of saga-age Iceland – who in 'The Norsemen in Iceland' (1858) Dasent labels the 'bravest warriors, the boldest sailors'[12] – or 'the hair-breadth escapes and deeds of daring' that Frederick Metcalfe celebrates in his discussion of *Friðþjófs saga* in *The Englishman and the Scandinavian* (1880),[13] to the Victorian, the image of the Norseman was frequently characterised by invulnerability, as well as what Matthew Townend describes as associations of 'political liberty'[14] that comprised a refusal to entertain impotence or abasement. Wawn has emphasised the fact that Georgian enthusiasts of Old Norse literature were primarily drawn to legendary and mythological material, which may in part explain how the association of indomitability became pervasive. It was only with the appearance of Dasent's translations of the 1860s that the flawed and fallible heroes of the sagas of Icelanders became more widely known to the British public.

This construction of unassailable Norse manliness, in fact, corresponds with more widespread conceptions of masculinity that endured from the eighteenth century into the nineteenth and associated male

[9] Preface to *Five Pieces of Runic Poetry Translated from the Islandic Language*, trans. Thomas Percy (London: Dodsley, 1763), p. i.

[10] Ingrid Hanson, *William Morris and the Uses of Violence, 1856–1890* (London: Anthem Press, 2013), p. 68.

[11] 'Preliminary Dissertation' preceding Snorri Sturluson, *The Heimskringla; or, Chronicle of the Kings of Norway*, trans. Samuel Laing, 3 vols (London: Longman, Brown, Green and Longmans, 1844), I, p. 7; Wawn, *Vikings*, pp. 98–99.

[12] George Webbe Dasent, 'The Norsemen in Iceland', in *Oxford Essays, Contributed by the Members of the University* (London: John W. Parker and Son, 1858), p. 214; Wawn, *Vikings*, p. 149.

[13] Frederick Metcalfe, *The Englishman and the Scandinavian; or, A Comparison of Anglo-Saxon and Old Norse Literature* (London: Trübner, 1880), p. 287; Wawn, *Vikings*, p. 131.

[14] Matthew Townend, *The Vikings and Victorian Lakeland: The Norse Medievalism of W.G. Collingwood and His Contemporaries*, Extra Series, 34 (Kendal: Cumberland and Westmorland Antiquarian and Archaeological Society, 2009), p. 9.

virtue with autonomy.[15] When in 1839, for example, Carlyle wrote – in reference to the Englishman's attitude to the degradation of the Irish labourer – that 'the Saxon man if he cannot work in these terms, finds no work. He too may be ignorant; but he has not sunk from decent manhood to squalid apehood: he cannot continue there',[16] it was defiance of abasement that he implied was the cornerstone of manliness. Similarly, when in 1867 Charles Kingsley (who considered the Norse Vikings 'the great male race') wrote that 'all true manhood consists in the defiance of circumstances' and 'if any man be the creature of circumstances, it is [...] because he has ceased to be a man, and sunk downward to the brute', it was submission to impotence that he deemed the root of effeminacy.[17]

With such conceptions of manliness prevalent in the period that led up to Morris translating the sagas, it is all too easy to confuse his acclamation of the courage of the Icelanders with the intrepid invincibility of those 'notions of a pre-feudal gentry, of brave and free men sailing away from king and court' that Aho has argued were 'nourished by Scott, Carlyle, Kingsley and Dasent'.[18] Yet if, rather than concentrating on his later recollections, one looks closely at the construction of masculinity that Morris created in his saga translations, journals and short poems from 1868–76, it becomes clear that what he revered as courageous in Old Norse literature was something quite different from the spurning of impotence or abasement that Carlyle and Kingsley promoted as manly, and that correlate with hackneyed images of sea-bound Viking valour. By contrast, the analysis of these texts in this chapter reveals that it is frequently the protagonist's vulnerability that impresses Morris as heroic: his ability to experience debility, fragility and failure. While perseverance in the face of difficulty is integral to the type of courage that Morris admires, inviolability and vanquishment are not (and, indeed, his beloved Icelandic heroes rarely accomplish either). In translations of sagas such as *Grettis saga*, *Gunnlaugs saga* and *Kormáks saga*, each of which are renowned in their own way for the titular character's fallibility, it is often the hero's incapacity that Morris highlights, rather than his invincibility.

A major theme in *Grettis saga* is the hero's gradual descent into

---

[15] David Alderson, *Mansex Fine: Religion, Manliness and Imperialism in Nineteenth-Century British Culture* (Manchester: Manchester University Press, 1998), pp. 10–14.

[16] Thomas Carlyle, *Chartism*, 2nd edn (London, 1840), p. 28.

[17] Quoted in Hanson, p. 76, from Charles Kingsley, *Three Lectures Delivered At The Royal Institution On The Ancien Regime: As It Existed On The Continent Before The French Revolution* (London: Macmillan, 1867), p. 88

[18] Aho, 'Iceland', p. 112.

incapacitation. He begins as a young man of extraordinary stature and prowess – the strongest man in all Iceland – and, yet, by the end of the saga has fallen victim to frailty and fear. Hunted through the wilds as an outlawed itinerant, he eventually dies the ignoble death of a pariah. A creature of contradiction, Grettir is simultaneously foul tempered and kind, oversized and sensitive, spending most of life struggling to find a place in a society that often seems paltrier than him. Though it is fundamentally ambiguous to what extent his lack of restraint leads to his downfall or is simply coincident with bad luck, his remarkable tenacity in spite of his inability to assimilate has made him an icon of integrity. In translating *Grettis saga*, Morris was particularly struck by the hero's determination to remain galvanised in the face of increasing loss, a capacity that he deemed morally virtuous. Sending Charles Eliot Norton a copy of the newly published translation in May 1869, he commented that 'there underlies all the rudeness a sentiment and a moral sense that somehow made the hopeless looking life of our hero endurable; at any rate he did endure it in a kind of way that is a lesson I think to us effete folk of the old World'.[19] The question arises as to what precisely Morris saw in Grettir's outlook that he felt could be instructive to him.

A clue to the answer to this question lies in the nuance of the passages of Morris's translation of *Grettis saga* in which the hero experiences the gradual depletion of his strength. At these points the prose style often rises from one that is frequently opaque and halting to something more lyrical, emotionally clear and, on occasion, majestic. In the episode in which the diminution of Grettir's powers begins, for example, Morris imbues the moment in which the hero is awe-struck at the sight of the monster Glámr glancing at the moon with a grave serenity that intimates a sort of veneration for the scene:

> Tunglskin var mikit úti, ok gluggaþykkn; hratt stundum fyrir, en stundum dró frá. Nú í því, er Glámr fèll, rak skýit frá tunglinu, en Glámr hvessti augun upp í móti, ok svá hefir Grettir sagt sjálfr, at þá eina sýn hafi hann sèt svá, at hánum brygði við. Þá sigaði svá at hánum af öllu saman, mœði ok því, er hann sá at Glámr gaut sínum sjónum harðliga, at hann gat eigi brugðit saxinu, ok lá náliga í milli heims ok heljar. (*GRE*, p. 85)[20]

---

[19] Letter to Charles Eliot Norton, dated 13 May 1869, in Kelvin, I, p. 76.
[20] 'Outside the moonlight was strong and there was dense cloud with openings it, sometimes drifting over and sometimes away [from the moon]. Just as Glámr fell, the clouds swept away from the moon and Glámr looked up intently at it. And Grettir has said so himself that this is the only sight that he

Morris translates this passage as:

> Bright moonlight was there without, and the drift was broken, now drawn
> over the moon, now driven from off her; and, even as Glam fell, a cloud
> was driven from the moon, and Glam glared up against her. And Grettir
> himself says that by that sight only was he dismayed amidst all that he ever
> saw.
>
> Then his soul sank within him so, from all these things, both from
> weariness, and because he had seen Glam turn his eyes so horribly, that he
> might not draw the short-sword, and lay well-nigh 'twixt home and hell.
> (*CW*, VII, p. 90)

Instead of translating *Tunglskin var mikit úti* as 'the moonlight was bright
outside' or even 'there was bright moonlight outside', Morris chooses
'Bright moonlight was there without', generating a quality of stateliness and gravity. By inverting the conventional English word order and
choosing 'without' for *úti* (literally 'out' or 'outside') he creates a sense
of portent that is less apparent in the Old Norse text. His translation
of the complicated syntax describing cloud drifting across the moon is
especially measured. The almost untranslatable compound noun *glug-
gaþykkn* (literally [implied: 'there were] thickness-openings' or 'thick-
ness-windows') becomes 'the drift was broken', and *hratt stundum fyrir
en stundum dró frá* (literally 'sometimes cast over and sometimes drew
off from') becomes 'now drawn over the moon, now driven from off her',
maintaining the syntactic parallelism and increasing the alliteration that
underpins the Old Norse passage. Morris's version evokes the lumines-
cence of the cloud-strewn night sky, with the feminine personification
of the moon (in Old Norse the word is neuter) heightening the stately
cadence of the passage. The stateliness is intensified by his decision to
move his translation of *hafi hann sèt svá* ('he has ever seen') from the
middle to the end of the second sentence. Similarly, while the Old Norse
text does not mention anything resembling a 'soul' (*Þá sigaði svá at
hánum af öllu saman* literally means 'it sank so that everything left him'
but has the sense of 'he was so overwhelmed'), Morris's insertion of 'his
soul sank within him so' imbues the last image of Grettir lying exhausted
í milli heims ok heljar ('between earth and hel', which Morris translates as
'"twixt home and hell') with a gravity that is more matter of fact in the Old

---

has seen that has ever unnerved him. He was then so overwhelmed both with
exhaustion and seeing Glámr cast his eyes up so intensely that he was unable to
draw his sax and lay almost between earth and the next world.'

Norse prose. The amplification of the portentous quality in this passage suggests that, far from considering it unfortunate or regrettable, Morris in some way revered Grettir's initial experience of incapacitation.

This apparent stylistic reverence becomes even more explicit in the solemn tone that permeates Morris's translation of Glámr's subsequent curse:

> en þat má ek segja þèr, at þú hefir nú fengit helming afls þess ok þroska, er þèr var ætlaðr, ef þú hefðir mik eigi fundit; [...] Þú hefir frægr orðit hèr til af verkum þínum, en hèðan af munu falla til þín sektir ok vígaferli, en flest öll verk þín snúast þèr til úgæfu ok hamingjuleysis. Þú munt verða útlægr gjörr, ok hljóta jafnan úti at búa einn samt; þá legg ek þat á við þik, at þessi augu sè þèr jafnan fyrir sjónum, sem ek ber eptir, ok man þèr þá erfitt þykja einum at vera, ok þat man þèr til dauða draga. (*GRE*, p. 85)[21]

He translates this passage as:

> and this must I tell thee, that thou now hast got half the strength and manhood, which was thy lot if thou hadst not met me: [...] Hitherto hast thou earned fame by thy deeds, but henceforth will wrongs and manslayings fall on thee, and the most part of thy doings will turn to thy woe and ill-hap; an outlaw shalt thou be made, and ever shall it be thy lot to dwell alone abroad; therefore this weird I lay on thee, ever in those days to see these eyes with thine eyes, and thou wilt find it hard to be alone – and that shall drag thee unto death. (*CW*, VII, p. 90)

Despite the fact that they denote the familiar form of the second-person pronoun, the archaism of words such as 'thou', 'thee' and 'hadst' in this passage contributes to a formal register that is lacking in the Old Norse text. In translating *Þú munt verða útlægr gjörr* ('you shall be made an outlaw' or literally 'you shall become an outlaw made') as 'an outlaw shalt thou be made', and *Þú munt [...] hljóta jafnan* ('You will always be allotted') as 'ever shall it be thy lot', Morris chooses an even more archaic word order than he would have created by simply mirroring the

---

[21] 'And I may say this that you have now received half of the power and the manhood which would have been expected for you if you had not met me; [...] You have become renowned here for your deeds but henceforth will fall into outlawry and man-slayings and most of your deeds will now turn back on you into ill-luck and lack of fortune. You will be made an outlaw and condemned always to be [exposed/outdoors] and live alone. Then I lay this upon you: that these eyes which I possess might forever be in your sight, and it will seem difficult for you to be alone. And this will drag you to your death.'

Old Norse, reinforcing the quality of solemnity, and perhaps even sanctity. Indeed, it is possible that nineteenth-century readers would have heard biblical echoes in this syntax: 'Blessed shalt thou be in the city, and blessed shalt thou be in the field' (Deuteronomy 28.6 KJV). Similarly, Morris's insertion of 'this weird' (a cognate of Old Norse *urðr* 'fate') where there is no equivalent word in the Norse text (*þá legg ek þat á við þik* means simply 'Then I lay this upon you') heightens the degree of omen. Altogether the intensified sombreness suggests that Morris empathised with Grettir, perceiving no conflict between the hero's incapacity and his status as an icon of masculinity. On the contrary, the tone of Morris's translation implies that he regarded the moment when Grettir's incapacitation begins as something monumental and even venerable. In Morris's eyes, Grettir's ability to suffer vulnerability had the potential perhaps to make him a greater man.

Morris's association of Grettir's incapacity with courageous masculinity contrasts with Maria H. Frawley's assertion that nineteenth-century conceptions of invalidism were frequently associated with an epitome of femininity.[22] Rather than deeming the prospect of incapacitation 'a debilitating posture of submission bound to the feminine' (which is how Frawley interprets Robert Louis Stevenson's description of physical resignation as 'the cowardice that apes a kind of courage'),[23] here Morris seems to conceive of it as an almost hallowed opportunity for a man. To this extent his translation contests the orthodoxy expressed by Stevenson that accommodation of infirmity inevitably implies effeminacy. As Frawley demonstrates, however, even if submission to infirmity was associated with women, many nineteenth-century invalids concurred with the notion that it might be embraced as a hallowed opportunity. Affliction could offer the sufferer the 'priceless opportunity to experience and exhibit grace'[24] if it were conceived of as 'an essentially

---

[22] Maria H. Frawley, *Invalidism and Identity in Nineteenth-Century Britain* (Chicago: University of Chicago Press, 2004), pp. 24–25. Although Frawley concentrates primarily on sociological attitudes to prolonged sickness rather than on literary portrayals of injury or abasement, the differing notions of infirmity that she provides are helpful in considering Morris's particular attitude to incapacity.

[23] Frawley, pp. 156–57; Robert Louis Stevenson, 'Health and Mountains', in *Sketches, Criticisms: Lay Morals, and Other Essays* (London: Heineman, 1923), pp. 473–79 (p. 458).

[24] Frawley, pp. 157–58.

ahistoric, transcendent experience'.[25] In many invalid-written texts of the period, Frawley contends, incapacitation provided sufferers with the higher purpose of enduring 'the comforts of consolation, the virtues of resignation',[26] so that a certain quality of dignified acquiescence became desirable. While Morris was almost certainly an atheist by the time that he met Eiríkur (see Chapter 1, p. 51), and so would be unlikely to have invoked the theological concept of grace here, he seems nevertheless to have felt that incapacitation offered a valuable chance to exhibit a form of gracious acquiescence to fortune in which the sufferer accommodates incapacity wholeheartedly, rather than rejecting it.

This respect for a kind of courage that embraces vulnerability is intimated in the lyrical tone of dignity that Morris confers on those moments of *The Story of Grettir the Strong* that portray the hero's growing fear of the dark. Soon after he has been cursed, for example, Grettir reports a new susceptibility to fear, 'Á því fann hann mikla muni, at hann var orðinn maðr svá myrkfœlinn, at hann þorði hvergi at fara einn saman, þegar myrkva tók; sýndist hánum þá hvers kyns skrípi' (*GRE*, p. 86),[27] which is translated as 'but that herein be found the greatest change, in that he was become so fearsome a man in the dark, that he durst go nowhither alone after nightfall, for then he seemed to see all kinds of horrors' (*CW*, VII, p. 91). The archaism of 'was become' and use of 'fearsome' to mean 'afraid' rather than 'frightening' in Morris's choice of 'he was become so fearsome a man in the dark' for *hann var orðinn maðr svá myrkfœlinn* ('he had become a man so afraid of the dark' or literally 'he was become a man so dark-afraid'), and of 'durst' and 'nowhither' in his choice of 'he durst go nowhither alone' for *hann þorði hvergi at fara einn saman* ('he in no way dared to go out alone'), imbues Grettir's attitude towards his newly found fear with a stature that is less pronounced in the Norse text. In addition, the choice of 'then he seemed to see all kinds of horrors' for *sýndist hánum þá hvers kyns skrípi* ('then all kinds of spectres appeared to him') intensifies the hero's vulnerability, amplifying his bravery in enduring it. The combination of heightened dignity and vulnerability suggests that Morris esteemed Grettir's capacity to adapt to the more exposed circumstances in which he found himself. For Morris, this attitude of embrace

---

[25] Frawley, p. 166.

[26] Frawley, p. 162.

[27] 'The great difference he found was this: that he had become a man so afraid of the dark that he in no way dared to go out alone after dark; then all kinds of spectres appeared to him.'

is valuable not because it holds the potential for divine grace but because the attitude is by itself courageous and masculine. It is, in fact, potentially the best consolation available to a man in what appears to be, for Grettir at least, a godless world.

If Morris did not see the possibility of divine grace in Grettir's embrace of incapacitation, then perhaps he saw something that might, for want of a better phrase, be termed earthly acquiescence: a quality that combines dignified acceptance with the reality of human vulnerability. This quality is discernible in the lucid simplicity of the episodes in *The Story of Grettir the Strong* that touch on the protagonist's relentless endurance of ill luck, epitomised by the passage in which the local grandee Þorbjörg in digra discovers that the outlawed Grettir has been captured by the local farmers and asks him why he has caused them such disruption. This moment possesses a particularly simple transparency that allows Grettir's gracious humanity in accepting his vulnerability to shine through. The poignant meekness of his reply, 'Eigi má nú við öllu sjá; vera varð ek nokkurstaðar' (*GRE*, p. 119),[28] is captured in the plainness of Morris's rendering: 'I may not look to everything; I must needs be somewhere' (*CW*, VII, p. 129). In recognising the impossibility of his position (as a living man he has to be somewhere but as an outlaw he is allowed to be nowhere), Grettir openly acknowledges the burden of his reduced situation. By frankly admitting to his new limitations and working within the reality of this incapacitation, he exhibits a quality of grace that amounts to an accepting, even equanimous, approach to frailty. Far from seeing weakness in this attitude, in the simplicity of his translation here Morris shows Grettir's unassuming acceptance of fallibility to be touching, commendable and manly.

If, for Morris, incapacitation in the sagas presents an opportunity for the hero to embrace his circumstances with dignity, more pragmatically it also offers him the chance to test himself and uphold his ideals in a manner reminiscent of Arthurian gallantry. In this way, undergoing affliction or injury becomes what Hanson calls 'a kind of crucible for the forging of identity',[29] because is only when the hero becomes vulnerable that he can demonstrate the strength of his determination to remain courageous. Something of this demonstration of integrity is apparent in Morris's translation of the scenes in *Grettis saga* that recount the hero's

---

[28] 'One may not look to everything; I have to be somewhere.'

[29] Hanson, p. 13. Hanson employs the phrase cited here in relation to 'combat' in Morris's early short stories, but its relation to affliction or injury is implicit.

descent into death, in which Morris emphasises the nobility that Grettir maintains as he gradually succumbs. In the passage in which the leg wound that so weakens Grettir is discovered to have festered, for instance, the register of Morris's translation has the effect of ennobling the hero's integrity in enduring fatal debility:

> Kveiktu þeir þá ljós; ok er til var leyst, sýndist fótrinn blásinn ok kolblár, en sárit var hlaupit í sundr, ok miklu illiligra, enn í fyrstu. Þar fylgdi mikill verkr, svá at hann mátti hvergi kyrr þola, ok eigi kvam hánum svefn á augu. (*GRE*, p. 179)[30]

Morris translates this passage as:

> Then they kindled a light, and when the swathings were undone, the leg showed all swollen and coal-blue, and the wound had broken open, and was far more evil of aspect than at first; much pain there went therewith so that he might not abide at rest in any wise, and never came sleep on his eyes. (*CW*, VII, pp. 194–95)

The lyrical choice of 'showed all' for *sýndist* (literally 'appeared') adds a faint poetic quality to the moment when Grettir's wound is revealed, which a reader might experience as more dignified than in the original version. Similarly, the gentle archaism of phrases such as 'much pain there went therewith' (for *Þar fylgdi mikill verkr* [literally 'there/from it followed/arose great pain']), 'abide at rest' (for *kyrr þola* ['experience calm/rest']), 'not […] in any wise' (for *hvergi* ['by no means/not at all/in no way']) and the literal 'on' for the preposition *á* to translate *eigi kvam hánum svefn á augu* (literally 'sleep did not come to his eyes') endow Grettir's final decline with a quality of almost courtly decorum that is lacking in the Norse text. In contrast to a Carlylean or Kingsleyan ideal of the vigorous male body as an instrument of productivity or work, in this scene, Morris appears to portray Grettir's incapacitated body as a vehicle for manly resolve.

In Kenneth Hodges's analysis of the value of chivalric wounding in *Le Morte d'Arthur* he argues that within Malory's text 'wounds increase masculine worth'. In his view, scholarly assumptions that the Malorian ideal of masculinity is synonymous with invulnerability disrupt 'the

---

[30] 'They then kindled a light; and when it was untied the leg appeared swollen and coal-blue, but the wound was split apart and much worse than it had been at first. It caused so much pain that he could not experience rest, and sleep did not come to his eyes.'

whole system of meaning that makes masculine combat significant' in the poem.[31] Morris's translation of the final fight that leads to Grettir's death appears to confirm that he shares a similar attitude. In this scene, he heightens the resolve with which the hero and his brother Illugi respond to Grettir being mortally wounded (after having already been reduced to fighting on his knees due to almost total debilitation), so that the event of the injury becomes an opportunity to achieve masculinity, rather than to lose it. Where the 1853 edition has 'Þá mælti Grettir: berr er hverr á bakinu, nema sèr bróður eigi. Illugi kastaði skildi þá yfir hann, ok varði hann svá Gretti röskliga, at allir menn ágættu vörn hans' (*GRE*, p. 185),[32] Morris chooses 'Then cried Grettir, "*Bare is the back of the brotherless.*" And Illugi threw his shield over Grettir, and warded him in so stout a wise that all men praised his defence' (*CW*, VII, p. 201). Morris's 'Bare is the back of the brotherless' is pithier than the Norse phrase *berr er hverr á bakinu, nema sèr bróður eigi* (literally 'Bare is each one on the back, if he does not have a brother'), so that the close succession of alliterating [b] sounds imbues it with a proverbial quality that is more spirited and exultant. The phrase 'warded him in so stout a wise' to translate *varði hann svá Gretti röskliga* (literally 'warded' or 'protected Grettir so bravely') also amplifies Illugi's bravery, rendering him nobler and more gallant. Despite the fact that Grettir's wounds mean that his situation is hopeless – Illugi and he are utterly outnumbered and Grettir is, in any case, already dying from the festering leg injury – he behaves with integrity and valour in the direst of circumstances. Hodges's suggestion that the heroes of *Le Morte d'Arthur* show their courage and moral integrity by choosing to fight despite 'knowing themselves to be vulnerable' is equally true of Grettir and his brother.[33]

Hodges's further opinion that Malory does not ultimately present 'inviolate masculinity as an intact narrative goal' appears also to be true of the author of *Grettis saga*, and certainly of Morris as translator of *The Story of Grettir the Strong*. In Morris's more valiant translation of Grettir's death, he underscores the irrelevance of inviolability to masculinity by stressing the hero's worth in defeat and the worthlessness of his attackers'

[31] Kenneth Hodges, 'Wounded Masculinity: Injury Gender in Sir Thomas Malory's "Le Morte Darthur"', *Studies in Philology*, 106 (2009), 14–31 (p. 17).

[32] 'Then Grettir said: each one's back is bare unless he has a brother. Illugi then threw a shield over [Grettir] and guarded him so bravely that everyone praised his protection.'

[33] Hodges, p. 28.

victory. Once Illugi has himself been incapacitated in the fight, Grettir is left entirely vulnerable to his soon-to-be killers who finally turn their sole attention on him:

> Eptir þat gengu þeir at Gretti; var hann þá fallinn áfram. Varð þá engi vörn af hánum, því at hann var áðr kominn at bana af fótarsárinu. (*GRE*, p. 186)[34]

Morris translates this passage as:

> Thereafter they went up to Grettir, but he was fallen forward on to his face, and no defence there was of him, for that he was already come to death's door by reason of the hurt in his leg. (*CW*, vii, p. 202)

Here, Morris makes Grettir's position more precarious and degrading by having him fall 'onto his face' where his Norse counterpart simply falls forward. Subsequently, Morris's translation venerates the once vital hero during the final moments of Grettir's degradation when his attackers behead his lifeless body, which in the Norse text is described in an almost shockingly matter-of-fact register:

> Þá tók Öngull saxit tveim höndum, ok hjó í höfuð Gretti; varð þat allmikit högg, svá at saxit stózt eigi, ok brotnaði skarð í miðri egginni; ok er þeir sá þat, spurðu þeir, því hann spillti svá grip góðum. Öngull svarar: þá er auðkenndara, ef at verðr spurt. Þeir sögðu þessa eigi þurfa, þar sem maðrinn var dauðr áðr. At skal þó meira gjöra, segir Öngull; hjó hann þá á háls Gretti tvau högg eðr þrjú, áðr af tœki höfuðit. (*GRE*, p. 186)[35]

Morris translates this passage as:

> Then Angle took the short-sword in both hands and smote at Grettir's head, and a right great stroke that was, so that the short-sword might not abide it, and a shard was broken from the midst of the edge thereof; and

---

[34] 'After this they went at Grettir; he had then fallen forward. There was then no defence in him because he was already near death from his leg-wound.'

[35] 'Then Öngull took the sax with two hands, and hewed at Grettir's head; it was such a great blow that the sax did not withstand it, and a shard broke off from the middle of its blade; and when they saw this they asked why he was spoiling such a good treasure. Öngull replied: so it will be easier to recognise if anyone asks. They said that there was no need for this as the man was already dead. Nevertheless, more shall be done, said Öngull; he then hewed two or three blows at Grettir's neck, before taking off his head.'

when men saw that, they asked why he must needs spoil a fair thing in such wise.

But Angle answered, 'More easy is it to know that weapon now if it should be asked for.'

They said it needed not such a deed since the man was dead already.

'Ah! but yet more shall be done,' said Angle, and hewed therewith twice or thrice at Grettir's neck, or ever the head came off. (*CW*, vii, pp. 202–03)

Morris's choice of 'a right great stroke' for *allmikit högg* ('a very big blow', literally 'an all/entirely great hew'), 'in such wise' for *svá* ('so/such'), 'fair' for *góðr* ('good'), 'hewed [...] twice or thrice' for *hjó [...] tvau högg eðr þrjú* ('hewed two or three blows'), 'or ever' for *áðr* ('before') and 'spake' for *sagði* ('said') imbues this passage with an archaic intensity that is lacking in the Norse text. The demeaning treatment of Grettir's body becomes something more deliberate, even ceremonial in Morris's translation. Whereas in the Norse text the dispute over the damage to the sword alludes more clearly to the shamefulness of unnecessarily beheading a man who cannot defend himself, in Morris's translation, the slightly convoluted, elevated quality of the exchange masks the ethical point at stake and augments more generally the build-up to the crucial instant when the hero is beheaded. By suffering such degradation to the end so doggedly, even willingly, despite his fragility, it seems that, in Morris's view, Grettir achieved true manhood, triumphing over those whom he considered lesser, more grasping and, as he saw them, 'effete' men (see this chapter, p. 85, above). For Morris, Grettir appears to have been most courageous when most incapacitated, valiantly striving to embrace his circumstances even in the knowledge that victory is impossible. If Grettir adheres to a 'religion of courage' in which endurance is the ultimate act, it is not inspired by Christ's passion nor explicitly by any pre-Christian deity but by an effectively non-theist belief that this form of vulnerability-embracing stoicism is simply the most heroic attitude to take to life.

Grettir is by no means the only character to be devastated by incapacity in the sagas. Amongst the sagas of Icelanders that Morris began to read in 1868 were a number of stories that centre on a hero who is portrayed as fundamentally incapable of fulfilling a romantic commitment to a beloved, leading to conflict with a rival and the development of a torturous love triangle as the hero continues to covet his lost love. In *Kormáks saga* and *Gunnlaugs saga* (and to a lesser extent *Laxdæla saga* and the legendary *Völsunga saga*), it is this peculiar incapacitation in the hero that is the source of a cycle of pained longing, inertia and inhibition that dominates the central narrative. Gunnlaugr, for example, fails to return from abroad to marry his beloved Helga after he is delayed by the threat of war. Missing a ship so that he lands in the wrong part of Iceland, and subsequently twisting his foot, he arrives home after her wedding to Hrafn and is unable to win a comprehensive victory in the duels that follow. Likewise, Kormákr fails to attend his wedding to Steingerðr after their relationship is cursed. He subsequently ruins the attempts of a prophetess to lift the spell and even refuses Steingerðr when his rival Þorvaldr Tinteinn offers her to him, claiming that the union is not fated to happen. As with *Grettis saga*, in neither *Kormáks saga* nor *Gunnlaugs saga* is it evident to what extent the flaws in the hero's character lead to his failure or simply coincide with greater fateful forces. As Diana Whaley has asserted: 'The reader is left to wonder how the saga author meant his Christian audience to view the balance of fate and human responsibility.'[36]

A preoccupation with this *romantic* rather than *corporeal* incapacity is apparent in Morris's rendering of the love triangles in his translations of *Gunnlaugs saga* and *Kormáks saga*. If in his translation of *Grettis saga*, it is the diminution of the hero's physical strength that Morris foregrounds – the progress of his fear, vulnerability and invalidity – in these sagas it is the inert longing of his romanticised sexual frustration, his almost castrated impotence and spiritual separation from his intended. In scene after scene in Morris's translations of these sagas, he augments and romanticises the quality of non-carnal yearning that the hero feels for the heroine, with the result that the endurance of the sexually incapacitated state is idealised.

In his translation of the scene in *Gunnlaugs saga*, for example, in which Gunnlaugr chances on Helga on the opposite bank of a river after she has married Hrafn, Morris idealises the quality of romantic pining. This is clear in the initial verse that the hero speaks in both the 1869 *Fortnightly Review* version of the saga and the version that he reworked for *Three Northern Love Stories* in 1875 once his appreciation of skaldic verse had considerably improved:

> Alin vas rýgr at rógi,
> runnr olli því gunnar,
> lág var ek auðs at eiga
> óðgjarn, fíra börnum;
> nú er svanmærar síðan,

[36] Introduction to *Sagas of Warrior-Poets* (London: Penguin, 2002), p. xix.

svört augu mèr bauga,
lands til læsi gunnar
lítil þörf at líta. (*GUN*, p. 260)[37]

In his 1869 rendering of *Gunnlaugs saga*, Morris translated this verse as:

For what but end of mirth
Didst this damsel come on earth?
I, the grove of fight, so wrought
That to mad love I was brought;
Henceforth can it profit me
Those dark eyes with eyes to see,
Or the swan-like to behold
Closing round her arms the gold?[38]

In his 1875 rendering of *Gunnlaugs saga*, he translated the same verse as:

Born was she for men's bickering:
Sore bale hath wrought the war-stem,
And I yearned ever madly
To hold that oak-tree golden.
To me then, me destroyer
Of swan-mead's flame, unneedful
This looking on the dark-eyed,
This golden land's beholding.[39]

In the first two lines of the 1869 version Morris romanticises the heartache that Helga causes Gunnlaug. She is a 'damsel' rather than a *rýgr* ('lady/ woman'), 'come on earth' (a romantic and aggrandising image lacking in the Norse stanza) for 'end of mirth' rather than *róg* ('strife/discord/ quarrel'). Though in the 1875 translation Helga is no longer a 'damsel'

---

[37] Prose word order of stanza: *Rýgr vas alin at rógi fíra börnum, Gunnar runnr olli því; var ek óðgjarn at eiga auðs lág; nú er síðan svört augu mèr lítil þörf at líta til svanmærrar baugalands læsi gunnar.* 'The lady was born for strife amongst the children of men, the shrub of the valkyrie (Gunn) [> warrior > Hrafn or Þorsteinn] caused this; I was desperately eager to marry the log of wealth [> woman]; now my black eyes are seldom needed to me in looking on the swan-glorious light-valkyrie (Gunn) of the ring-land [> woman].'

[38] 'The Saga of Gunnlaug the Worm-Tongue and Rafn the Skald', trans. William Morris and Eiríkr Magnússon, *Fortnightly Review*, January 1869, 27–56 (p. 51).

[39] *Three Northern Love Stories, and Other Tales*, trans. William Morris and Eiríkr Magnússon (London: Ellis & White, 1875), p. 51.

and is now born for 'men's bickering' (closer to *róg fíra börnum* ['strife for the children of men']), she is still described more sentimentally as having wrought 'sore bale', which has no equivalent in the Norse stanza. Similarly, in the third and fourth lines of the 1869 translation Gunnlaug is more headily brought 'to mad love', rather than being simply *óðgjarn at eiga* ('vehemently/madly keen to marry') Helga. While in the 1875 rendering the translation of *var ek óðgjarn* ('I was vehemently/madly eager') is modified to the more literal 'I yearned ever madly', Morris introduces the particular quality of pining or aching that is suggested by MnE 'yearned', since the Old Norse cognate *gjarn* simply means 'eager for/desirous of/willing' here (with the prefixed *óð* indicating 'madly/violently').[40] Moreover, in choosing to translate *eiga* ('to own/hold' but in the context of relationships 'to marry') as 'hold' rather than 'marry' in the 1875 version, he chooses to stress the pain of the thwarted romantic or spiritual bond between the lovers, rather than the specific loss of the legal union.

Though Morris's word choices in the later version of this verse were perhaps influenced by a clearer attempt to reflect the alliteration in the Old Norse stanza, and the more ardent tone might be in part the result of switching to unrhymed lines (which create greater opportunity for sustained energy through enjambment), his tendency to romanticise Gunnlaugr's pining for Helga may also indicate that he deemed the hero's ability to endure romantic incapacitation to be as virtuous as Grettir's ability to endure physical incapacitation. Since Morris chose to rework this verse six years after he first translated it, it seems unlikely that the increased intensity of the quality of romantic inertia was due to lack of experience with the language. Indeed, his sustained tendency to idealise the hero's impeded longing in the 1875 version, despite his increased ability to translate Old Norse, suggests that he was attracted to something about the endurance of romantic pain.

This possibility is supported by Morris's various renderings of the subsequent verse that Gunnlaug speaks, which he happened to translate on three separate occasions over the 1868–76 period (once each for the

---

[40] While *gjarn* is etymologically related to MnE *yearn* via Middle English *yernen* ('to wish for, long for'), OE *geornan/giernan* ('to strive for, be eager for, desire'), *georn* ('desirous, eager') and ON *girna* ('to desire'), it does not suggest the quality of plaintive tenderness that the modern word does. See *Chambers Dictionary of Etymology*, ed. Robert K. Barnhart (Edinburgh: Chambers, 1988), p. 1252.

1869 and 1875 versions of *Gunnlaugs saga*, and on a further occasion when the same stanza is spoken by the hero of *Kormáks saga* also):

> Brámáni skein brúna
> brims af ljósum himni[41]
> Hristar hörvi glæstar
> haukfrán á mik lauka;
> en sá geisli sýslar
> síðan gullmens fríðar
> hvarma túngls ok hrínga
> Hlínar óþurft mína. (*GUN*, p. 261)[42]

In his 1869 rendering of *Gunnlaugs saga*, Morris translated this verse as:

> How the lash-girt moon and bright
> Of the linen-hid delight
> From the calm heaven shone on me
> Eager bright as hawk's-eyn be!
> Ah, that that lash-tempered ray
> Of the golden-gleaming may,
> Still such evil hap should move
> Both for me and for my love![43]

In his version of *Kormáks saga* (c.1871–72), he translated it as:

> The bright moon of the brow
> Brake out of that light heaven
> Of that goddess linen-girded
> Eager glad to shine upon me:
> But that beam of the goldbearer,

---

[41] The verse appears with a slightly different wording in the edition of *Kormáks saga* that Morris used, reading 'brims und ljósum himni', 'hauk-frán', 'síðan gollhríngs Fríðar' and 'hvarmatúngls ok hrínga'. See *KOR*, p. 14.

[42] Prose word order of stanza: *Haukfrán brámáni hörvi glæstar lauka brims Hristar skein á mik af ljósum brúna himni; en sá hvarma túngls geisli gullmens fríðar sýslar síðan óþurft mína ok hringa Hlínar.* 'The hawk-gleaming lash-moon [> eye] of the valkyrie (Hrist) of leek-surf [leek surf > ale, valkyrie of ale > woman] adorned with linen shone on me from out of her brow's bright sky [> forehead] but that ray of the moon of the eyelid [moon of the eyelid > eye, ray of the eye > gaze] of the goddess (Fríð) of the golden necklace [> woman] henceforth will bring/has brought trouble for me and for the goddess (Hlín) of rings [> woman] as well.'

[43] Morris and Eiríkr Magnússon, 'Saga of Gunnlaug (1869)', p. 51.

> Bright cheeks moon-beam, bringeth surely
> Henceforth harm enough upon me
> Yea on her too, red rings' goddess. (*SoK*, p. 78)

In his 1875 rendering of *Gunnlaugs saga*, he translated it as:

> Moon of linen-lapped one,
> Leek-sea-bearing goddess,
> Hawk-keen out of heaven
> Shone all bright upon me;
> But that eyelid's moonbeam
> Of gold-necklaced goddess
> Her hath all undoing
> Wrought, and me made nought of.[44]

In his 1869 translation Morris significantly increases the sense of idealised ardour, which has the effect of rendering Gunnlaug less sexually charged than his Norse counterpart. Helga is not simply *hörvi glæstar* ('adorned/ shining with linen'), she is a 'linen-hid *delight*'. The archaism of 'eyn' and 'may' places the verse in the realm of romantic enchantment; an effect that is accentuated by the fact that both *helmings* work as exclamations of wonder concurrent to the incident they are describing (rather than, as in the Norse verse, as thoughtful acknowledgements of a moment that has just occurred). While in the translation of circa 1871–72 Morris follows the Old Norse more closely[45] – the heroine is now a 'goddess linen-girded' (connected to the kenning that utilises the valkyrie, Hrist) and the exclamatory sentences have been replaced by simple observations – there are still touches of romanticisation. The heroine's gaze is 'Eager glad' (for which there is no equivalent in the Norse stanza) and the archaism of 'brake', 'girded' and 'Yea' heightens the register in which Gunnlaug laments his separation from Helga.

In the 1875 translation, it is evident that Morris understands the way in which the verse (and the kennings in particular) work more clearly, so that *lauka brims Hrist* ('Hrist [valkyrie] of the surf of the leek > valkyrie of ale > woman'), for instance, now becomes 'Leek-sea-bearing goddess', and *gullmens Fríðr* ('goddess (Fríðr) of the golden-necklace > woman') goes from 'gold gleaming may' to simply 'goldbearer' to 'gold-necklaced

---

[44] Morris and Eiríkr Magnússon, *Three Northern Love Stories* (1875), p. 51.
[45] He does, however, choose a slightly different word order: *brúna* ['of the brow'] is now part of the first kenning rather than the second, for instance.

goddess'. Nevertheless, even though the first *helming* is now particularly close to the Norse stanza, Morris cannot resist rhapsodising the experience of romantic incapacitation by translating *sýslir síðan ópurft mína ok ok hringa Hlínar* ('henceforth trouble occurs/will occur for me and for the goddess (Hlín) of rings as well') to a more histrionic image of destruction in 'hath all undoing | Wrought, and made me nought of'. This sustained inclination to idealise the aspect of incapacitated romantic longing in the various translations of these verses suggests that the element of the love triangle that particularly attracted Morris is the way in which it imprisons the protagonist in a position of frustration, and thereby challenges him to respond prudently to the testing situation. Gunnlaugr's romantic impotence thereby actually becomes a productive experience for a man.

One further way to examine Morris's idealisation of romantic incapacitation in the sagas is to consider this propensity in relation to the newly erotic phase of Pre-Raphaelitism that had gained momentum during the 1860s. This impulse is perhaps most conspicuous in the 'virile form of aestheticism' of Rossetti's self-contained female portraits,[46] which in the years leading up to Morris's saga translations had, according to Jan Marsh, 'increasingly displaced the earlier religious and literary subjects of his work'.[47] In paintings such as *Bocca Baciata* (1859), *Monna Pomona* (1864), *The Bride* (1865) and *Monna Vanna* (1866), Rossetti radically portrayed the sensuality of his 'carnal beauties' as both positive and powerful,[48] so that 'far from being deleterious' the female subject's sexual experience became, in J. B. Bullen's words, 'an enhancing virtue'.[49] The vulva-like lips of the subject of *Bocca Baciata*,[50] the enticing fingers and full-throated neck of the subject of *Monna Pomona*, the unswerving, enthralling gaze of the subject of *The Bride* and luscious luxuriance of the subject of *Monna Vanna* concentrate the intense seductiveness of the woman in question while simultaneously compelling the (ostensibly male) viewer into a posture of voyeuristic fascination.[51] By contrast, in Morris's translation of the scene in *Kormáks saga* when the hero spends

[46] Robert Upstone, *The Pre-Raphaelite Dream: Paintings and Drawings from the Tate Collection* (London: Tate, 2003), p. 28.

[47] Jan Marsh, *Pre-Raphaelite Women: Images of Femininity in Pre-Raphaelite Art* (London: Phoenix Illustrated, 1998), p. 23.

[48] Marsh, p. 86.

[49] J. B. Bullen, *The Pre-Raphaelite Body: Fear and Desire in Painting, Poetry, and Criticism* (Oxford: Clarendon Press, 1998), p. 93.

[50] Bullen, p. 129.

[51] Upstone, pp. 147–57.

a sexually charged night with Steingerðr separated only by a partition, he places Kormákr in a constrained position of chaste innocence, minimising the powerfully erotic allure of the heroine, as well as the frustrated libidinous urges of the hero:

> um nóttina hvíldi sínum-megin bríkar hvârt þeirra. Þa kvað Kormakr vísu:

> Hvílum handar bála
> hlín, (valda sköp sínu
> þat sjám reið at ráði)
> rík, tveim megin bríkar;
> nærgi er oss í eina
> ángrlaust sæng gaungum
> dýr Sköfnúngi drafnar
> dyneyjar við freyja. (*KOR*, p. 184)[52]

Morris translates this verse as:

> and they slept a-night with the panel of the bed between them, each on their own side. And Kormak sang:

> Lady, that arm's-light bearest,
> Here are we laid together,
> Nought but the bed's board betwixt us.
> Sure this the fates have brought forth,
> That, with the sword's dear sweetling,
> Goddess of soft down islands,
> All sorrow slaked for ever
> I should at last be lying. (*SoK*, p. 117)

While the Norse verse is ultimately a declaration of both Steingerðr's

---

[52] Prose word order of stanza: *Hvílum, handar bála hlín, tveim megin bríkar; valda rík sköp sínu; þat sjám at ráði reið; nærgi er gaungum oss ángrlaust í eina sæng, drafnar freya, dýr Sköfnúng[i/a] dyneyjar við.* 'During the night they slept one each side of a screen: Then Kormákr spoke a verse: we sleep, Hlín of the fires of the arm [fires of the arm > gold, goddess (Hlín) of gold > woman], one on each side of a screen; the powerful fates rule their way; we see that they are wrathful in their plan; whenever we get into the same bed carefree, Freya of the foaming sea [goddess (Freya) of the foaming sea > woman], you are dear to the mast/tree [> man] of the island's din of the swords [island > shield, din of shields > battle, man of battle of the swords > warrior] or (possibly, although grammatically unclear) you are dear to the sword of the mast/tree of the din of islands [island > shield, din of shields [> battle], mast/tree of battle > warrior, sword of the warrior > his penis].'

sexual power (which is almost fetishised in two vividly sensual kennings) and Kormákr's physical frustration at being continually forced into a posture of detachment because he finds her so sensually alluring, Morris's stanza suggests Kormak's innocent pleasure at lying in the same bed as Steingerd, with neither character being overtly eroticised. Though in the Norse text it is not clear exactly how the partition separates the sleepers from one another, and specifically whether they are sharing the same bed, as O'Donoghue has highlighted, Morris imagines the panel explicitly 'down the middle of the [*same*] bed',[53] consciously placing his lovers in the position in which their separation is most equally symmetrical and, therefore, romantically symbolic. The partition becomes an emblem of division in Morris's text rather than a genuine hindrance to carnality.[54] The role of the fates is also altered so that, whereas in the Norse stanza they represent potent and vigorous forces that prevent the sexual union of hero and heroine, in Morris's verse they become a kindly and decorous version of providence that allows Kormak and Steingerd to lie blissfully beside one another in a naive pose of purity. Where Rossetti's paintings offer 'explicit testimony to the power of sexual attraction and an embodiment of [his] feelings of erotic yearning for the opposite sex',[55] Morris's stanza proposes an almost androgynous affirmation of respectful companionship and decency, with the hero apparently taking pleasure in his endurance of frustration.

The contemporary of Morris who is perhaps best known for portraying androgyny in his artistic work was his close friend Burne-Jones. In *Days of Creation* (1872–76) and *The Golden Stairs* (1876–80) the ethereal, alabaster spirits of his paintings are imbued with an epicene quality that, as Bullen has emphasised, led to censorious accusations of unmanliness when they were first shown.[56] Bullen argues that Burne-Jones's androgynes were in part created to defy 'a certain kind of masculinity',[57] which

---

[53] Heather O'Donoghue, *The Genesis of a Saga Narrative: Verse and Prose in Kormaks Saga* (Oxford: Clarendon Press, 1991), p. 126.

[54] On the same page O'Donoghue directs readers interested in the sexual interpretations of this verse by earlier scholars to Peter Hallberg, *Old Norse Poetry: Eddic Lay and Skaldic Verse* (Lincoln: University of Nebraska Press, 1975), pp. 151–52.

[55] Upstone, p. 147.

[56] Bullen, p. 154. See also Henry James, 'The Picture Season in London, 1877', in *The Painter's Eye: Notes and Essays on the Pictorial Arts*, ed. John L. Sweeney (London: Hart Davis, 1956), pp. 130–51.

[57] Bullen, p. 185.

he identifies as a 'set of values which privileged the active, the material, and the unreasonable at the expense of the non-material, and the intuitive.'[58] Since, in Bullen's view, many Victorian men (and especially those who had 'bisexual or homoerotic leanings or those who attached great importance to intuitiveness and sensitivity') were burdened by the stresses of 'a highly masculinized culture', representations of androgyny became a way of pushing against the strictures of normative masculinity.[59]

It is possible that Morris's own employment of androgyny in his saga translations was intended to have a similar effect. In the subsequent stanza that Kormak speaks while lying next to Steingerd, Morris stresses the impassive neutrality of his hero over the ruttish frustration of his Norse counterpart:

> Sváfum hress í húsi
> horn þeyjar við freyja
> fjarðar legs en frægja
> fimm nætr saman grimmar;
> ok hyrketils hverja
> hrafns æfi gnoð stafna
> lags á lítt of hugsi
> lá ek andvana banda. (*KOR*, p. 184)[60]

Morris translates this verse as:

> Soft in the house I slept,
> And she who sets horns flowing,
> We slept, we twain together
> Through five nights' bitter torment.

---

[58] Bullen, p. 193.

[59] Bullen, p. 194.

[60] Prose word order of stanza: *við [vit] sváfum hress, en frægja horn þeyjar fjarðar legs freyja, í húsi grimmar nætr fimm saman; ok lá ek andvana banda lags hverja hrafns æfi á lítt of hugsi hyrketils stafna gnoð.* 'We two slept on, fit and well, renowned Freya of the froth of the horn's land of the fjord [froth of the horn > ale, land of the fjord > horn/vessel, goddess (Freya) of the ale-horn > woman], in a house five grim nights together; and I lay deprived of the binding companionship [> sexual intercourse] each age of the raven [> night] with little on my mind, on the prow of the ship of the fire-kettle [> bed, although Einar Ól. Sveinsson points out that this looks more like a kenning for *fire-place*']. See *Vatnsdæla Saga; Hallfreðar Saga; Kormáks Saga; Hrómundar þáttr halta; Hrafns þáttr Guðrúnarsonar*, ed. Einar Ól. Sveinsson, Íslenzk Fornrit, 8 (Reykjavík: Hið íslenzka fornritafélag, 1939), pp. 273–74.

> Blank on the bed I lay
> Through the black day of ravens
> Empty of every thought
> All hope of love's embracing. (*SoK*, p. 118)

Where Kormákr is *andvana banda lags* ('deprived of the binding companionship [> sexual intercourse]') for five *grimmar nætr* ('grim' or 'dire nights', with the adjective 'grimmr' here perhaps suggesting something of his physical discomfort at being sexually aroused but obstructed), Morris's Kormak is 'blank' and 'empty of thought | All hope of love's embracing'. Rather than being sexually frustrated he simply lacks sensual desire. Morris's translation does not distinguish as clearly between the femininity of the kennings associated with Steingerðr and the masculinity of the imagery associated with Kormákr's arousal. Instead, his hero and heroine are set in mutual equivalence beside one another. There is more of a nuance of shared fellowship in Kormak and Steingerd sleeping 'we twain together' 'Soft in the house' than in the Norse stanza's *við [vit] sváfum hress* ('we two slept, healthy'). As well as idealising the courage of endurance that he perceived in Kormákr's impotent separation from Steingerðr, in his augmentation of the almost androgynous sexual innocence of the hero it is plausible that, like Burne-Jones, Morris was using art to defy a construction of masculinity associated with the prevailing ethos of materialism, commerce and conquest.

There is, of course, the possibility that Morris had more personal reasons to admire the courage of the saga heroes to endure incapacitation. Critics have often noted the preponderance of love triangles in his writing (*TEP*, II, pp. 284–85; *LOT*, p. 130), with many linking his attraction to them to the triangular relationship in which he found himself with his wife and Rossetti.[61] Yet, while it is conceivable that Morris gained some kind of catharsis in translating the sagas of Gunnlaugr and Kormákr during a period when he was perhaps himself feeling emotions of betrayal, conflicted devotion and pining, he had in fact been drawn to the trial of integrity and loyalty that the motif presents – what Boos has termed 'fidelity-in-rejection' (*TEP*, II, p. 284) – from his youth. He was already contemplating the Palomydes–Iseult–Tristram story in the spring before either he or Rossetti met the young Jane Burden in the summer of 1857 (when Morris based his portion of the Oxford Union murals on 'Sir Palomydes's Jealousy of Sir Tristram and Iseult') (*LOT*, p. 130).

---

[61] See Wilmer, 'Maundering Medievalism', pp. 214–15.

Moreover, 'Gertha's Lovers', the even earlier 1856 story written for *The Oxford & Cambridge Magazine*, had also centred on a love triangle (*TEP*, II, pp. 284–85.) It seems more likely, therefore, that Morris was attracted to the triangular relationships in the poets' sagas because he was already interested in the endurance that comes with being constrained, than that in the early 1870s he chose the Norse love triangles as vehicles to reflect his unhappy private life. As he began to translate the sagas, the romantic incapacitation that is intrinsic to their love triangles spoke directly to his developing ideal of the heroic, informing his conviction that the embrace of fallibility is both brave and manly.

Even though I have suggested that Morris's attraction to incapacity in the sagas did not derive primarily from his potential position as a cuckold, there is no doubt that in a form of homage to his heroes – 'I was quite ready to break my neck in my quality of pilgrim to the holy places of Iceland (*CW*, VIII, p. 67) – he approached the Icelandic journeys as tests of what appear to have been his own private feelings of inadequacy, which possibly (though not certainly) arose at a time when unhappiness in his marriage was approaching a climax. Throughout the first journal, for example, he regularly registers apprehension at the physical require-ments of the trek, so that a picture emerges of a man who deems himself rather incapable and cowardly. He is as 'nervous as might be' riding through his first lava field (*CW*, VIII, p. 30), confesses 'trepidation' on fording his first river (*CW*, VIII, p. 39) and admits 'to [his] shame, how [he has] had the pass of Búlandshöfði on [his] mind for some days' (*CW*, VIII, p. 122).

Morris also repeatedly contrasts his own intrepidness negatively with that of his rugged companion W. H. Evans, who had been attracted to Iceland primarily for the 'shooting and fishing' (Introduction to *CW*, VIII, p. xv). When Evans points out the small size of ship on which they will sail to Iceland, Morris pretends 'not to care', though his flesh creeps as he expects 'firstly to die of sea-sickness, secondly to be drowned' (*CW*, VIII, p. 6). Once trekking, he records Evans riding hard in front while he loiters behind (*CW*, VIII, p. 56), choosing to sleep on the parlour floor while he takes a fold-out bed (*CW*, VIII, p. 63), managing to light the fire after he fails (*CW*, VIII, p. 78), and even turning down one of his worms in favour of fishing without bait (*CW*, VIII, p. 72). Criticising himself for his own 'milksopishness' during a severe storm, Morris reckons Evans to have withstood it better (*CW*, VIII, p. 87), and goes on to remark that he is the only one of the party not to dismount on the precarious shale of Búlandshöfði (*CW*, VIII, p. 133).

Almost as frequently as he acknowledges his own incapacity, Morris challenges himself to overcome it. On one occasion after giving up while climbing into the cave of Surtshellir, he berates himself for having missed (to his 'great shame and grief' 'by [his] lachesse') a great pillar of ice and a frozen waterfall: 'they said that it was hard enough to get there, and Evans had an ugly fall on his knee which he felt for many days afterwards. Nevertheless, why didn't I try it' (*CW*, VIII, p. 84). Later, as he approaches the hazardous pass of Búlandshöfði he mulls over his own capacity not to panic. Though he does not 'really think [the pass] dangerous for capable people', he frets about what would happen if his head 'gave way half way across' and decides at first on a circuitous route. However, in the end, 'it would be mean to shirk Búlandshöfði as one of the marvels of our pilgrimage' prevails (*CW*, VIII, p. 122–23), and he later records that when it came to navigating the pass he 'discounted [his] fear', merely suffering 'a beating of the heart, not unpleasant, and a little trembling about the knees' (*CW*, VIII, p. 133). Afterwards, seeing that Faulkner was 'rather disappointed' and Evans 'scornful of the whole affair', Morris eventually decides that he 'ought not to have spoken of it as a perilous pass at all' (*CW*, VIII, p. 134). The reader repeatedly sees him struggling to locate courage in his own incapacity.

A comparable process of seeking courage is apparent in several of Morris's short poems on Icelandic themes. In these verses Morris (as speaker) longs to discover his own courageousness by entreating the medieval Icelanders to commune with him. His various attempts to draft the last line of the sonnet that begins 'Grettir, didst thou live utterly for nought' (1869), for example, show him experimenting with ways to express an almost desperate desire to receive some measure of Grettir's tenacity:

> ~~Reach~~, Grettir, through the dark, ~~I shall not fear.~~
> Speak   for I can hear.
>   I am anear[62]

Initially emphasising both the speaker's desire for Grettir to embrace him through the darkness, and his resolution to be brave, Morris twice changes the end of the sonnet in order to emphasise the speaker's solidarity, if not kinship, with the hero. There is the sense that the speaker wants most to keep Grettir company in the darkness that he so fears and, in doing so,

---

[62] William Morris, 'B. L. Add. MS 45318' (British Library, London, [n. d.]), p. 91a.

benefit from his courage. In this poem, Morris envisions Grettir (who seems to possess even greater humility than in the saga translation) as a model of vigorous living, even in the face of adversity, succeeding to maintain an 'eager life in ill luck's meshes caught'.[63] Similarly, in 'To the Muse of the North' (c.1869–70) the speaker pleads with the muse to allow him a share in the shouldering of the burden of the Icelandic people: 'Let some word reach my ears and touch my heart, | That, if it may be, I may have a part | In that great sorrow of thy children dead'. He yearns to know what it is to be able to endure their adversity: 'for sure I am enough alone | That thou thine arms about my heart shouldst throw, | And wrap me in the grief of long ago'.[64]

In Morris's other sonnet to the Icelandic heroes beginning 'A life scarce worth the living' (1869), the speaker stresses the living example of tenacity that, in their dejection, the heroes have presented him with: 'that which carried him through good and ill, | Stern against fate [...] strives | With wasting time, and through its long lapse gives | Another friend to me'. Though Morris portrays reality as a godless abyss here (when the inhabitants of Iceland die they 'fare without an aim | Unto the dull grey dark from when they came'), their steadfastness inspires the speaker to discover the value of courageousness in the emptiness of his own life.[65] In the same way that Morris's engagement with Iceland involved a personal dimension that allowed him to challenge himself in the same terrain in which he imagined the saga characters to have lived and breathed, his engagement with Icelandic literature and poetry involved a personally didactic element: he literally attempted to draw inspiration from the lives of the heroes for how to live his own life.

By the time that Morris returned from the second Icelandic trip in 1873, it is clear that he had discovered some form of courage for himself. In the almost twenty-two months since September 1871 when he arrived back from the first voyage, he had endured an interval of deep melancholy that coincided with Jane spending extended periods of time with Rossetti (see Introduction, pp. 19–20). By November 1872, he declared of his friendship with the artist that 'it is really a farce our meeting when we can help it', but such pragmatism had not stopped him from admonishing himself for his own dejection: 'When I said there was no cause for my feeling low

---

[63] William Morris, 'B. L. Add. MS 45318', p. 91a; *CW*, VII, p. xix.
[64] William Morris, *A Book of Verse: A Facsimile of the Manuscript Written in 1870* (London: Scolar, 1980), p. 43.
[65] William Morris, *Book of Verse*, p. 36.

[...], I am afraid that it comes from some cowardice or unmanliness in me.'[66] In this frame of mind, the chance of returning to Iceland represented a remedy to him for such supposed weakness. In February 1873, he confessed 'Iceland gapes for me still this summer: [...] if I can only get away in some sort of hope and heart I know it will be the making of me.'[67] In many ways, the trip proved to be just that. His daughter, May, asserts that the second visit touched him 'even more closely than the first visit had': as 'all that first excitement gave place to an exaltation of spirit peculiarly intense, expressed in some degree by the sort of detachment the diary conveys' (Introduction to *CW*, viii, p. xxxiii).

Throughout the second journal Morris comments repeatedly on a newly discovered assuredness where he would once have been fearful. He notes proudly that 'it said something of my feeling at home [...] that when a horse ran over stock and stone about here and the two boxes came down with a crash my heart never rose to my mouth' (*CW*, viii, pp. 188–89) and, subsequently, on fording the deepest river that he has ever crossed in Iceland, he boasts: 'Nevertheless the whole thing had got unfrightful to me now and I crossed it pipe in mouth (*CW*, viii, p. 225).[68] A newly dispassionate quality to the prose is certainly evident in the second journal. The excitability, rumbustiousness and self-depreciation of the first expedition give way to a grounded contemplation of the changing contours of the landscape that renders Morris more self-assured and resilient. In the words of Purkis: 'The contrast between the two journals is clear; by the end of the second Morris has achieved his quest: Iceland has been wrestled with and conquered – now it is like a friend to be treated familiarly and without fear'.[69] He had embraced his own incapacity and in doing so somehow surmounted it.

The return from Iceland in September 1873 marks a fundamental watershed in Morris's life: 'Do you know I feel as if a definite space of my life had passed away now I have seen Iceland for the last time', he wrote almost immediately that he was back in London.[70] Though it is unclear why he was so resolved on the fact that he would never see the island again, it appears that it had already fulfilled its function in his mind and he was now able to move forward keenly with a new confidence: 'I am

[66] Letter to Coronio, probably dated 12 November 1872, in Kelvin, i, p. 172.
[67] Letter to Coronio, dated 11 February 1873, in Kelvin, i, p. 178.
[68] See also *CW*, viii, pp. 196, 201.
[69] Purkis, p. 27.
[70] Letter to Coronio, probably dated 14 September 1873, in Kelvin, i, p. 198.

wanting to settle down now into a really industrious man: for I do not mean to go to Iceland again if I can help it', he wrote in October.[71] Indeed, even though he would always remain prone to passing gloomy moods, in the autumn of 1873 a new maturity (or perhaps even a newly heroic attitude) seems to have become available to him that by and large sustained his generally buoyant disposition for the rest of his life. Kindly offering encouraging advice to Burne-Jones's school-age son in December 1874, he reassured him that 'you may take it as a certain rule both in fisticuffs and all manner of fighting that if you are not afraid of being hit you can hit your enemy, and then the rest is a matter of endurance only'.[72] By March 1875, he was remarking 'I must needs call myself a happy man on the whole: and I do verily think I have gone over every possible misfortune that may happen to me in my own mind, & concluded that I can bear it if it should come'.[73]

While the two years between the voyages of 1871 and 1873, when Morris was at his lowest ebb during his wife's affair with Rossetti, certainly overlap with the gradual emergence in his mind of a new ideal of courageous living, this chapter has shown that the signs of a new attitude towards heroic masculinity in Morris are visible in the saga translations made in 1868 and 1869, indicating that a wider process of development was in progress that was not necessarily linked as narrowly to the strain of his marriage as some critics have suggested. It may be that there is something ultimately inscrutable about how Iceland and its literature informed Morris's own private sense of manhood, and subsequently sustained him on his return. James Morris alludes rather romantically to him having been guided by 'the mystique of the North',[74] while Charles Harvey and Jon Press describe the conversion that Morris underwent during this time as 'something at once more vague and more substantial' than 'any specific creed' to which 'it is impossible to put a name'.[75]

Whatever motivated Morris's newfound definition of courageousness (in Chapter 1, I suggested that it may have developed as his faith in a

[71] Letter to Louisa Macdonald Baldwin, dated 22 October 1873, in Kelvin, I, p. 203.
[72] Letter to Philip Burne-Jones, probably dated 7 or 14 December 1874, in Kelvin, I, p. 242.
[73] Letter to Macdonald Baldwin, dated 25 March 1875, in Kelvin, I, p. 247.
[74] William Morris, *Icelandic Journals*, ed. James Morris (Fontwell, Sussex: Centaur Press, 1969), pp. xv–xvi.
[75] Charles Harvey and Jon Press, *Art, Enterprise and Ethics: The Life and Works of William Morris* (London: Frank Cass, 1996), p. 80; Preston, p. 25.

mystical reality waned [see pp. 50–52]), it is clear that the embrace of human vulnerability was integral to it. For Morris, enduring incapacity in the sagas provided a means by which a hero was able to grow into true manliness because it offered an authentic trial of courage that the Romantic image of the indomitable Viking denied. The experience of incapacitation provided the sufferer with an opportunity to locate the courage to retain integrity, thus allowing for a process of heroic maturation as he grew in moral determination. It is this determination born of incapacity that Morris describes as the 'sentiment and moral sense' that made Grettir's 'hopeless looking life' endurable, and that represented for him a 'lesson' to the 'effete folk' of the present (see this chapter, p. 85, above).

It was also something like this determination that Morris hoped to find for himself through his voyages to Iceland and in the hopes he expressed in his short Norse-inspired poems. It was an attitude to life that endeavoured to engage eagerly in the world despite the meshes of fortune, to move forward like Grettir with, in Hanson's words, 'a kind of active passion that stands in contrast to mental or emotional detachment'.[76] In creating what Hanson calls a 'more holistic vision of manliness' in his Icelandic heroes,[77] one that she suggests may involve the vulnerability of 'abandonment to destiny, rather than defiance of it',[78] Morris rejected the category of heroism based on the ideal of inviolability in favour of a new ideal in which the felt experience of vulnerability and fallibility was integral to a manly life. It was paradoxically through the embrace of incapacity that Morris located the courage to live more heroically.

---

[76] Hanson, p. 79.
[77] Hanson, p. 70.
[78] Hanson, p. 76.

4

Heimskringla, Literalness and the Power of Craft

ESCRIBING THEIR WORKING practice as they translated *Heim-skringla* (Volumes 3–6 of The Saga Library) (see Introduction, pp. 12–15), Eiríkur Magnússon commented that Morris emended the style 'throughout in accordance with his own ideal' (Preface to TSL, 6, p. VII).[1] This remark raises the question of what constituted Morris's ideal of style and why he created it. Though Barribeau has highlighted the fact that in his translations from Old Norse Morris 'attempted to point out to his English audience the common Germanic roots of Icelandic and English',[2] and Aho has suggested that 'when Morris chose English words that were cognate to the original Icelandic, perhaps he was hoping that his readers would somehow thereby sense that old association',[3] no scholar has satisfactorily shown how the literal style that Morris gradually insisted upon for his saga translations was meant to bridge the temporal and cultural gap between the imagined medieval Icelandic society that he celebrated in the sagas and the degraded British one that he lamented in the present. This chapter, therefore, examines Morris's gradual insistence on literalness in translation and proposes that it represents an increasingly diligent attempt to reconnect his readers with an erstwhile kindred culture, but that this attempt was undermined by a misjudgement on his part of what his audience would recognise as familiar.

---

[1] Material in this chapter first appeared with a slightly differently wording as 'The Old Norse Sagas and William Morris's Ideal of Literal Translation', *Review of English Studies*, 67 (2016), 220–36. See http://res.oxfordjournals.org/content/early/2016/03/10/res.hgw022.full.

[2] Barribeau, 'Saga-Translation', p. 252.

[3] Introduction to *Three Northern Love Stories and Other Tales*, trans. William Morris and Eiríkr Magnússon, William Morris Library, 11 (Bristol: Thoemmes, 1996), p. xxiv.

The literal style into which Morris chose to translate Old Norse, which first evolved between 1868 and 1876 during the two collaborators' initial translation project but was further refined in the early 1890s when they redrafted earlier material for The Saga Library, proved controversial from its first appearance. In the broadest terms, its admirers considered it an appropriate register with which to impart the spirit of the sagas to a modern audience, while its detractors felt the opposite. Morris himself denounced it as 'something intolerable' to have 'the simple dignity of the Icelandic saga' rendered into the 'dominant literary dialect of the day – the English newspaper language' (Introduction to *CW*, VII, p. xvii). In his daughter May's view, it was necessary that he emend Eiríkur Magnússon's 'unconsidered journalese' into a language 'more worthy of the subject', since 'the terse grim language of the Sagas' was 'far better rendered into [Morris's] more direct phrasing than in the looser speech of modern life'.[4] An anonymous reviewer of *Three Northern Love Stories* (1875) concurred that the style was integral to enabling a successful encounter between the strange world of the sagas and the contemporary English audience, deeming the translation 'a work of art, not only satisfying the just demands of the foreign original, but also gratifying the ear and the taste of the native reader', who 'feels [...] as one who has been transferred from a relaxing to a bracing air'.[5]

By contrast, Albany F. Major complained that 'the archaic words and phrases' that came 'so closely to the words and idioms of the original Icelandic' were precisely what had given 'fresh currency to the ignorant idea that Sagas are something strange and weird'.[6] In a thinly veiled attack on the strangeness of Morris's translation style, Guðbrandur Vigfússon went as far as declaring that '[there] is one grave error into which too many English translators of old Northern and Icelandic writings have fallen, to wit, the *affectation of archaism*, and the abuse of archaic, Scottish, pseudo-Middle-English words'. For him, this 'abominable fault' made a saga sound 'unreal, unfamiliar, false'; far from capturing an authentic voice, Morris's translation style, in fact, made the sagas inauthentic and alien, stifling the diverse subtlety of the literature with a sham

[4] May Morris, *Artist*, I, p. 455.
[5] *William Morris: The Critical Heritage*, ed. Peter Faulkner (London: Routledge,1973), p. 211.
[6] Albany F. Major, review of *The Saga Library. 6 Vols. London: Bernard Quaritch*, by William Morris and Eiríkr Magnússon, *Saga-Book of the Viking Society for Northern Research*, 4 (1904), 468–70 (p. 468).

facade of rhetorical artifice. Ironically, in Guðbrandur's view, an attempt at authenticity destroyed one of the most characteristic features of the sagas: the bare and wholly unfussy narratorial voice whose effect, he felt, might only be imitated in translation by an idiomatic rendering.[7]

Almost twenty years after the publication of Guðbrandur's attack on Morris (sixteen after the death of Guðbrandur and nine after that of Morris), Eiríkur loyally defended his collaborator against this criticism:

> Anyone in a position to collate the Icelandic text with the translation will see at a glance that in the overwhelming majority of cases these terms are literal translations of the Icel. originals, *e.g.*, by-men – býar-menn = town's people; cheaping – kaupangr = trading station; earth-burg – jarð-borg = earth-work; show-swain – skó-sveinn = page; out-bidding – út-boð = call to arms, etc. It is a strange piece of impertinence to hint at '*pseudo*-Middle-English' scholarship in a man who, in a sense, might be said to be a living edition of all that was best in M. -E. literature. The question is simply this: is it worthwhile to carry the closeness of translation to this length, albeit that it is an interesting and amusing experiment? That is a matter of taste; therefore not of dispute. (Preface to TSL, 6, pp. vii–viii)

Eiríkur was adamant that what Guðbrandur deemed 'pseudo-Middle-English' was never cursory affectation but rather the result of a conscious and deliberate resolution to pursue a 'literal' rendering over idiomatic expression consonant with Morris's ideal of translation. In Eiríkur's view, the distinctive style was achieved with careful attention to the Old Norse text, rather than with the flippant or untutored attitude that the charge of inventing a 'pseudo' language might suggest. Considering him a 'living edition of all that was best' in Middle English literature (and thereby hinting at an opinion close to that of May that Morris possessed some kind of quasi-mystical capacity to intuit the voice of the Middle Ages), Eiríkur felt that his collaborator's experiment with literalness should at least be taken seriously, if not admired. If the value of such an endeavour was primarily in the undertaking, he argued, the success of the final product was a question of personal preference rather than the legitimacy of the project itself.

---

[7] Introduction to *Corpus Poeticum Boreale: The Poetry of the Old Northern Tongue from the Earliest Times to the Thirteenth Century*, ed. Gudbrand Vigfusson and F. York Powell, 2 vols (Oxford: Clarendon Press, 1883), I, p. cxv. Guðbrandur's irritation and Eiríkur's vexed response were surely influenced by the two Icelanders' antipathy for one another, see Wawn, *Vikings*, p. 356.

It is clear from Morris's own words that he did not translate literally by accident. As he wrote to Eiríkur while they were preparing *Three Northern Love Stories* (1875): 'I am deeply impressed with the necessity of making translations literal, only they must be in English idiom, and in undegraded English at the same time: hence in short all the difficulties of translation.'[8] While this comment demonstrates that Morris was somewhat out of touch with what the public considered readable English (being unidiomatic was precisely what his detractors criticised him for; a problem exacerbated by his pursuit of 'undegraded' words that were sometimes so archaic as to be obsolete), it also shows that his literal style was the result of a considered rationale involving deliberate choices that might even be claimed to approach a theory of translation. What, therefore, were these deliberate choices that created and, in Eiríkur's eyes, legitimised the style of Morris's translations from Old Norse?

In his discussion of the manuscript of *The Story of King Magnus, Son of Erling* in the Huntingdon Library, San Marino, California (which, like the manuscript of *The Story of Olaf the Holy* in the Brotherton Library, Leeds, is in Eiríkur's hand but littered with scores of corrections by Morris), Barribeau has demonstrated that the emendations to Eiríkur's initial translation that produced Morris's literal style fall broadly into three categories. First, Morris prefers to mirror Norse syntax, so that, for instance, verbs in Old Norse remain verbs in English, tenses are imitated and constructions mirrored. Amongst several examples, Barribeau highlights: Morris's correction of Eiríkur's 'took for king Sigurd' (*tóku ... Sigurð til konungs*)[9] to 'took Sigurd to king', so that the preposition *til* (literally 'to' but here 'as') is reflected more closely; his correction of Eiríkur's 'I deem' (*þykki mér*)[10] to 'methinketh', so that the impersonal voice is emulated; and his correction of Eiríkur's 'did not fasten the boat' (*festu þeir ekki bátinn*)[11] to 'made not the boat fast', so that the periphrastic auxiliary

---

[8] Letter to Eiríkur Magnússon, dated 29 January 1874, in Kelvin, I, p. 213. By 'in English idiom' I understand Morris to mean the kind of English that a nineteenth-century British English speaker would deem grammatically comprehensible or 'standard' in the widest sense of the word. By 'undegraded' I understand him to mean English words that derive from Old English or Old Norse rather than the 'post-Conquest' language of Anglo-Norman French (or arguably Latin).

[9] As in 'Took Sigurðr as king'.

[10] 'It seems to me.'

[11] 'They did not fasten the boat' or, more literally, 'They fastened not the boat.'

'did' (which only came into common usage in Early Modern English and is not a feature of Old Norse) is eliminated. Second, Morris frequently chooses to emulate Old Norse word order to create parallel constructions in English. Thus, Eiríkur's 'for this many gave good cheer' (*tóku margir vel undir þetta ráð*)[12] is altered to 'Many took well to this rede', and 'then the host on the bridge thinned' (*þá þynntisk lið á bryggjunum*)[13] is emended to 'then thinned the host on the bridge'. Third, Morris consistently selects cognate words in English, choosing 'fare' rather than 'go' for *fara* ('to go' or 'to travel'), 'flock' for *flokkr* ('a group of men') rather than Eiríkur's 'band', and the Germanic 'rede' rather than Eiríkur's French-derived 'counsel' or 'advice' for *ráð*.[14]

An examination of a passage in the 1891 manuscript of *The Story of Olaf the Holy* such as the following, in which King Óláfr prepares to attack London Bridge, corroborates Barribeau's observations on the elements of Morris's literal style:

> Ólafr konungr lét gera flaka stóra af viðartágum ok af blautum viði, ok taka í sundr til vandahús, ok lét þat bera yfir skip sín svá vítt, at þat tók af borðum út; þar lét hann setja undir stafi svá þykt ok svá hátt, at bæði var hœgt at vega undan ok ýrit stint fyrir grjóti, ef ofan væri á borit. En er herrinn var búinn, þá veittu þeir atróðr neðan eptir ánni, ok er þeir koma nær bryggjunum, þá var borit ofan á þá bæði skot ok grjót svá stórt, at ekki hélt við hvárki hjálmar né skildir [...]. (*HEI*, p. 225)[15]

Having written out the Old Norse, Eiríkur translated this passage in the same manuscript as:

> King Olaf had great hurdles made of willow twigs and raw/pliable wood, and let sheds of wicker-work be taken to pieces, and all this he had put up over his ships, so widely thatching them that they over-shaded the gunwales. Under this thatch he let props be placed so thickly and so high

---

[12] 'Many took well to this counsel.'

[13] 'Then the troop on the bridge became thinner.'

[14] Barribeau, 'Saga-Translation', pp. 244–46.

[15] 'King Óláfr had great wicker shields/hurdles made from willow strands and from soft wood, and huts made of wands taken apart, and had them put over the ships so widely that they reached over the sides; there he had staves/props set underneath so thick and high that it was both easy to fight under and stiff enough against any rocks that might be thrown from above. And when the retinue was prepared, they rowed in attack up the river, but when they came near to the bridge, the shot and stones thrown from above were so great that nothing protected them whether helmets or shields.'

that one could both fight easily from under it, and it was amply stout to stand stones being hurled upon it. Now when the host was arrayed they fell to the onset-row up the river; and when they came near to the bridge, there were hurled upon them both shot and stones so great that nothing could stand them neither helms nor shields. (SOH, p. 12)

Morris then emended Eiríkur's translation in the manuscript to:

King Olaf had great flake-hurdles made of willow-twigs and green wood, and let sheds of wicker-work be taken to pieces, and all these he let lay over the ships, so widely that they went right out-board. Thereunder he let set staves so thick and so high that it was both handy to fight from under, and it was full stout enough against stones if they were cast down thereon. Now when the host was arrayed they fell on a-rowing up the river; and when they came near to the bridge, there was cast down on them both shot and stones so great that nought might hold, neither helms nor shields. (SOH, p. 12)

In this passage Morris emends Eiríkur's translation several times to reflect the syntax of Carl Rikard Unger's edition more closely. Eiríkur's 'and all this he had put up over his ships' becomes 'and all these he let lay over the ships', emulating the verbal construction *lét þat bera* ('had it conveyed') and his helpful, illustrative addition of 'thatching' and 'this thatch' is removed altogether. Eiríkur's 'that one could both fight easily under it' becomes 'that it was both handy to fight from under', creating an empty subject to reflect the subjectless clause of *at bæði var hœgt at vega undan* ('that it was both possible to fight under'). His 'and it was amply stout to stand stones being hurled upon it' becomes 'and it was full stout enough against stones if they were cast down thereon', mirroring both the dative case of *fyrir grjóti* ('against rocks') and the if-clause in *ef ofan væri á borit* ('if they might be thrown from above'). Finally Eiríkur's 'to the onset-row' becomes 'on a-rowing', with Morris preferring to reflect the gerundive quality of *atróðr* by replacing a simple noun.

Morris revises Eiríkur's translation to follow the word order of Unger's edition in a couple of instances in this passage. By correcting 'that they over-shaded the gunwhales' (*at þat tók af borðum út* 'that they reached over the sides') to 'that they went right out-board' he ensures that the final two words of the sentence include the preposition *út* 'out' as well as the cognate *borð* ('board', 'side', 'planking') to reflect the position of *borðum út* ('over the sides'). Additionally, by changing 'he let props be placed' (*lét hann setja [...] stafi* 'he had staves placed') to 'he let set staves', Morris gives full voice to the auxiliary verb *láta*, allowing both parts of 'let set' to precede the object in imitation of *lét hann setja*. In terms of cognates, Morris emends Eiríkur's 'hurdles' to 'flake-hurdles' in order to incorporate *flakar* ('wicker-work shields'), his 'props' to 'staves' to incorporate *stafir*, his 'thickly' to 'thick' to reproduce more closely the inflection of *þykt*, and his 'nothing could stand' to 'nought might hold' to emulate *ekki hélt við* ('nothing held against' or 'nothing withstood'). Morris twice changes Eiríkur's 'hurled' (for *á borit* and *borit* [...] *á*, literally 'borne onto' or 'thrown onto') to 'cast down', selecting a cognate of another Norse verb *kasta* ('to throw') instead of a word that derives from Middle English *hourle*, for which there is no Norse cognate. Having presumably considered *borne onto* to be too inexplicit a translation of *á borit*, in 'cast down' Morris opted for a word that clearly meant 'threw' but was older than 'hurl', and had an explicit connection to Old Norse.

In replacing Eiríkur's 'easily' with the somewhat peculiar 'handy' in this passage, Morris appears to be erroneously connecting the etymology of Modern English *hand* and Norse *hœgr* ('easy'), a connection that he also makes earlier in the manuscript when he translates *úhœgt* ('not easy') (*HEI*, p. 220) as 'unhandy' (*SOH*, p. 4). One explanation for this is that Morris wanted to emphasise as a nuance of the Norse word for 'easy' or 'easeful' the quality of dexterous skill with a tool or weapon that led the adjective 'handy' in English to be affixed onto words such as 'handicraft' or 'handiwork', and thereby to stress the union of dexterity and ease in Norse culture. Another is that he referred to the entry for *hœgr* ('easy') in the *Icelandic–English Dictionary*, which gives *ykkr er þat hœgst um hönd* ('it is most at hand for you') and *til hœgra vegs* ('on the right hand') as examples of usage and mistakenly connected *hœgr* with *hönd* ('hand').[16] Either way, Morris's employment of 'high' and 'handy' here (followed by 'stout' and 'stones') creates a moment of alliterative archaism in his rendering.

In addition to the three categories of emendation that Barribeau highlights, a fourth may be added that is fundamental to the creation of Morris's distinctive style.[17] As Aho has emphasised, in his translations Morris regularly introduces ancient-sounding subordinating conjunctions and pronominal adverbs such as 'sithence', 'thereto' or 'whereunder',

---

[16] Cleasby and Vigfusson, p. 305.
[17] Strictly speaking this category is a subdivision of the first in which Morris attempts to mirror Old Norse syntax.

which are associated with the syntax of Middle English.[18] In comparing the translations to the editions, it is striking that such words often lack an explicit counterpart in the Old Norse prose. In the passage above, for example, Eiríkur's 'Under this thatch he let props be placed' (*þar lét hann setja undir stafi* 'there he had staves set under') becomes '*Thereunder* he let set staves' [my italics] with Morris excising the supplementary indirect object 'this thatch' that Eiríkur has added to allow the English to make sense. The Old Norse phrase does not provide an indirect object for *setja undir* ('set underneath') because *undir* ('under' or 'underneath') is able to qualify *setja* ('to set'), creating what is effectively a phrasal verb. In this instance, such a construction cannot easily exist in English, which requires an indirect object to follow the preposition *under*, so rather than invent a noun for the English prepositional phrase (as Eiríkur had done), Morris adds an archaic pronominal adverb, thereby mimicking the Old Norse structure with the closest equivalent that has ever existed in English.[19] Similarly, Morris has excised the supplementary object 'it' from Eiríkur's 'being hurled upon it' (*ef ofan væri á borit* 'that might be thrown onto [it] from above'), correcting the clause to mimic the phrasal verb-like construction of *á borit* ('thrown onto [it]') to give 'if they were cast down *thereon*' [my italics].

Thus, even these instances, which appear to show Morris introducing words or constructions lacking in the Old Norse text, arise from him paying extremely close attention to the edition in front of him. Not only does he mirror wherever possible the Norse syntax, word order and lexis in Modern English, but where it is impossible (such as in the case of a phrasal verb in Old Norse that simply has no equivalent in Modern English) he employs the closest word or construction that has ever existed in English, whether or not it remains in current usage. In the instances in which he has to find the closest grammatical fit, Morris pursues literalness so determinedly that he creates archaism where he could avoid it if he were to follow Eiríkur's more idiomatic rendering; this, to the frustration of certain readers, such as Stevenson: 'For the love of God, my dear and honoured Morris, use *where*, and let us know *whereas* we are, wherefore our gratitude shall grow, whereby you shall be the more

---

[18] Introduction to Morris and Eiríkr Magnússon, *Three Northern Love Stories* (1996), p. xx.

[19] It seems to me that this ability to mine Middle English for lexical and syntactical counterparts in Old Norse is part of the quality that led Eiríkur to call Morris 'a living edition of all that was best' in its literature.

honoured wherever men love clear language, whereas now, although we honour, we are troubled.'[20]

As Barribeau stresses, the aspect of Morris's literal style that has proven most contentious, evoking 'admiration in some' but 'fury in many', is the extension of his preference for cognates to include 'extremely archaic, sometimes dialectal, often obscure English words', so that in *The Story of Magnus, Son of Erling*, for example, Morris translates: '*týnt*, "lost", as "tyned", choosing a northern dialectism originally borrowed from Old Norse. [...] "enemies", *óvinir*, is translated literally [...] (the Icelandic prefix *ó-* is a negative element) as "unfriends"; also *ófrelsi* ("tyranny") becomes "unfreedom", and *ófriðr* ("war"), becomes "unpeace".[21] This tendency to employ a word that had either evolved in Modern English to mean something distinct from its cognate in Old Norse or had become so scarce as to be unintelligible to any but the most philologically alert or regionally attuned reader is already striking in the earliest saga translations. In *The Story of Grettir the Strong* when Bardi Gudmundson predicts that Grettir's boundless rashness will cause future trouble, the narrator explains that 'Grettir thought ill of his spaedom' (*CW*, VII, p. 78), with Morris employing a rare cognate of Old Norse *spár* ('prophecies') from northern English dialect.[22]

Later in the saga, when Glam begins to haunt Thorhall-stead, Thorhall comes upon the following scene in his shed: 'There he saw where lay the neatherd, and had his head in one boose and his feet in the other.' While an erudite mind or speaker of dialect might well have recognised *neat* as a word for oxen (from Old Norse *naut* 'cattle'), and a *neatherd*, thus, as an English rendering of *nautamaðr* (literally a *cattle-man*, or *cowherd*), Morris's choice of 'boose' (cognate with Old Norse *báss* 'a stall for an animal') was evidently so obscure that, even in the first edition of their translation, Eiríkur was permitted to add an infrequent gloss to clarify

---

[20] Quoted in John M. Simpson, 'Eyrbyggja Saga and Nineteenth Century Scholarship', in *Proceedings of the First International Saga Conference. Edinburgh, 1971* (Viking Society for Northern Research: London, 1973), pp. 360–94 (p. 371).

[21] Barribeau, 'Saga-Translation', p. 246.

[22] For the Old Norse scene on which Morris based his translation, see *GRE*, p. 74. For the regional distribution of words related to *spaedom*, see the entry for *spae* in Joseph Wright, *The English Dialect Dictionary*, 6 vols (London: Frowde, 1898–1905), V, pp. 640–41.

the translation: 'Boose, a cow-stall'.[23] Though such uncommon words, in Townend's view, 'nearly always turn out to be historically correct or philologically justified',[24] Morris surely cannot have intended his use of what sometimes bordered on obsolete vocabulary to have rendered these passages incomprehensible.

In Aho's comparison of the verse in Morris's 1869 rendering of *Gunnlaugs saga* that begins 'To this close-fist the right I gave | A new mark, grey of face to have'[25] and its reworked form in the 1875 translation of *Three Northern Love Stories* that begins 'Bade I the middling mighty | To have a mark of waves' flame',[26] he has emphasised Morris's increasing resolve to reproduce more explicitly in the later version both the sense of the *dróttkvætt* verse and its intricate prosody. Although he argues that the meaning of the earlier verse is 'clear enough', he points to a remarkable shift in the 1875 interpretation towards fidelity to the composition of the Old Norse stanza: 'What is impressive here is that Morris has replicated most of the original's structure: alliteration binds odd and even lines [...] the even lines have the requisite interior full rhyme [... and] the odd lines make a stab at another standard feature of "drottkvaett" stanzas: internal half rhymes.'[27]

Aho also highlights here the more literal rendition of the kennings in the 1875 stanza.[28] Whereas in the 1869 verse Morris tends to provide the referent of a kenning without any periphrastic allusion, in the 1875 version he provides the base-word and determinant without interpretation, so that, for example, 'a new mark' in the earlier stanza becomes 'a mark of waves' flame' [waves' flame > gold, golden mark] in the later one. Morris's 1875 readers are, therefore, put in a position much like that of a medieval Icelandic audience in which they are required to decipher the allusions themselves. Aho argues that the attendant ambiguity is a typical

---

[23] *Grettis Saga: The Story of Grettir the Strong*, trans. William Morris and Eiríkr Magnússon (London: Ellis and White, 1869), p. 103. For the regional distribution of words related to *neat*, see Wright, IV, pp. 238–39, and for words related to *boose*, see Wright, I, pp. 342–43.

[24] Matthew Townend, 'Victorian Medievalisms', in *The Oxford Handbook of Victorian Poetry*, ed. Matthew Bevis (Oxford: Oxford University Press, 2013), pp. 166–83 (p. 177).

[25] Morris and Eiríkr Magnússon, 'Saga of Gunnlaug (1869)', p. 34.

[26] Morris and Eiríkr Magnússon, *Three Northern Love Stories* (1996), p. 16.

[27] Introduction to Morris and Eiríkr Magnússon, *Three Northern Love Stories* (1996), p. xxvi.

[28] For the verse in Old Norse, see *GUN*, p. 211.

trait of skaldic verse, whose composers were celebrated for displaying ingenuity and inventiveness rather than lucidity. In revising the stanzas to be as literal as possible and, thereby, increasing the degree of obscurity for his audience, in Aho's words, 'we can watch the Victorian skald matching wits with Gunnlaug and Raven' (the supposed composers of the saga's verses).[29]

If we compare the verses in Morris's early 1870s translation of *Eyrbyggja saga* to those in the published saga of 1892, it becomes even clearer that, over the twenty-seven years between 1868 when Morris started Norse lessons with Eiríkur and the eventual publication of Volume III of *Heimskringla* (Volume 5 of The Saga Library) in 1895, he developed more exacting requirements for their literal translation:

Ek skar 'sýlda svana-fold: *hafit* austan súðum með hlaðit flaust, þvíat 'gœi-brúðr: Þuríðr leiddi oss fast *með* ástum || ek gat híngat víða vásbúð – 'hugfullr víglundr: (*ek*) byggir nú um stund helli fyrir konu-bíng – .[30]

Morris translated this verse in the late 1860s or early 1870s as:

> Through the cold meadows of the swan
> Into the west my good ship ran;
> The boarded bow threw up the sea
> Because loves bonds were fast on me
> The longings of the goodly bride
> Drew me across wetways and wide;
> Now in stone cave must I be laid
> For pillows sweet by fair limbs made.[31]

He then rewrote it in the early 1890s for publication in The Saga Library as:

---

[29] Introduction to Morris and Eiríkr Magnússon, *Three Northern Love Stories* (1996), p. xxvi.

[30] 'I cut the frozen-stiff earth of swans [frozen-stiff earth of swans > earth of swans > sea, frozen sea] from the east with boards with a loaded ship, because that pretty maid led me strongly with love. I became tired from widespread wetness on the way here, the brave battle-tree [battle-tree > warrior, brave warrior] dwells now a while in a cave instead of a woman's bed.' The Old Norse text is quoted from *Eyrbyggja Saga*, ed. Guðbrandr Vigfússon (Leipzig: Vogel, 1864), pp. 134–35. This is the prose word order that he gives of of Verse 73. For the stanza in verse form, see the same edition, p. 73.

[31] 'Eyrbyggia Saga', trans. William Morris and Eiríkr Magnússon (Fitzwilliam Museum, Cambridge, 1868), William Morris Collection, Morris/ Eyrbyggia, p. 95.

With the boards was I shearing the icy cold swan-field;
From the East in the laden keel fared I erewhile;
So hard and so hard there the dear bride she drew me;
So fast and so fast in her love was I bounden.
Weary wet-worn I was as we wended thereover
The highway of waves; and now all heart-heavy
The grove of the battle in cave hath abiding
Instead of the fair woman's bolster beneath him. (TSL, 2, p. 107)

The correlation between the Norse original and the stanza of the early 1870s is appreciably more rudimentary than that between it and the stanza of the early 1890s. Quite unlike the quality of calm endurance expressed in the medieval verse, the tripping tetrameter and rhyming couplets of the earlier translation imbue it with a sanguine, jaunty quality that is reinforced by somewhat hackneyed, effusive adjectives ('*good* ship', '*goodly* bride', 'pillows *sweet*', '*fair* limbs') and sentimental phrasing: the ship runs 'into the west' rather than *austan* ('from the east'); rather than simply *með ástum* ('with love') the narrator is impelled by the typically torturous early Morrisian affliction of love's 'bonds'; and the image of the woman's bed from which the speaker is separated is romanticised.

There is little sense of corporeal suffering in the earlier verse. It is the romantic draw of the lover across the water that is emphasised rather than the arduousness of the sea journey or the speaker's deprivation. While Morris has evidently made some attempt to be literal in the earlier verse (the first kenning *sýlda svana-fold* ['frozen-stiff earth of swans'] is rendered fairly closely as 'cold meadows of the swan' and in translating *gœi-brúðr* ['pretty bride' or 'maid'] as 'goodly bride' he both incorporates a cognate of *brúðr* and reproduces the first consonants of each Norse word), in general he does not follow the syntax of the Old Norse stanza scrupulously.[32] The lines *gœi-brúðr leiddi oss fast með ástum* ('the pretty maid led me strongly with love') and *ek gat híngat víða vásbúð* ('I became tired from widespread wetness on the way here'), for example, are conflated into 'The longings of the goodly bride | Drew me across wetways and wide', and the final kenning *hugfullr víglundr* ('courageous battle-tree') is excised altogether, with Morris simply providing the referent 'I'.

In the later translation, however, Morris goes out of his way to follow the syntax of the Old Norse stanza, frequently employing cognates: *Ek*

---

[32] It is also possible that 'in stone' in the earlier translation is a mistaken literal translation of *um stund* ('for a time').

skar ('I sheared' or 'I cut') now becomes 'was I shearing'; the dative *súðum* ('with boards/planking') becomes 'With the boards'; *austan* is now rendered directly as 'From the East'; the vessel is 'laden' (*hlaðit*, 'laden') rather than 'good'; and the speaker 'Weary wet-worn' (*vásbúð* 'tired from wetness'); *fyrir* becomes more specifically 'instead of' rather than 'for'. As in the Norse verse, it is now the 'bride' (*brúðr*) herself that draws the speaker across the sea rather than her 'longings', and the image of her bolster becomes less sentimental.

Though Morris does slip into slightly cloying ardour in lines three and four with the archaic 'bounden' and repetition of 'so hard' and 'so fast' (which may have helped him to fill the longer lines), the diction of the later stanza is generally plainer and more terse, frequently including single-syllable words and lacking the mawkish adjectives of his first attempt. The later verse refers more clearly to the personal suffering and endurance of the speaker as he attempts to return to his love, simply contrasting the lonely discomfort of the coastal cave with the comfort of his lover's bed, rather than presenting an idealised picture of romantic yearning. Morris also attempts some alliteration in a glance towards the Old Norse stanza as it stands in verse rather than prose form.

Perhaps most noticeably, in the 1892 version Morris translates both kennings as directly as possible with *sýlda svana-fold* ('frozen-stiff earth of swans' or 'swans'-earth') becoming 'icy cold swan-field' (Morris presumably considers 'fold' to mean a pen or paddock here, as in a *sheep-fold*), and *hugfullr víglundr* ('heart-full/courage-full battle-tree/battle-grove') becoming 'all heart-heavy | The grove of the battle'. Of Morris's relationship to the kennings in *Eyrbyggja saga*, Eiríkur would later write:

> Morris was so taken with the workmanship of the 'kenning' that once – we were doing the verses of the Eredwellers' saga – he said it was a task we must address ourselves to bring together a corpus of the kennings with a commentary on their poetical, mythical, legendary, and antiquarian significance, when we should find leisure in it. Through his manner of dealing with the 'kennings' in this saga, it is easy to see that his own version meant to be a forerunner to such a work, for it is both a translation and a sort of commentary throwing out their picturesque points to the fullest extent; hence their choice of the long metre in order to have a freer play with this element in the verses. (Preface to TSL, 6, pp. ix–x)

Eiríkur makes it clear that Morris came to see the kennings not simply as charming metaphors that he might sometimes choose to translate as they stood, or otherwise eliminate, but as a form of medieval workmanship integral to the poetry. Indeed, they had become so important to him that, despite the brevity of the original *dróttkvætt* lines, in his published version of *Eyrbyggja saga* Morris chose a longer line length that created the syllabic space necessary for the morphologically simpler nineteenth-century language to allow the kennings 'the same force in the translation as they bear in the original' (Preface to TSL, 2, p. xlvii). In addition, in the 1892 stanza above, he appears to go as far as creating his own kenning, introducing 'highway of waves' [> *the sea*] (again presumably to make up the necessary syllabic space in the line) for which there is no counterpart in the Old Norse verse.

The translation history of this stanza shows how Morris's commitment to literal translation became paramount over time. In respect of his eventual attitude to kennings, in 1905 Eiríkur explained: 'The quaint vividness of fancy that manifests itself in these "kennings" appealed greatly to Morris' imaginative mind, and he would on no account slur over them by giving in the translation only *what they meant*, instead of *what they said*.' Indeed, by the time the two collaborators came to publish *Heimskringla*, Morris's dedication to present *what they said* as literally as possible was such that Eiríkur later felt the need to account for the resultant impairment of Morris's poetic fluency:

> It will, no doubt, be remarked, how, in a great number of cases the rendering of the verses of Heimskringla presents a certain stiffness that was altogether foreign to Morris' fluent versification. The reason for this is twofold: In the verses he wanted to be as honestly literal as the prose: The principle involved in literal rendering, as far as possible, of the various links that served to make up the 'Kennings,' or the poetical periphrases. (Preface to TSL, 6, p. ix)

In Eiríkur's view, literalness in translation had by this time become so important to Morris that he prioritised it above all else. This intense commitment to a literal rendering of saga verses is unmistakeable in his workings of the 1891 manuscript of *The Story of Olaf the Holy* (published in 1894), which shows Eiríkur providing Morris with the stanzas in Old Norse in prose word order, as well as a parallel translation into English. As Morris works these translations into verse he crosses out Eiríkur's versions and inserts his new stanzas. On pages twelve and fourteen of the manuscript, for example, Eiríkur has provided Morris with the prose word order and a translation of the tenth stanza of the saga. Morris has then crossed these out and inserted his own verse rendering, which is subsequently published with slightly different wording in *The Saga*

Library. In the 1891 manuscript, Eiríkur's transcription of the Old Norse verse in prose word order and subsequent translation beneath reads:

> Gunn-Þorinn kennir éla Yggs, þú brauzt enn Lunduna
> bryggjur;
> *Fight-daring knower of the squalls of Ygg, thou didst brake still*
> *further London bridge;*
>
> þér hefir snúnat at vinna linns lönd
> *to thee it has turned (come)*
> *thou hast had the good luck to winn the serpent's lands.*
>
> Hart um krafðir skildir höfðu gang;
> *Hard be-craved shields had roar;*
> *challenged did roar*
>
> enn gamlir járnhringar gunn-þinga = byrny
> *but old iron-rings of fight-gear*
>
> sprungu. Við þat óx hildr
> *sprang in sunder. At that waxed the fight.* (SOH, pp. 12, 14)

In the same manuscript, Morris has then versified Eiríkur's translation as:

> O battle-bold, the cunning
> Of Ygg's storm! Yet thou brakest
> Down London Bridge: it happed thee
> To win the land of ling-worm.
> Hard shields be-craved had roar there;
> There too they sprang asunder,
> Hard iron-rings of the war-coats.
> Therewith the battle waxèd. (SOH, p. 13)

In 1894 the verse was published as:

> O battle-bold, the cunning
> Of Ygg's storm! Yet thou brakest
> Down London Bridge: it happed thee
> To win the land of snakes there.
> Hard shields be-craved had roar there;
> There too they sprang asunder,
> Hard iron-rings of the war-coats.
> Therewith the battle waxèd. (TSL, 4, p. 15)

Eiríkur's translation is lucid and follows the syntax of the Norse prose carefully. It seems that he is partially anticipating the style that Morris will favour, frequently employing cognates himself: *þér* ('to you') becomes 'to thee'; *vinna* ('to gain, prevail against, win in battle') becomes 'to winn' (with the spelling error indicating just how closely Eiríkur was following the Old Norse); *krafðir* ('desired') becomes 'be-craved'; *sprungu* ('sprang' or 'burst') becomes 'sprang in sunder'; and *óx* ('grew', from *vaxa* 'to grow' or 'wax') becomes 'waxed'. Eiríkur also glosses several of his more literal renderings, demonstrating that, even to Morris, the sense of this style of translation is not necessarily explicit: by 'be-crafted' Eiríkur means 'challenged', by 'had roar' he means 'did roar' (despite the fact that the Norse verse uses *höfðu* ('had'). Though Eiríkur's translation possesses a certain degree of archaism ('to thee', 'thou hast', 'be-crafted', 'waxed'), it avoids any glaringly obsolete words and there is no obvious attempt to forge an overtly poetic diction. By providing a translation that is syntactically close and points out relationships between Old Norse and English, it is evident that, to some extent, he is anticipating Morris's proclivities. However, it is difficult to tell to what degree Eiríkur's style reflects his own inclination or whether he is effectively translating to order for Morris (see Conclusion, p. 173). It is also evident that English is not his first language. The error mentioned above and the peculiar '*in* sunder' suggest a hesitancy that ultimately gives Morris the authority to decide what should be right in English.

In comparison to Eiríkur's translation, Morris's versification is characterised by an even stronger attempt to follow the Old Norse syntax, greater concision (and thus a tighter, punchier effect) and a tendency towards more archaism and idiosyncrasy. Eiríkur's 'thou has had the good luck to' is transformed into the archaic 'it happed thee to', with Morris employing the highly obscure impersonal form of the Middle English verb *to hap* ('to enjoy good fortune') in order to emulate the impersonal construction of the Old Norse phrase *þér hefir snúnat* at ('it has befallen you to or it has come about for you that') and shorten Eiríkur's version so that it fits into the newly versified line. Retaining all of Eiríkur's cognates, including 'had roar' rather than the gloss 'did roar' and 'be-craved' (which Morris may have linked etymologically in his mind to *crafted* with the sense of 'forced' or 'exacted'), Morris increases the degree of archaism by choosing 'Therewith' instead of Eiríkur's 'At that' to translate *Við þat* ('with that' or 'at that'), and adding an augment to his 'waxed' to create 'waxèd'.

The relationship between Eiríkur's syntactically faithful, somewhat archaic but rarely obscure idiom and Morris's etymologically exacting, often eccentric and sometimes arcane style is also apparent in the translation of the kennings in this verse. In both the 1891 manuscript and 1894 published version Morris has turned Eiríkur's translation of the first kenning *Gunn-Þorinn kennir éla Yggs* (which Eiríkur translates as 'Fight-daring knower of the squalls of Ygg') into 'O battle-bold, the cunning | Of Ygg's storm!'[33] While Eiríkur's translation is direct and clear, it lacks any overtly poetic qualities such as alliteration. Morris immediately makes his 'Fight-daring' more lyrical with the vocative, alliterative and pithy 'O battle-bold' and exchanges the noun 'knower' (which evidently refers to a person) for the cryptic 'the cunning' (which does not).

Though he presumably wants to make an etymological connection here between the verb *kenna* ('to know') in Old Norse (which provides Eiríkur's *kennir* 'knower') and the obsolete English sense of *cunning* ('knowledge, erudition'),[34] the fact that the noun does not explicitly allude to a sentient being means that the reader has to rely on the explanation appended to the 1894 publication – 'The cunning of Ygg's storm': "*kennir Yggs éla*": Yggr = Odin, his *él*, squall. storm = battle, the cunning one thereof, a warrior, King Olaf' (TSL, 4, p. 472) – to discover that 'the cunning *one*' is actually intended. Although Morris translates the rest of the kenning directly as he finds it (despite making *éla* ['showers'] singular not plural), he does not attempt to help the reader understand that Ygg (ON *Yggr*) is another name for Odin, preferring to leave this to the explanation in the index too (or perhaps presuming that his readers would recognise *Yggr* from the name of the great ash tree *Yggdrasil* ['Yggr's horse > Óðinn's tree > a gallows']). The growing obscurity of these literal verse translations makes an explanatory index increasingly necessary, so that the reader's experience becomes less like an audience member deliberating on the words of a skáld and more like a student studying the words of scholar.

By emending Eiríkur's 'serpent's lands' (*linns lönd* 'lands of the serpent > gold') to 'land of ling-worm' in the manuscript, Morris appears eager to forge a link between the word *linnr* ('serpent'), and the *lyngormur*

---

[33] Based on Eiríkur's translation and the explanation given in the index to their published version *Gunn-Þorinn kennir éla Yggs* can be understood as 'Fight-daring knower of the squalls of Ygg [> Yggr > Óðinn, Óðinn's squalls > battle, fight-daring knower of battle > brave warrior > King Óláfr]. See TSL, 4, p. 472.

[34] See 'cunning, n.1', *OED Online*, Oxford University Press, March 2017 [Accessed 25 April 2017].

('heather or ling worm')[35] of *Ragnars saga Loðbrókar* and Jón Árnason's Victorian collection of Icelandic legends (both of which are snakes that grow monstrously when gold is placed beneath them).[36] Though *ling* and *linnr* are not etymologically related, it may be that Morris linked the two via the closely connected Germanic legend of the *linn-ormr* ('snake-worm'),[37] which appears as a gold-associated serpent in Saxo's version of the Ragnar Loðbrók story, the *Nibelungenlied* and *Þiðreks saga af Bern*.[38] In making this emendation he seems to have favoured crafting bridges between English and some (or all) of the old stories over philological accuracy. The fact that the 1891 publication of the kenning gives 'land of snakes' instead (with the explanatory note in the appendix reading 'Land of snakes: "linns land" = gold)' suggests that in the end the allusion in the manuscript was considered too obscure or unstable to include.

What was the motivation for this increasing insistence on literalness in his translations from Old Norse? A clue to the purpose behind Morris's emergent theory of literal translation lies in what Barribeau calls '[one] of the most extreme examples of [his] persistence in maintaining cognates', namely: 'his revision [in the manuscript of *The Story of Magnus, Son of Erling*] of Magnússon's translation of *kraptr*, as in *með fjanda kraptr*, "the power of the fiend", to "the craft of the fiend" – in this case somewhat confusing the actual meaning'.[39] The etymology of *craft* became especially important to Morris as, throughout the late 1870s and afterwards, his understanding of the word began more explicitly to embody the unification of work and personal agency that he deemed fundamental to a thriving society.[40] In an 1882 lecture to students of the Leek School of

---

[35] Guðbrandur Vigfússon gives the translation of *lyngormr* as: 'a "ling-worm", snake'. See Cleasby and Vigfusson, p. 401. *Lyng* is the Old Norse word for 'heather'.

[36] See *Saga af Ragnari konúngi Lodbrók ok sonum hans*, in *Fornaldar sögur nordrlanda*, ed. Carl Christian Rafn, 3 vols (Copenhagen: Popp, 1829), I, 235–99 (pp. 237–43); *Íslenzkar þjóðsögur og æfintýri*, ed. Jón Árnason, 2 vols (Leipzig: Hinrich, 1862), I, pp. 638–41. The volume that contains *Ragnars saga Loðbrókar* and Jón Árnason's collected tales were both sold in the auction of Morris's books that followed his death. See 'Catalogue (1898)', pp. 3, 84.

[37] Guðbrandur Vigfússon gives *linn-ormr* as a cognate to German *lind-wurm* ('lindworm'). See Cleasby and Vigfusson, p. 390.

[38] Katharine M. Briggs, *A Dictionary of British Folk Tales in the English Language*, 2 vols (London: Routledge and Paul, 1970), I, p. 373.

[39] Barribeau, 'Saga-Translation', p. 246.

[40] See Morris's public lectures 'The Lesser Arts' (1877) and 'Making the Best of It' (c.1879) in *CW*, XXII, pp. 3–27, 81–118.

Art he invoked the definition of the Old Norse cognate *kraptr* to explain that:

> the right meaning of the word craft is simply *power*: so that a handi-craftsman signifies a man who exercised a power by means of his hands, and doubtless when it was first used was intended to signify that he exercised a certain kind of power; to wit, a readiness of mind and deftness of hand which has been acquired through many ages, handed down from father to son and increased generation by generation.[41]

Holding Morris's understanding of the word in mind, it seems unlikely that in correcting 'power' to 'craft' in *The Story of Magnus, Son of Erling*, he was simply encouraging his readers to decipher the modern cognate's former connotation intellectually. Rather, it seems plausible that, in making this correction, Morris was hoping that his readership might be inspired more potently by an encounter with the vestigial resonance of the old word and, perhaps implicitly through it, with those heroic speakers of Old Norse who had exercised that 'certain kind of power' that he wished to revive. Indeed, from the beginning of their collaboration, Morris and Eiríkur appear to have used cognates as nodes that opened something like a metaphysical conduit between their own consciousness and that of medieval Iceland: 'The dialect of our translation was not the Queen's English, but it was helpful in penetrating into the thought of the old language. Thus, to give an example, *leiðtogi*, a guide, become load-tugger (load=way, in load-star, load-stone; *togi* from *toga* to tug (on), one who leads on with a rope' (Preface to TSL, 6, p. xiv). In 'penetrating into the thought' of Old Norse by pursuing literalness, the two collaborators continually crafted these moments of encounter in which some kind of mutual communion might occur.

While the pursuit of such points of mutuality may have begun simply as a pleasurable method of study during the Old Norse lessons that Eiríkur initially gave to Morris, it is too pat to assume, as Swannell and Quirk have done, that Morris's primary goal in continuing to craft literalness was to share with his audience the pleasure of the reciprocal mechanics

---

[41] From 'Art: A Serious Thing', in LeMire, pp. 36–53 (p. 45). Morris's definition of *craft* here appears to derive directly from his acquaintance with Old Norse *kraptr* or *kraftr*, the definition for which appears in Guðbrandur Vigfússon's 1874 dictionary as '*might, strength, power*'. See Cleasby's and Guðbrandur Vigfússon's 1974 dictionary, p. 354.

of the two languages.[42] In 1884 in Morris's second lecture on the Gothic Revival he suggested, echoing Ruskin's insistence that art cannot grow out of modern society, that the architects involved in its early stages had failed to understand that, if they wanted to realise the vitality of the old architecture in their new buildings, it was necessary to create an animate dialogue between the nature of the old time and that of the present: 'at first we imitated the outward aspects of it without understanding its spirit much as the Renaissance artists had done with the old classical art, but without infusing any of the spirit of our own times into it as they had done so as to make a living style'.[43] Similarly, in his preference for literalness, Morris appears to have attempted a 'living style' of translation by forging repeated points of cultural confluence between Old Norse and English.

Lamenting the fact that Old English had preserved no tales of how 'the folk of Middlesex ate and drank and loved and quarreled and met their death in the 10th century',[44] by the time he delivered 'The Early Literature of the North – Iceland' in 1887, Morris had come to regard the island as an isolated 'casket' in which the last bastion of early Teutonic culture had survived, isolated from the tyrannical influence of the Latinate Mediterranean. When he called it an 'Isle of Refuge'[45] he did not mean that it had served as a refuge for *him* – a retreat from which to escape the alleged torments of his marriage or the moral horrors of High Victorian capitalism – but as a refuge for the cultural ideal of the Gothic that now made '[a]ll the northern countries, and England too [...] the spiritual colonies of Iceland'.[46]

It followed, therefore, that the idiom that allowed the possibility of a living encounter between Old Norse and English comprised only the consanguineous 'Teutonic element in our speech' (Introduction to *CW*, VII, p. xviii), that is, English words derived from Old Norse (and sometimes Old English), and Middle English constructions and vocabulary that otherwise came the closest to thirteenth- and fourteenth-century Icelandic. Although the result resembled an imaginary dialect that might have survived had the Norman Conquest never occurred, as Eiríkur

[42] Swannell, 'Interpreter', pp. 375–76; Quirk, p. 76.
[43] From 'The Gothic Revival II', in LeMire, pp. 74–93 (p. 82).
[44] From 'Early England', in LeMire, pp. 158–78 (p. 167).
[45] From 'The Early Literature of the North – Iceland', in LeMire, p. 181.
[46] Quoted in Ruth Ellison, 'Icelandic Obituaries of William Morris', *The Journal of the William Morris Society*, 8.1 (1988), 35–41 (pp. 40–41).

asserted, it was born of no frivolous diversion to create a phony language but was rather an earnest attempt to achieve a convergence of Old Norse and its most closely related constituent parts in English, in which the spirit of the Gothic might most effectively be conveyed: 'It is not "pseudo-Middle English," as some critics have thought. It is his own, the result of an endeavour by a scholar and a man of genius to bring about such harmony between the Teutonic element in English and the language of the Icelandic saga as the not very abundant means at his command would allow' (Introduction to *CW*, VII, p. xviii). As Morris's confidence in the society that he imagined had produced the sagas grew, it seems that he increasingly insisted on creating such linguistic meeting places in the hope that the reader might encounter a vital transmission of the medieval Gothic culture that was their rightful inheritance.

Several critics have argued that Morris's primary motivation in forging these repeated moments of encounter was to expose his audience to the strangeness of the Icelandic material. Dudley L. Hascall proposes that the archaic words and constructions were necessary in creating the antique quality that a Modern Icelander would perceive in Old Norse, as well as the 'by-gone Germanic heroes of the Middle Age',[47] while Durrenberger and Durrenberger maintain that the free use of archaisms was designed to generate 'a spirit of an earlier time'.[48] Waithe suggests that Morris 'wanted to make the invigorating strangeness of heroic society known to his readership'[49] and, thus, 'responded to the challenge of representing strangeness by devising a strange language' in the hope that 'a text "in translation" would allow its readers to appreciate the alterity of the original'.[50] In his analysis of Morris's approach to translating both the sagas and *Beowulf*, Waithe draws on Lawrence Venuti's concept of translatory 'foreignisation' to argue that by rejecting the practice of rendering his translations into an 'invisible' modern idiom, Morris intended to disrupt the assimilation of the antecedent text into the dominant cultural values of contemporary Victorian English.[51] By 'recruiting what seemed unfamiliar or uncanny in the already-known',[52] in Waithe's view, Morris

---

[47] Dudley L. Hascall, '"Volsungasaga" and Two Transformations', *The Journal of the William Morris Society*, 2.3 (1968), 18–23 (p. 19).

[48] Introduction to Durrenberger and Durrenberger, p. 48.

[49] Waithe, p. 90.

[50] Waithe, p. 94.

[51] Waithe, p. 93; Lawrence Venuti, *The Translator's Invisibility: A History of Translation* (London: Routledge, 1995), p. 203.

[52] Waithe, p. 93.

hoped that 'an authentic link between the heroic past and the Victorian present might momentarily be opened'.[53]

In my view, scholarly emphasis on Morris's employment of strangeness in the style of these translations risks too strong an implication that he consciously used literalness as a sophisticated technique to create a jarring encounter for the reader, one that might perhaps startle them into discerning what remained of the two cultures' mutuality in the degraded present. While I agree that he hoped that the language of his translations would open a link for his audience between past and present, it seems more likely to me that in repeatedly pursuing literalness Morris was simply presenting an idiom that he hoped his readership would experience more straightforwardly as related to them, rather than uncanny. The extraordinary 'intuition' with which Morris 'saw through the language' from the beginning of his work with Eiríkur (Preface to TSL, 6, p. xiv), coupled with the 'personal feeling' that his collaborator felt 'may have unduly affected his judgement' on the potential popularity of the sagas in Britain (Preface to TSL, 6, p. x), does not suggest a mind that would adopt literal rendering as a calculated tactic to create literary shocks. The degree of literalness in his translations may, therefore, reflect a misjudgement on Morris's part of the scale of his audience's linguistic tolerance and vocabulary: where he hoped that they would see the related and familiar, they may more often have simply seen the alien.

What is so peculiar about Morris's entire Icelandic project is that he seems to have employed a technique in his translations whose effect is fundamentally foreignising in the apparent hope that it would achieve the largely 'domesticating' goal of relaying the remnants of consanguinity between the culture of the target and host text. Venuti's assertion that foreignisation 'assumes a concept of human subjectivity that is very different from the humanist assumptions underlying domestication' is helpful in clarifying the paradoxically domesticating aspect of the motivation behind Morris's project.[54] Despite the potentially alienating provocation of his diction, his wish, in Waithe's words, to 'bring the good news home' was ultimately humanist.[55] Morris saw authentic human nature as essentially stable across time and perhaps hoped his translations might act as vehicles for its transmission from medieval Iceland and rejuvenation in the present. His literal rendering might, therefore, be regarded

[53] Waithe, p. 96.
[54] Venuti, p. 24.
[55] Waithe, p. 90.

as an endeavour to bring the cultural authenticity of the progenitor-text at least part of the way to his readers, who, encumbered, as he deemed them, with a corrupted post-Norman Conquest, post-Renaissance industrialised idiom of English, might be enthused to meet their ancestor part of the way, as though embracing a relative they had not seen for some time.

To illustrate this encounter between reader and ancestor, Waithe has employed the image of a host welcoming a stranger into his home, suggesting that Morris 'believed in the possibility of accommodating a comparable strangeness within the "house" of the target language', in which the source text 'retains its integrity' but 'resists assimilation'.[56] An alternative image that incorporates the degree of kinship that Morris perceived between reader and ancestor might be the meeting of two distant relatives at a guesthouse somewhere between the modern traveller's crumbling home and his ancient cousin's native country. In building a linguistic medium to accommodate the reunion (newly constructed at some Middle English midway point between modern Franco-English journalese and medieval Icelandic), Morris hoped his reader-traveller might quickly recognise his ancient kinsman, breaking through 'whatever entanglement of strange manners or unused element may at first trouble him' to find 'such close sympathy with all the passions that may move himself to-day' (*CW*, vii, p. 286).

It must be admitted that this hope was not necessarily achieved. By employing literalness so rigidly, Morris risked alienating his readers with an idiom that he simply did not see as alien. As several critics have highlighted, a flaw in his attitude as a translator is that he appears to have considered his readership in only the most abstract and optimistic way. Swannell suggests that Morris 'became so skilful at this transmuting process that he sometimes forgets his readers and becomes unintelligible';[57] Wawn that 'it is sometimes difficult to resist the sense that Morris was reaching out to an audience of initiates rather than seeking to win converts';[58] and Ruth Ellison that 'if he considered his wider readership at all, it was with the assumption that the readers' tastes and abilities matched

---

[56] Waithe, p. 94.
[57] Swannell, 'Interpreter', p. 376.
[58] Wawn, *Vikings*, p. 260.

his own.'[59] Although Litzenberg was certainly accurate in demonstrating that the diction of the translations was not a 'conglomerate mass of linguistic quackery' scattered with neologism,[60] the degree to which Morris pursued an idiom 'combining the literary English of his own day with words dug from the depth of English literary history'[61] meant that he created what Ellison and Waithe both call a 'private language',[62] inaccessible to those of his readers who lacked the eyes of a 'living edition of all that was best' in Middle English literature. By translating his Old Norse editions so literally, Morris may have inadvertently prevented his audience from seeing the wood for the trees or, in this case, the sagas for the words.

It is true that those readers looking for the sagas may not easily find them in Morris's translations. The literal choices frequently reduce the pace of the text, complicate the laconic economy of the narrative, bury the comedy, and sometimes confuse the sense altogether. At its worst, the style undermines the quality of stark vividness for which the sagas of Icelanders have been so celebrated with a quaintness that, as George Johnston argues, gives the impression that they 'belong in a never-never land' that is 'marvellously consistent' but 'never quite real.'[63] Yet, for those readers interested in the development of Morris's ideology, the literal style upon which he gradually resolved in his Icelandic translations offers insight into a period that has frequently been presumed to predate the materialisation of his political philosophy. Far from becoming what E. P. Thompson called a 'sub-trade' that was 'incompatible with the fullest concentration of his intellectual and moral energies,'[64] Morris's literary output at this time shows that he was, in fact, attempting to reconnect Victorian Britain with what he deemed to be a more authentically virtuous phase of their culture (in which *craft* had meant a skilled, versatile and dependable kind of power) well before he began to speak on the matter in public.

---

[59] Ruth Ellison, '"The Undying Glory of Dreams": William Morris and the "Northland of Old"', in *Victorian Poetry*, ed. Malcolm Bradbury and David Palmer (London: Arnold, 1972), pp. 138–75 (p. 143).

[60] Litzenberg, 'Diction', pp. 327–28.

[61] Litzenberg, 'Diction', p. 359.

[62] Ellison, 'Undying Glory', p. 143; Waithe, p. 101.

[63] George Johnston, 'On Translation – II', *Saga-Book of the Viking Society for Northern Research*, 15 (1957), 394–402 (pp. 394–96).

[64] E. P. Thompson, p. 188.

5

Sigurd the Volsung and the Fulfilment of the Deedful Measure

URING THE CLIMACTIC final exchange between Sigurd and Bryn-hild in Morris's adapation of the Sigurðr cycle *The Story of Sigurd the Volsung and the Fall of the Niblungs* (1876), after the heroine has been overcome by grief at the hero's betrayal of her, Sigurd attempts to console her with an exhortation to resolute activity. Initially associating the dawning of a new day with the opportunity for optimistic endeavour – 'Awake, arise, O Brynhild! for the house is smitten through | With the light of the sun awakened, and the hope of deeds to do' – he subsequently offers himself as the embodiment of an ideal of action that might serve as an antidote to despair: 'It is I that awake thee, and I give thee the life and the days | For fulfilling the deedful measure, and the cup of the people's praise' (*CW*, XII, p. 222). In an image that evokes a heroic Germanic lord providing drink for his retainers, Sigurd implies that the accomplishment of a certain kind of purposeful conduct (the fulfilment of the 'deedful measure') for the general good of the community (the cup of the people's praise) is a fundamentally hopeful and valuable approach to life.

As inspiration for this scene, Morris had drawn on the episode in *Völsunga saga* that depicts the last conversation between Sigurðr and Brynhildr, which in 1869 he had declared to have touched him more than anything he had ever met with in literature: 'there is nothing wanting in it, nothing forgotten, nothing repeated, nothing overstrained'.[1] Yet, despite the remarkable esteem in which Morris held the episode in the saga, a close inspection reveals that it contains no such invocation to heroic action. When the saga's Sigurðr encourages Brynhildr to rise from her bed, he does not seem motivated by any explicit reason other than perhaps the broad intimation that cheerful behaviour is preferable to misery: 'vaki þú, Brynhildr! sól skín um allan bæinn, ok er ærit sofit; hritt

---

[1] Letter to Norton, probably dated 21 December 1869, in Kelvin, I, p. 99.

af þèr harmi ok tak gleði' (*VÖL*, p. 194).² By contrast, in the hero's appeal to Brynhild in *Sigurd,* Morris appears to offer an entire ethos that has the potential to invigorate life with new meaning and might be described as 'deedfulness'. In light of this, in this chapter I examine the significance of the 'deedful measure' in *Sigurd* as a whole, arguing that Morris created an ethos of action in the poem that he hoped his audience would embrace as distantly familiar. Although he believed he was faithfully reforging the lost epic of Sigurðr, this ethos was in fact not in his sources. I conclude that Morris discovered a confidence in 'deedfulness' that had, despite his audience failing to embrace it, evolved through his engagement with Old Norse literature, and by which he subsequently attempted to live.

As Hanson has asserted, deeds 'define the characters' in *Sigurd*.³ In the far-flung Dark Age world of his epic Morris creates a model of manliness that 'rests on action and heroism expressed in deeds'.⁴ At the simplest level, to be 'deedful' in the poem is to be accomplished in exploits. Sigurd is described in passing as 'full fair of deed and word' (*CW*, XII, p. 155) and Gunnar and his brothers as 'the deedful Niblungs' (*CW*, XII, p. 303), suggesting their previous successes in warfaring and feats of daring. Compared to those of their saga counterparts, however, the heroic deeds that Morris's heroes perform are rarely as acquisitive, self-serving or explicitly violent. Like their medieval Icelandic descendants, in Morris's translation of the sagas of Icelanders, the 'deedful' heroes of *Sigurd* behave with more dignity than their Norse equivalents and are less motivated by the attainment of prestige and wealth (see Chapter 2, pp. 57–73). Where, for example, the saga's Sigmundr and Sinfjötli are shown to act with merciless covetousness when it is explained that they 'fara nú um sumrum víða um skóga, ok drepa menn til fjár sèr' (*VÖL*, p. 130),⁵ the Sigmund and Sinfiotli of Morris's adaptation are shown to act

---

² 'Wake up, Brynhildr! The sun is shining throughout the whole town, and you have slept enough; throw off your sorrow and cheer up.' The motivations for the characters' responses are convoluted in the section of *Völsunga saga,* which suggests that there were competing versions in its sources. Sigurðr goes from implying Brynhildr's underhand nature by predicting that she is plotting against them to telling her that he loves her more than himself, and Guðrún taunts Brynhildr by showing her the ring only to express her sorrow at her grief once she has taken to her bed, see *VÖL*, pp. 194–96.
³ Hanson, p. 68.
⁴ Hanson, p. 70.
⁵ 'Travel now widely through the forest in the summers, and kill men for their goods.'

congruently with their community, so much so that a kind of conscientiousness is implied on their part:

> And all the deeds of the sword he learned him, and showed
>   him the feats of war
> Where sea and forest mingle, and up from the ocean's shore
> The highway leads to market, and men go up and down,
> And the spear-hedged wains of the merchants fare oft to the
>   Goth-folk's town. (*CW*, xii, p. 32)

Though Sigmund teaches Sinfiotli the 'deeds' of weaponry and warfare, the target and purpose of the 'feats of war' remain indistinct. Instead, Morris alludes to the importance of gaining accomplishment and emphasises the idyllic context of the instruction. Sigmund teaches Sinfiotli to fight on the seashore at the edge of the community to which they are connected by the roads that the farmers and merchants use to travel to market. Whether the reference to the coastline implies that father and son are fighting raiders or raiding themselves is ambiguous, but the deeds of these characters are coloured with a more abstract idealised benevolence than the frequently materialistic endeavours of the saga's protagonists (who are adept at plundering).

This 'deedful' benevolence imbues *Sigurd* with a paternalistic quality at points that does not appear in the saga. When Sigmund is 'set on his father's throne' it is said that he 'hearkened and doomed and portioned, and did all the deeds of a king' (*CW*, xii, p. 49), but no similar comment is made about the saga's Sigmundr. Similarly, when Hogni overhears the wails of the thrall who is about to have his heart cut out,[6] he calls for clemency because he values the meek dignity of the slave's life: 'O fools, must the lowly die | Because kings strove with swords?' (*CW*, xii, p. 293). His saga counterpart, on the other hand, intercedes only to halt the feeble cries of Hjalli, who is portrayed as a figure of ridicule due to his cowardice (*VÖL*, p. 218). As well as generally gaining accomplishment, therefore, an aspect of fulfilling the 'deedful measure' is to place oneself in symbiotic relationship with the community. Like the heroic lord's relationship with the *comitatus*, a conscientious hero takes the welfare of his people upon himself to advance popular cohesion.

Again like the heroes of Morris's translation of the sagas of Icelanders, the 'deedful' heroes of *Sigurd* (or those women who support them)

---

[6] The slave is called Hjalli in *Völsunga saga* and 'Atlakviða' ('The Lay of Atli') but is unnamed in *Sigurd*.

indulge less in overtly brutal or aberrant behaviour than their counterparts in *Völsunga saga*. As Hascall has noted, in *Sigurd* Morris tones down Sigmundr and Signý's cruelty towards her sons with Siggeir by excising the instances in *Völsunga saga* in which she has her brother kill them, after first testing their mettle by sewing their sleeves to their wrists.[7] Whereas in his poem Morris has Sigmund humanely lead his feeble charge from the wild wood back into the care of his mother once he realises he is too timid to foster (*CW*, XII, pp. 26–27), the author of *Völsunga saga* describes a more ruthless fate for the boy: 'Signý mælti: tak þú hann þá ok drep hann; eigi þarf hann þá lengr at lifa; ok svâ gerði hann' (*VÖL*, pp. 127–28).[8]

Similarly, while towards the end of *Sigurd* Gudrun tells Atli euphemistically 'Thou hast swallowed the might of the Niblungs, and their glory lieth in thee' (*CW*, XII, p. 302) and it is, thus, uncertain whether either infanticide or cannibalism has been committed,[9] in the Old Norse text Guðrún explicitly slits her sons' throats and feeds them to their father (*VÖL*, p. 221). In Morris's poem, Signy's incest with her brother is also made more palatable by rendering it an explicit sin that she takes on herself for the sake of her avenging her father – 'Alone I will bear it; alone I will take the crime' (*CW*, XII, p. 27) – where no such comment is made in the saga (p. 128). Morris goes on to portray Sinfiotli as more explicitly unnatural than the saga's hero, so that his incestuous begetting becomes more clearly deviant. While the saga character is described simply as 'bæði mikill ok sterkr ok vænn at áliti, ok mjök í ætt Völsúnga' (p. 129),[10] Morris's Sinfiotli becomes the outlandish 'huge-limbed son of Signy with the fierce and eager eyes' (*CW*, XII, p. 32). The hero who fulfils the 'deedful measure' must, thus, not only be accomplished in humane and considerate exploits and act in synergy with the people, but he must also refrain from activities that in *Völsunga saga* Morris considered 'of the monstrous order'.[11]

More than this, however, to be 'deedful' in *Sigurd* is to uphold a broad ethical attitude: a spontaneous, almost unthinking, eagerness to embrace

---

[7] Hascall, p. 22.

[8] 'Signý said: Take him now and kill him; there is no need for him to live any longer; and so he did.'

[9] In Morris's version, Gudrun may simply be referring here to the fact that Atli has 'devoured' her brothers by killing them.

[10] 'He was both tall and strong, handsome in appearance and much like the line of the Völsungs.'

[11] Letter to Webb, probably dated 15 August 1869, in Kelvin, I, p. 89.

and subsequently make the most of the circumstances allotted to you. In Morris's adaptation, for example, Sigurd's resolution to bear the pain of his lost union with Brynhild privately, once the effect of the potion of forgetfulness has worn off, is described in much more momentous terms than in the saga. Whereas Sigurd demonstrates that, in David Ashurst's words, 'acceptance is the appropriate moral response to his circumstances'[12] when he determines to suffer the 'burden till the last of the uttermost end' (*CW*, XII, p. 201), his Old Norse counterpart merely resolves not to let it become known that he has recognised Brynhildr (*VÖL*, pp. 187–88). Similarly, when King Volsung arrives in the Land of the Goths only to discover that Siggeir intends to wage war on him, he chooses to embrace the situation wholeheartedly rather than to retreat. While, for the Völsungr of the saga, this decision is based purely on the breach of honour that would be involved in breaking his vow never to take flight ('þat munu allar þjóðir at orðum gèra, at ek mælta eitt orð úborinn, ok strengda ek þess heit, at ek skylda hvârki flýja eld nè járn fyrir hrædslu sakir') (*VÖL*, p. 123),[13] for the Volsung of the poem, the act of embracing the battle provides the glorious potential for immortal commemoration in 'the deed that dies not, and the name that shall ever avail' (*CW*, XII, p. 14). It is not avoidance of shame that motivates Morris's Volsung so much as the desire to become a symbol of virtuous living in the history of his people, by openly and instinctively embracing fortune.

The incentive to become part of the ongoing tale of the people marks a crucial distinction between the ethos of shame that exists in the saga and the ethos of deedfulness that Morris invents for *Sigurd*. In the Old Norse text, the characters mostly work from primal desires to obtain honour and avoid dishonour: Signý is talked into travelling home with Siggeir after their betrothal because it would be dishonourable to break the agreement (*VÖL*, p. 122); the dispute that leads to Brynhildr recognising Guðrún's ring is sparked by the petty insult of Brynhildr assuming precedence over Guðrún (*VÖL*, p. 118); Brynhildr brings about her and Sigurðr's death primarily because of the insupportable shame that has arisen from him making her an *eiðrofa* ('oath-breaker') (*VÖL*, p. 192).

[12] David Ashurst, 'Wagner, Morris and the Sigurd Figure: Confronting Freedom and Uncertainty', in *Revisiting the Poetic Edda: Essays on Old Norse Heroic Legend*, ed. Paul Acker, Carolyne Larrington and T. A. Shippey (New York: Routledge, 2012), pp. 219–37 (p. 232).
[13] 'All peoples will bear witness to it that I spoke one word before I was born and made the vow that I would never flee fire nor iron for the sake of fear.'

In *Sigurd*, however, Morris replaces this honour code with one in which 'deedful' characters are inspired to subordinate their private desires to the glory of the popular narrative in which their lives play a small but integral part. No sooner, for instance, has Volsung entreated his daughter to consider the importance of the public tale and marry 'that our name may never die' (*CW*, xii, p. 2) than Signy agrees despite the 'wrack and the grief' that she knows it will bring her. Morris conceives of her marriage as a feat of self-abnegation for the sake of the people's story, rather than as a necessary step in upholding the family honour. As the titular hero, Sigurd epitomises the life led for the sake of the greater ongoing narrative. His potential deeds are linked to the future glory of the people's tale as soon as he is born: 'O thy deeds that men shall sing of! O thy deeds that the Gods shall see!' (*CW*, xii, p. 66). As he grows up he deems his destiny to be a 'deedful' life in the communal story: 'the world is wide, and filled with deeds unwrought; | And for e'en such work was I fashioned lest the song-craft come to nought' (*CW*, xii, p. 73). Unlike their saga counterparts, the 'deedful' heroes of *Sigurd* are alive to the fact that their deeds are simply stitches in the tapestry of the popular history that quite literally surrounds them.[14] They strive, in the words of Herbert F. Tucker, to become 'worthy of the tale by living up to an original greatness'.[15]

By contrast, characters that are 'deedless' or otherwise frustrate 'deedful' behaviour in *Sigurd* show no concern for the ongoing account of their people embodied in the popular tale. Rather than seeking to enhance the story and thereby strengthen its capacity to provide solace

---

[14] Hiordis embroiders 'The deeds of the world that should be, and the deeds of the world that were of old' (*CW*, xii, p. 50) and Brynhild leads the disguised Sigurd into her bed-chamber in which the walls are hung with 'the deeds that were done aforetime, and the coming deeds of worth' (*CW*, xii, p. 193). While in the saga, there are references to the actions of specific heroes being woven into tapestries (Brynhildr, for example, is embroidering the deeds that Sigurðr has performed when he arrives at Heimir [*VÖL*, p. 175]), there is little indication of the importance of the wider history of the people as a whole. If anything the embroiderers consider reflecting on the deeds of the heroes to be mere amusement. Brynhildr suggests 'skemtum oss allar saman, ok ræðum um ríka konúnga ok þeirra stórvirki!' ('Let's have fun together, and talk about powerful kings and their bold deeds!') (*VÖL*, pp. 179–80) before she interprets Guðrún's dreams, and later Guðrún embroiders a tapestry with 'mörg ok stór verk ok fagra leikar' ('many bold deeds and fair games') when she is grieving Sigurðr's death (*VÖL*, p. 205).

[15] Herbert F. Tucker, *Epic: Britain's Heroic Muse 1790–1910* (Oxford: Oxford University Press, 2008), p. 515.

and inspiration for future generations, they indulge themselves in individualistic, self-seeking aspirations and attempting to manipulate the exigencies of fortune to their own ends. Sigurd labels Regin a 'deedless' man just as he has craftily begun to encourage him to win the gold (*CW*, XII, p. 73) and Grimhild repeatedly conspires to bend the course of destiny to her own desires: 'But Grimhild looked and was merry; and she deemed her life was great, | And her hand a wonder of wonders to withstand the deeds of Fate' (*CW*, XII, p. 166). Regin explains that when Fafnir took the gold he declared: 'Lo, I am a King for ever, and alone on the Gold shall I dwell | And do no deed to repent of and leave no tale to tell' (*CW*, XII, p. 86). Each of these characters becomes what Tucker describes as a 'blocking agent' who 'in seeking to thwart the tale, threatens to supplant *relation* with interventionist *cunning* and to crush epic narrativity into the apocalyptics of the quick fix'.[16]

To be 'deedless' in the poem can also signify the experience of psychological alienation from the surrounding environment. When Brynhild refuses to rise from her bed after discovering Sigurd's betrayal, Gudrun refers to the lapse of time that has passed as 'the deedless night' (*CW*, XII, p. 218). After Sigurd drinks the potion of forgetfulness and loses all memory of Brynhild he rides from the hall 'with no deed before him' (*CW*, XII, p. 168) into the 'deedless dark' (*CW*, XII, p. 169).[17] Similarly, when Gudrun is grieving for Sigurd it is said that 'Her heart was cold and dreadful; nor no good from ill she knew, | Since her love was taken from her and the day of deeds to do' (*CW*, XII, p. 234). In *Sigurd* it is, thus, possible to become 'deedless' not only as a patently bad character who indulges in egocentric endeavour but also as a well-intentioned character who deviates from the honourable path. To be 'deedful' is, therefore, not shown to be an unchanging state but a way of acting that must be continually reaffirmed and defended against becoming 'deedless'. A hero must continue to work diligently through the deeds of his life to remain heroic.

Overall, Morris's portrayal of 'deedfulness' and 'deedlessness' shapes the ethical foundation of *Sigurd* as a whole. Characters who are 'deedful' are shown to be morally virtuous, while characters who are 'deedless' are shown to be either morally corrupt or otherwise to have become estranged from their former moral integrity. While Morris liked the

---

[16] Herbert F. Tucker, 'All for the Tale: The Epic Macropoetics of Morris' *Sigurd the Volsung*', *Victorian Poetry*, 34 (1996), 373–96 (p. 380).

[17] Sigurðr experiences no such sense of disorientation at the equivalent point in the Old Norse text. See *VÖL*, pp. 185–87.

instinctive, unthinking embrace of values associated with the shame culture portrayed in the sagas, as I showed in Chapter 2, he did not like the ruthless behaviour that came with it (see p. 80). Rather than presenting a shame culture in *Sigurd* in which honour is sought in a relatively narrow-minded, crude manner, Morris, therefore, portrays an ethos in which it is virtuous to embrace earthly conditions without the possibility of any consolation, other than the knowledge that to live whole-heartedly as part of the wider narrative of the people is to live heroically. To win a part in the popular tale replaces honour as the cherished asset. Sigurd is a hero because he 'would utterly light the face of good and ill' (*CW*, XII, p. 106). In other words, he wishes to encounter the extant world as it is, with what Ashurst describes as 'all its violence, its potential for peace and plenty, its good and its evil',[18] and then to proceed resolutely within these conditions.

Unheroic characters, on the other hand, wish to reject the extant world by confusing or equating the good and the ill. Grimhild creates the 'eyeless tangle' (*CW*, XII, p. 222) and Regin aspires to a prelapsarian existence in which 'there shall be no more dying, and the sea shall be as the land | And the world for ever and ever shall be young beneath [his] hand' (*CW*, XII, p. 89). Sigurd's preference (and we may presume that of Morris too) is, by contrast, for a world in which human life is accepted as temporal and transitory, and must, therefore, be embraced unreservedly, allowing: 'Bright end from bright beginning, and the mid-way good to tell, | And death, and deeds accomplished, and all remembered well!' (*CW*, XII, p. 104). Ultimately, in the 'deedful' ethos that Morris presents in *Sigurd*, he celebrates the story of human existence on earth, with all its fallibilities and weaknesses, as more heroic than any divine existence of 'changeless mirth' in which 'battle and murder shall fail, | And the world shall laugh and long not, nor weep, nor fashion the tale' (*CW*, XII, p. 80).

As well as structuring the ethos of *Sigurd*, the aspiration to fulfil the 'deedful measure' structures the fabric of the poem itself. In its unyielding prosody, the scale of its vision and impermeable diction, the poem becomes what Tucker calls 'an order of aesthetic enactment'[19] in which Morris performs the 'deedful' attitude that he endorses in its narrative.

---

[18] David Ashurst, 'William Morris and the Volsungs', in *Old Norse Made New: Essays on the Post-Medieval Reception of Old Norse Literature and Culture*, ed. David Clark and Carl Phelpstead (London: Viking Society for Northern Research, 2007), pp. 43–61 (p. 57).

[19] Tucker, 'Macropoetics', p. 382.

At the simplest level, the attitude of embrace associated with 'deedful-ness' is enacted in *Sigurd*'s material design. With its long lines 'crowding the margin' and 'each new book and chapter pressed up flush with its predecessor', the poem's almost overwhelming appearance in both the Ellis & White edition of 1876 and the Kelmscott edition of 1898 alerts the reader to the fact that, in Tucker's words, to 'enter this text imaginatively is to court engulfment'.[20] Indeed, *Sigurd* is so visually commanding that it necessarily imposes on the reader the determined deed of undertaking to read it.

The emphatic prosody is also instrumental in enacting the unreflec-tive, instinctive aspect of 'deedful' embrace. Basically iambic but with 'with substitutions of anapaests and dactyls occurring so frequently as to be almost regular',[21] Morris selects for his epic what Tompkins terms a 'rushing metre' that is so indefatigable that it can 'stun thought'.[22] So visceral that it 'soaks into the bones',[23] *Sigurd*'s hexameter, in which 'after three voiced beats comes a rest where the heart beats four', creates an unremitting dynamic that, combined with the relentless couplet rhymes and reverberating alliteration, must be embraced almost bodily. Pulsating with an energy that Tucker labels 'communal performativity',[24] the poem demands to be either read aloud or with nothing less than whole-hearted determination. In the same way that 'deedfulness' must be affirmed continually or lost, the relentlessness of the versification requires the reader to affirm the act of reading continually or cease altogether. The poem, thus, puts the reader in the position of committing to be 'deedful'.

The increased space and energy that *Sigurd*'s hexameter lines allow not only invigorate the experience of reading the poem but they also invigorate the speech of the characters, in a manner that suggests their increased steadfastness in comparison to their equivalents in the sources. Particularly in the instances in which Morris draws on the twenty or so poems of the *Poetic Edda* that relate to the Völsung cycle, in his hexam-eters (which may contain as many as sixteen syllables),[25] he frequently

[20] Tucker, *Epic*, p. 515.
[21] Hascall, p. 20.
[22] Tompkins, p. 228.
[23] Tucker, 'Macropoetics', p. 384.
[24] Tucker, *Epic*, p. 512.
[25] Geoffrey B. Riddehough's contention that in his 'attempt at a line-for-line rendering' of the *Aeneid* 'he found a long verse necessary' raises the possibility that Morris chose the longer lines of *Sigurd* simply to allow enough space to fit in the detail that he desired from his sources. See 'William Morris's

adapts what Hoare calls the 'compressed, allusive'[26] *fornyrðislag* or *málaháttr* lines (which may contain as few as four) into bolder prolonged vociferations. In transforming the moment in 'Sigrdrífumál' ('The Lay of Sigrdrífa'), for instance, in which Sigurðr wakens Brynhildr, Morris changes the heroine's brief, perplexed questions into an extended resonant inquiry:

> Hvatt beit brynju?
> hví brá ek svefni?
> hverr feldi af mèr
> fölvar nauðir? (*EDD*, p. 115)[27]

In *Sigurd*, Morris adapts this verse as:

> O, what is the thing so mighty that my weary sleep hath torn,
> And rent the fallow bondage, and the wan woe over-worn?
> (*CW*, XII, p. 124)

In comparison to her eddic counterpart, Morris's Brynhild speaks with a more determined demanding tone. While the succinct, almost delicate, clarity of Brynhildr's queries evokes bewilderment at who has woken her – as she recalls the cutting of her mail-shirt, her subsequent awakening and release from confinement – the longer, more resounding lines spoken by Brynhild create a dramatic sense of her liberation, invoking Sigurd's might, as well as employing a vital image of being both torn and rent from sleep. Similarly, in his adaptation of the verse in 'Guðrúnarkviða hin fyrsta' ('The First Lay of Guðrún') – in which, grieving for Sigurðr's loss, Guðrún compares her reduced situation to a tiny leaf blowing amongst the wild sedge – the greater length and impetus of Morris's lines transform the heroine's complaint from one of tender vulnerability to declarative lament:

Translation of the "Aeneid"', *The Journal of English and Germanic Philology*, 36 (1937), 338–46 (p. 338). It is certainly possible to see the translation of the *Aeneid*, on which Morris worked from the autumn of 1874 to the spring of 1875 before beginning work on *Sigurd* in October 1875, as a dry run for the creation of his own epic. See letter to Macdonald Baldwin, dated 25 March 1875, in Kelvin, I, p. 248.

[26] Hoare, p. 56.

[27] 'What bit into my burnie? | why was I brought from sleep? | who has released me from | pale fetters?'

Ek þótta ok
þjóðans rekkum
hverri hæri
Herjans dísi;
nú em ek svá lítil,
sem lauf sè
opt jölstrum,
at jöfur dauðan. (*EDD*, p. 125)[28]

In *Sigurd*, Morris adapts this verse as:

> O might of my love, my Sigurd! how oft I sat by this side,
> And was praised for the loftiest woman and the best of Odin's pride!
> But now am I as little as the leaf on the lone tree left,
> When the winter wood is shaken and the sky by the North is cleft. (*CW*, xii, p. 236)

While the Norse prosody is remarkable for its breviloquence, with its unadorned *fornyrðislag* lines lending the verse a blunted restraint that suggests something of the emotional numbness of Guðrún's grief, in Morris's sustained hexameter the terseness is exchanged for a more forceful quality of impassioned misery. Morris's Gudrun also recalls Sigurd's extraordinary power, and her comparison of herself to a leaf now becomes a more expansive image that includes a wood, the north wind and the great sky above. In both of these extracts, the increased scale and energy of Morris's chosen metre generates a more vigorous, emphatic quality in the speech of the heroines that evokes the heroic fortitude of 'deedfulness'. Whereas in these moments in the eddic sources the heroines are portrayed as vulnerable and exposed, in Morris's version they become awesome figures of primitivist epic.

Throughout *Sigurd*, Morris fashions the primitivist scale integral to the enactment of 'deedful' fortitude not only by enlarging the lines to hexameters but also by drastically inflating the size of the overall narrative to monolithic dimensions that generate what might be described, in the

---

[28] 'I considered myself | amongst the warriors of a king | higher than any | of the maidens of Herjan [Óðinn] [> valkyries]; | Now I am as little, | as a leaf is | often amongst the wild sedge | at the death of a king.'

words of Jeffrey Skoblow, as an 'irreducible totality'.[29] The circumstances of Sigurd's birth, for instance, are given in two or three sentences in the saga (*VÖL*, pp. 148–49), which Morris expands to nearly six pages (*CW*, XII, pp. 61–67). Sigurd's arrival at the Niblung hall is similarly enlarged from a few sentences in *Völsunga saga* (*VÖL*, pp. 181–82) to over eight pages in his poem (*CW*, XII, pp. 149–57); and a single sentence in the saga that describes the raids that Sigurðr undertakes with Gunnarr and his brothers ('Þeir fóru nú víða um lönd, ok vinna mörg frægðarverk, drápu marga konúngasonu, ok engir menn gerðu slík afrek sem þeir' [*VÖL*, p. 184])[30] becomes six pages of glorious mutual warfaring in *Sigurd* (*CW*, XII, pp. 157–63). The correlation of awesome scale and the primitivist fortitude of 'deedfulness' is perhaps most apparent in Morris's transformation of Odin, who compared to the Óðinn of the saga is almost unrecognisable:

> ok er orrostan hafði staðit um hríð, þá kom maðr í bardagann með síðan hatt ok heklu blá; hann hafði eitt auga ok geir í hendi; þessi maðr kom ámót Sigmundi konúngi, ok brá upp geirnum fyrir honum. (*VÖL*, p. 145)[31]

In *Sigurd*, Morris adapts this passage as:

> But lo, through the hedge of the war-shafts a mighty man there came,
> One-eyed and seeming ancient, but his visage shone as flame:
> Gleaming-grey was his kirtle, and his hood was cloudy blue;
> And he bore a mighty twi-bill, as he waded the fight-sheaves through,
> And stood face to face with Sigmund, and upheaved the bill to smite. (*CW*, XII, p. 54)

In contrast to the Óðinn of the saga, who emerges as something of an inconspicuous figure (his elusive wiliness made all the more mysterious

[29] Jeffrey Skoblow, *Paradise Dislocated: Morris, Politics, Art* (London: University Press of Virginia, 1993), p. 49. Skoblow uses this phrase in relation to *The Earthly Paradise* but it also seems pertinent to *Sigurd*.
[30] 'They now travelled widely throughout the lands, performing many glorious deeds, killing many sons of kings, and nobody achieved such accomplishments as them.'
[31] 'And when the battle had been raging for a time, then a man came into the fight with a low-hanging hood and a dark cloak; he had one eye and a spear in his hand; this man went against Sigmundr, and raised the spear in front of him.'

by his nondescript appearance), Morris renders Odin here a 'mighty' man who *wades* through the 'hedge of war-shafts' [wall of swords/spears > battle/army] and 'fight-sheaves' [sheaves of battle > swords], emitting flame-like light from his face. His garments now gleam elementally and he carries a 'mighty twi-bill', rather than a simple spear. Overall, the monumental scale gives the impression of a primordial idol who advances with 'deedful' resolution rather than sly cunning.

In public scenes such as these, the increased scale of *Sigurd* is often created in part by the introduction of a social or civic perspective that is lacking in the Norse text (such as the emphasis on the surrounding retinue in the passage above). Private moments in the sources become public spectacle in the poem, and the interdependence between 'deedful' hero and the community is stressed where it is not in the Norse texts. Earlier in his adaptation of 'Guðrúnarkviða hin fyrsta' ('The First Lay of Guðrún'), for instance, Morris transforms the moment between the grieving Guðrún and her sister Gullrönd from an intimate exchange to a communal display:

> Svipti hon blæju
> af Sigurði
> ok vatt vengi
> fyr vífs knjám:
> 'Líttu á ljúfan,
> legðu munn við grön,
> sem þú hálsaðir
> heilan stilli!' (*EDD*, p. 124)[32]

In *Sigurd*, Morris adapts this verse as:

> All heed gave the maids and the warriors, and hushed was the
> spear-thronged place,
> As she stretched out her hand to Sigurd, and swept the linen
> away
> From the lips that had holpen the people, and the eyes that had
> gladdened the day;
> She set her hand unto Sigurd, and turned the face of the dead

---

[32] 'She swept the sheet | from Sigurðr | and turned the pillows | towards the woman's knees, | "Look at your loved one | lay mouth against lip | as you embraced | the king alive."'

> To the moveless knees of Gudrun, and again she spake and
>   said:
> 'O Gudrun, look on thy loved-one; yea, as if here living yet
> Let his face by thy face be cherished, and thy lips on his lips be
>   set!' (*CW*, xii, p. 235)

While there is no mention of any onlooker in the moment in
'Guðrúnarkviða hin fyrsta' when Gullrönd sweeps the cover from
Sigurðr, and it therefore seems comparatively personal (with the range of
focus limited and close), by including in his version a hushed assembly of
solemn witnesses that is spear-thronged with warriors, Morris expands
the martial grandeur of the scene, as well as emphasising Sigurd's place
within the heart of his society. The hero's dead lips are now described as
those that had once helped the people, and his great eyes stare up to the
'cloudy roof of the Niblungs', suggesting a scale of vision that, in the words
of Charlotte H. Oberg, takes in 'not only all levels of human society but
extends beyond the earth itself to include all of reality'.[33] In expanding
the public context of the scene to this extent, Morris transforms what is
essentially a passage about the nature of mourning into one that emphasises the fundamental worth of living 'deedfully' in the world for the sake
of the common good.

This tendency to expand the social context of *Sigurd* is crucial to
Morris's portrayal of 'deedfulness'. In order to make the ethos of the
poem appear coherent it was necessary for him to depict a culture that
could have credibly maintained it. Eschewing the Latinate vocabulary
and quasi-Arthurian imagery that survived into 'The Lovers of Gudrun',
Morris now experimented with auto-referential diction to create a
discrete cultural and ethical cocoon that, in the words of Simon Dentith,
is 'impermeable to the infiltration of contemporaneity'.[34] As well as
coining numerous kennings on traditional subjects like battle, the sea
and gold,[35] Morris experimented with circumlocutory ways of expressing

---

[33] Oberg, p. 89.

[34] Simon Dentith, 'Morris, "The Great Story of the North", and the
Barbaric Past', *Journal of Victorian Culture*, 14 (2009), 238–54 (p. 244).

[35] Kennings related to battle include: 'battle-acre' [> battlefield] (*CW*, xii,
p. 5) and 'battle-play' [> battle] (*CW*, xii, p. 32); 'bale-fires' light' [presumably,
bale-fire > sword, sword light > battle], blood-reeds' tangle [blood-reed > sword,
sword tangle > battle] and fallow blades of fight [> shining swords of fight >
battle swords] (*CW*, xii, p. 32). Kennings referring to the sea include: 'the field
of the fishes', 'from the bath of the swan' (*CW*, xii, p. 3); 'swan-bath', 'Ægir's acre'
(*CW*, xii, p. 13); 'sea-flood' (*CW*, xii, p. 23); and for mermen, sea-spirits or

less familiar subjects: shepherds become 'searchers of the thicket' (*CW*, XII, p. 6); sailors 'dealers with the oar'; wolves 'dogs of the forest' (*CW*, XII, p. 20); and snakes 'creeping-kin' (*CW*, XII, p. 31). In drawing on images from within its own frame of reference in this way, rather than using metaphors or similes that refer to classical mythology, the world of *Sigurd* remains insulated from any external culture or epoch. When, for instance, Sigurd disguises himself as Gunnar to ride the Wavering Flame, Morris creates the circumlocution 'Wildfire's Trampler that Gunnar's image bore' (*CW*, XII, p. 191), which describes the hero's intermediate state in terms of the context of the poem only, portraying him purely through his actions and outward appearance after his own person and past has been confounded by the magic draught.

Similarly, in his use of epic similes (which, as Dentith notes, have sometimes been employed elsewhere in the epic tradition to provide 'a point of comparison in the workaday world'),[36] Morris refuses to be diverted from the internal reality of the poem. When Signy agrees reluctantly to marry Siggeir, the clamour that follows her assent is compared to the waves sweeping over unseen rocks off the coastline:

> She spake, and the feast sped on, and the speech and the song
>   and the laughter
> Went over the words of boding as the tide of the norland main
> Sweeps over the hidden skerry, the home of the shipman's bane.
>   (*CW*, XII, p. 3)

In describing the feast by invoking the surrounding sea Morris 'seeks to find the grounds of comparison from within the heroic world he is seeking to create',[37] drawing from a store of images that refer to the internal poetic universe of *Sigurd* to portray the hubbub in the hall, while simultaneously contextualising it within the wider imaginary realm of the surrounding landscape. The broader context of this moment reinforces the authenticity of the epic universe, rendering it more comprehensive than the internal realities of the sources. With such details Morris creates something approaching a discrete secondary world that

---

raiders 'folk of fishy fields' (*CW*, XII, p. 9). Kennings referring to gold include: 'the flame of the sea' (*CW*, XII, p. 32); and 'flame of the Glittering Heath' [flame of Fáfnir's heath > gold] (*CW*, XII, p. 21).

[36] Dentith, 'Barbaric Past', p. 245.

[37] Simon Dentith, *Epic and Empire in Nineteenth-Century Britain*, Cambridge Studies in Nineteenth-Century Literature and Culture, 52 (Cambridge: Cambridge University Press, 2006), p. 75.

depicts what J. R. R. Tolkien would call 'the nameless North of Sigurd of the Völsungs'.[38] Neither the framed story-world of *The Earthly Paradise* tale, nor a saga explicitly set in Iceland, *Sigurd's* universe is more clearly defined and self-coherent than the legendary one of its saga source (see Chapter 6, pp. 169–70). In creating his own epic myth in *Sigurd*, Morris created a fantasy world via a design that was neither what Tolkien termed 'representation' nor 'symbolic interpretation of the beauties and terrors of the world'[39] but perhaps something more like that which he believed the author of *Beowulf* had used, one that 'glimpses the cosmic and moves with the thought of all men concerning the fate of human life'.[40] By creating such an immersive secondary world, Morris also provides a convincing context for the invented ethos of 'deedfulness' that can resonate with the real world of the reader but also act in contrast to it. In addition, the hermetic nature of the secondary world suggests something of the impossibility of transcending one's reality: there is nothing in *Sigurd's* universe but its particular worldly context and internal tale. 'Deedful' characters, therefore, have no choice but to embrace the world in which they find themselves and play their part in the continuing popular narrative.

The question arises as to what Morris was trying to achieve in writing a poem that rendered the ethos of 'deedfulness' both thematically and physically. Tucker has implied that his motivation for *Sigurd* was equivalent to that which inspired his translations *The Aeneids of Virgil* (1875), *The Odyssey of Homer* (1887) and *The Tale of Beowulf* (1895). Arguing that the ballad-based metre that Morris employed for all of these works highlights a belief that 'the epics he translated all had at bottom the same cultural work to do',[41] Tucker casts him as a renationalising bard, liberating these 'illegitimately privatized'[42] founding myths that hold the potential to sustain and direct whichever society embraces them 'as their own'.[43]

While it is no doubt true that, in coining an Icelandic epic in a measure that not only captured a rhythm of 'vernacular English balladry'

[38] J. R. R. Tolkien, *Tree and Leaf* (London: Allen & Unwin, 1964), p. 40.
[39] Tolkien, *Tree and Leaf*, p. 25.
[40] J. R. R. Tolkien, 'Beowulf: The Monsters and the Critics', *Proceedings of the British Academy*, 22 (1936), 245–95 (p. 277).
[41] Tucker, *Epic*, pp. 512–13.
[42] Tucker, *Epic*, p. 512.
[43] Tucker, *Epic*, p. 513.

but also a 'Greekish-Latinate hexameter',[44] Morris was partly seeking to restore a literature that, in Dentith's words, had been 'mistakenly overlooked in favour of the more prestigious material of Greece and Rome',[45] it is certainly not true that *Sigurd* was an equivalent project to these other translations. In the first place, there was no 'original' epic of Sigurðr for Morris to translate. With the closest thing to it (the missing 'Sigurðarkviða' ['Lay of Sigurðr']) lost to the Great Lacuna of the Codex Regius,[46] he did not assume the role of translator so much as epic skald. Taking the disjointed *Völsunga saga* as his frame, and reinforcing it with several heroic poems from the *Poetic Edda* and decoration from the *Prose Edda* and *Nibelungenlied*, Morris sought to reforge from the broken shards of the tradition the lost 'great Epic of the North' (*CW*, VII, p. 283).[47] Second, as the inheritance of not only the Icelanders, who had maintained 'the Gothic branch' of the great Teutonic race, but also of their English kinfolk (Preface to TSL, 1, p. vi), in Morris's eyes the Sigurðr story was not just *any* epic, it was *our* epic, 'which should be to all our race what the Tale of Troy was to the Greeks' (*CW*, VII, p. 286). Considering nineteenth-century culture to be fundamentally unconducive to the writing of poetry,[48] in filling the gap where the epic of Sigurðr should have been, Morris assumed a special ability to articulate the old culture in order to provide a poetic exemplar of the original values of the Germanic peoples for their English descendants.

In contrast to Tucker, Dentith has proposed that Morris's primary motivation in writing *Sigurd* was to confront his audience with a world so alien that they might deem it an 'antithesis to the degradation of

---

[44] Tucker, *Epic*, p. 512.

[45] Dentith, 'Barbaric Past', p. 252.

[46] In the section that contains the 'heroic' poems (which mostly narrate parts of the Sigurðr cycle) there are missing leaves between Sigurðr's meeting with Sigrdrífa and Brynhildr's demand that he be killed for betraying her. See *The Poetic Edda*, trans. Carolyne Larrington (Oxford: Oxford University Press, 1996), pp. 172–74.

[47] In 1869, Morris had hinted at his belief that there was an epic of Sigurðr that had been lost when he suggested that *Völsunga saga* had been 'put together from varying versions of the same song', letter to Norton, probably dated 21 December 1869, see this chapter, footnote 1, above. Years later he talked about 'Volsunga and even these Eddaic lays' being 'later than the original tale', which was 'told over and over again in them', May Morris, *Artist*, I, pp. 474–75.

[48] Letter to Norton, probably dated 21 December 1869, see this chapter, footnote 1, above.

contemporary civilisation':[49] Morris's 'admiration for *barbarism*'[50] led him to offer its values 'as a counterweight to the paltriness and ugliness of the contemporary world'.[51] Drawing on Waithe's argument that, in his translations, Morris 'adopted strategies designed to refuse translation in a total sense',[52] Dentith has argued that literary techniques were repeatedly employed in *Sigurd* that 'stress the radical otherness of his material'.[53] As I argued in Chapter 4, the suggestion that Morris consciously employed strangeness in his translations from Old Norse to create a jarring or uncanny experience for his readers seems unlikely. It is more probable that by presenting what Townend has called the 'communal story-world' of the 'Germanic-speaking peoples of Northern Europe' in an 'undegraded' idiom,[54] Morris was simply hoping that his readers would recognise it as related to them, without necessarily finding its effect uncanny (see Chapter 4, p. 132). Similarly, it seems that by presenting a world in *Sigurd* that expressed the uncorrupted, cultural foundations of the Teutonic people (and particularly the Gothic branch), Morris was hoping that his readers would spontaneously recognise the glorious founding values of their progenitors, without necessarily finding the alterity of this heroic society shockingly foreign.

Morris did not believe that British society had become entirely estranged from its Gothic past. In the 1870 Preface to their translation of *Völsunga saga*, he and Eiríkur Magnússon stressed the longevity of the saga's reception in Iceland. In their view, the author (whom Morris had previously described as an 'author-collector')[55] had assembled the saga from 'floating traditions' over time (*CW*, VII, p. 283). In 'The Early Literature of the North – Iceland' Morris argued that such traditions had then been passed down in an uninterrupted progression to the present day: 'the shepherd boy on the hill-side, the fisherman in the firth still chant

    [49] Dentith, 'Barbaric Past', p. 248.
    [50] Simon Dentith, 'Sigurd the Volsung: Heroic Poetry in an Unheroic Age', in *William Morris: Centenary Essays. Papers from the Morris Centenary Conference Organized by the William Morris Society at Exeter College Oxford, 30 June–3 July 1996*, ed. Peter Faulkner and Peter Preston (Exeter: University of Exeter Press, 1999), pp. 60–69 (p. 60).
    [51] Dentith, *Empire*, p. 83.
    [52] Waithe, p. 90.
    [53] Dentith, 'Barbaric Past', p. 247.
    [54] Townend, 'Victorian Medievalisms', p. 169.
    [55] Letter to Norton, probably dated 21 December 1869, see this chapter, footnote 1, above.

the songs that preserve the religion of the Germanic race'.[56] Even in the watered-down stock of the post-Norman Conquest English, he believed that a 'semi-Gothic feeling' had lingered 'in out-of-the-way corners of the country [...] much later'.[57] Contemporary Britons were not, therefore, *wholly* degraded. The dormant vestiges of their early roots still slumbered within them, holding the potential for cultural rejuvenation. Although it is true that Morris eschewed literary techniques that would entirely 'domesticate' either *Sigurd* or his translations into what he deemed the degraded part of the culture and idiom of his day, it seems likely that by portraying the 'first grey dawning of our race' in the 'deedful' ethos of *Sigurd* (*CW*, VII, p. 289), he hoped, in a less confrontational manner than some critics have suggested, to provide the conduit through which his audience would recognise, welcome and recover the extant part of that culture that endured in them. In this way, the hopes for cultural change that the pre-socialist Morris held were perhaps reformist, rather than catastrophic. He was encouraging the reinvigoration of that which he believed was already native to Britain.

It is possible that there is a scholarly bias towards viewing the effect of alienation that Morris achieved in *Sigurd* as intentional on his part, perhaps to protect him from accusations of misjudgement. Even if, as a late primitivist, Morris lamented the falling away of early Gothic culture, his passion for the sagas was something that he was basically excited by and wished to share. To this extent, it seems unlikely that he was attempting to create an aggressively provocative relationship with his readers in *Sigurd*. In portraying cultural alterity, he was surely imagining that his audience (if he imagined them at all) would find the ethos of their ancestors as inspirational as he did, recognising in it a buried familiarity. If *Sigurd* failed to gain the audience that its author desired,[58] it was probably because, as I suggested in Chapter 4, Morris did not write with an accurate view of his public in mind (see pp. 133–34).[59]

Indeed, Tucker goes as far as to claim that he can 'scarcely be said to

---

[56] From 'The Early Literature of the North – Iceland', in LeMire, p. 181.

[57] From 'The Gothic Revival I', in LeMire, pp. 54–73 (p. 68).

[58] Karl Litzenberg, 'William Morris and the Reviews: A Study in the Fame of the Poet', *The Review of English Studies*, 12 (1936), 413–28 (p. 419).

[59] As evidence for this argument in Chapter 4, I use the opinions of several other critics. However, as I state in the Conclusion (see p. 172), more work might be done on establishing who precisely Morris's readers were and what impact his translations and adaptations from Old Norse had on the general public.

have lifted a finger' to secure the kind of reception that he wanted for the poem.[60] It is presumable that many of Morris's readers did not read with the same awareness of early Germanic literature or English language that he did, and that the 'foreignness' that he hoped they would recognise as part of them may, therefore, have simply been disaffecting.[61] As a man who had the erudition and sensitivity to bridge the gap between the two cultures, it was up to him to act as an intermediary, and in this he did not succeed. But, how could he have? As this chapter has shown, to a large extent Morris invented the ethos from which the people of Iceland (and, in his view, England) sprang, elevating material to the status of founding myth that more than one critic has remarked is hardly comparable in terms of magnitude or sophistication to the *Iliad*.[62] If Morris essentially made up both the ethos and the original greatness of *Sigurd*, how could a nineteenth-century audience possibly have recognised any vestige of it in themselves?[63]

Even if Morris's ethos of 'deedful' action in the face of earthly temporality failed to inspire the same size of audience as *The Earthly Paradise*,[64] it did not fail to inspire him. Critics have commonly agreed that *Sigurd* marks the culmination of his poetic work, and especially of the period in which he engaged with Old Norse literature. Wilmer calls it 'the climax of Morris's prolific but intermittent poetic career',[65] Hartley S. Spatt 'his greatest achievement in poetry'[66] and Tucker 'in a sense his last turn of the screw'.[67] Dentith describes *Sigurd* as 'Morris's fullest poetic

---

[60] See Tucker, 'Macropoetics', p. 386.

[61] The failure of the audience to recognise the import of the poem may ironically have provided proof for the primitivist belief that the modern age was now too degraded to appreciate poetry.

[62] See Hartley S. Spatt, 'Morrissaga: Sigurd the Volsung', *ELH: A Journal of English Literary History*, 44 (1977), 355–75 (p. 355); Paul Thompson, p. 199.

[63] Morris himself felt that he had stuck 'very closely to the *Volsunga* in my poem of Sigurd: it is in fact the same story, modern amplification and sentiment accepted. I have invented nothing except detail'; quoted in May Morris, *Artist*, I, p. 474.

[64] See letter to Georgiana Burne-Jones, probably dated 27 January 1877, in Kelvin, I, p. 344.

[65] Clive Wilmer, 'Dreaming Reality: The Poetry of William Morris', in *The Oxford Handbook of Victorian Poetry*, ed. Matthew Bevis (Oxford: Oxford University Press, 2013), pp. 475–91 (p. 26).

[66] Spatt, p. 355.

[67] Tucker, *Epic*, p. 516.

engagement with the mythology of the old North'[68] while May Morris asserts: 'All his Icelandic study and travel, all his feeling of the North, led up to this, and his satisfaction with it did not waver or change to the last' (Introduction to *CW*, xii, p. xxiii). In this way, it can be argued that the Norse-related work that Morris produced in the years after meeting Eiríkur acted as a gradual preparation for the philosophy that he would express in *Sigurd*. Though in 1869 he had become exceptionally preoccupied with *Völsunga saga* and hankered to create an epic poem from it, at the time he did not believe himself capable of transforming the saga into anything worthwhile: 'I see clearly it would be foolish, for no verse could render the best parts of it, and it would only be a flatter and tamer version of a thing already existing.'[69] By October 1875, however, he had gained the confidence to begin the poem in which he would express his clearest enunciation yet of his ideal of heroism (Introduction to *CW*, xii, p. xxiii). Declaiming a heroic paradigm that was, in fact, not the Norse tale's moral code but his own (though one that Old Norse literature had clarified and confirmed in him), Morris attempted to restore the canon's missing epic, before putting the sagas, for the time being at least, to one side. For him, the moral code that he had expressed in the poem was vivid and personally graspable. *Sigurd*'s publication at the end of 1876 coincided with Morris starting to live 'not altogether deedless' himself,[70] as he embarked on a new period of practical activism and campaigning that would ultimately lead to him being celebrated as a hero of environmentalism, the Arts and Crafts Movement and revolutionary socialism (*LWM*, i, pp. 339–49).[71]

---

[68] Dentith, 'Barbaric Past', p. 238.

[69] Letter to Norton, probably dated 21 December 1869, see this chapter, footnote 1, above.

[70] From 'The Mythology and Religion of the North', (William Morris Gallery, London, [n. d.]), MS J 146, p. 2; quoted in *LWM*, i, p. 334 (see Chapter 6, p. 161).

[71] For the dates of Morris's earliest public lectures and campaign meetings in 1877, see LeMire, p. 234.

6

The Unnameable Glory and the Fictional World

SINCE MACKAIL WROTE of 'the long struggle, the deep brooding, through which [Morris] arrived at his final attitude' (*LWM*, II, p. 23), writers who have considered how his thought developed over the course of his life have tended to argue that the period of social campaigning and politicised writing that began in 1876 and continued throughout the 1880s until his death in 1896 emerged from what Kinna has called 'the Romantic impulses that inspired his artistic career'.[1] In other words, scholars have looked to Morris's art to explain the development of his politics, with the tension between his 'apparently regressive' veneration of the Middle Ages and the emergence of a 'progressive' desire for revolution often forming the 'starting-point for discussions of the political character and practicality of his socialist ideal'.[2]

Those scholars who have looked specifically to Morris's Norse-inspired medievalism to illuminate his social impulses after 1876 have typically concentrated on two questions: first, whether there is a relationship between his engagement with Old Norse literature and his particular formulation of socialism in his campaigning from the early 1880s onwards; and, second, whether his knowledge of the sagas shaped the socialistic themes of the 'late' romances in the late 1880s and the 1890s, particularly those that depict people of Germanic, though not explicitly Scandinavian, origin. This chapter considers the claims that have been made in relation to these two questions, specifically interrogating the possibilities that Morris's conception of the Norse Armageddon *ragnarök* influenced his model of the socialist revolution, that Iceland inspired his notions of ideal governance, and that the 'late' romances are an extension of his earlier saga-inspired works. It concludes by suggesting

---

[1] Kinna, p. 2.
[2] Kinna, p. 4.

that Morris's engagement with Old Norse literature was integral to his adopting an ideal of heroic action that coincided with the earliest stages of his campaigning but that it did not directly inspire either his socialism or the 'late' romances of the 1880s and 1890s.

There are reasons particular to Morris that have encouraged scholars to look to one phase of his life to explain another. Though many of his interests were consistent and enduring, his passionate nature meant that the focus of his work proceeded in discrete phases of intensity. In MacCarthy's words, his life 'unfolded in cycles' characterised by whatever he was currently focused on (*LOT*, p. 598). If 1856–68 were the years of Arthurian romance, a 'palace of Art' at Red House and the early work of 'the Firm', and 1868–76 were the years of Iceland and the sagas, difficulties in his marriage, and the reinvention of Morris & Co., then the years after *Sigurd* appeared in 1876 saw Morris's attention turning firmly towards social action, as he began to speak publicly on diverse matters that encompassed the preservation of ancient buildings, art's place in society and, after joining the Democratic Federation in January 1883, the need for a new order.

The fact that Morris's life evolved in discrete phases has lent itself to linear explanations of cause and effect concerning his motivations, especially where one phase follows another. The order in which his interests progressed means that it is possible to argue, for example, that his passion for socialism was inspired by his attraction to the Icelandic heroes. Such explanations can seem simplistic, especially when an attitude that Morris came to hold in a later phase of his life is read into an earlier one when he did not yet hold it. A second, more practical, reason why critics have tended to look to his earlier work to explain Morris's later preoccupations (and particularly the development of his political thought) is that fewer of his opinions were recorded before he began to write them into lectures from 1877 onwards. The fact that he did not lecture prior to this date has meant that writers looking for his social attitudes before then must try to glean them from his correspondence and journals, as well as from the implicit motivations of his artistic work.

Scholars who have looked to the earlier phase of interest in Old Norse literature to shed light on the later phase of socialist campaigning have typically made one of two claims: either that Morris's knowledge of *ragnarök* influenced his conception of socialist revolution, or that the ideal society that he imagined for Britain after the fall of capitalism was inspired by his familiarity with Iceland. Amongst those who have suggested the former, Mackail explains that Morris spoke of 'the new days as a thing which (as in Northern Mythology) can only arrive through some Night of the Gods' (*LWM*, II, pp. 24–25); Litzenberg proposes that 'Morris's ideal for the future, in its method of attainment, and in its result' was 'almost identical with the Doom of the Gods, the *ragna rök*, of the Elder and Younger Eddas';[3] and more recently O'Donoghue has suggested that, for Morris, 'inevitable revolution would be like Ragnarök, violence and destruction necessarily preceding a new world order of harmony and socialist justice'.[4] Though Morris's knowledge of *ragnarök* may well have influenced the language he employed to describe the coming revolution, in my view, any suggestion that his acquaintance with the mythological event somehow gave rise to his later model for a new order should be treated with caution because it risks, in Alessandro Zironi's words, attributing a 'yet-to-develop political agenda' to Morris's initial engagement with Old Norse literature, as though it were a kind of mythical 'foundation-stone of socialism'.[5]

Morris knew of *ragnarök* primarily from the *Poetic Edda* and *Prose Edda*, which he had already read in translation before he met Eiríkur Magnússon (see Introduction, p. 10) but came to know intimately at the time he translated *Völsunga saga* and wrote *Sigurd*. Both texts portray the mythical event as the end of the known world when the Æsir (the pantheon that includes Óðinn, Frigg, Þórr and Baldr) are called to do battle with their enemies. Óðinn is then swallowed by the wolf Fenrir. Þórr dies defeating the great sea-serpent Jörmungandr. The stars disappear, flames reach the heavens and the earth sinks into the sea. After the end of the world, there is a new beginning. The earth re-emerges from the waters, freshly green and, in a scene of rejuvenation, the surviving Æsir, joined from Hel by Baldr and his brother Höðr, discover the gods' golden chess pieces lying in the grass.

Morris was attracted to the imagery of *ragnarök* from comparatively early in his writing career, since he made passing references to it in four works written between about 1865 and 1871. The undated poem 'In Arthur's House' alludes to the time when 'Heimdall's horn | Screams out and the last day is born' and the heroine of a similarly undated play fragment 'Anthony' describes another character as 'Baldur come back to life

³ Litzenberg, 'Doom', p. 184.
⁴ O'Donoghue, *English Poetry*, p. 174.
⁵ Zironi, p. 212.

again' (*CW*, xxiv, pp. 323, 335).[6] There are also references to 'the Gods'-dusk' in 'The Lovers of Gudrun' (1869) (*CW*, v, p. 263),[7] and to the time 'when Balder comes back' in the poem 'Iceland First Seen' (1871) (*CW*, ix, p. 126).[8] While these brief allusions show that the myth of *ragnarök* clearly impressed Morris before he had started to read Old Norse, they do not advance any kind of political standpoint. Each of the instances above simply provides cursory colour for the cultural context of the particular scene in which they occur. Likewise, in *Sigurd*, the references to *ragnarök* largely reinforce the discrete cultural cocoon of the poem that Morris creates (see Chapter 5, p. 148,), rather than making any overtly political point. When Volsung vows that he shall have his sword in his hand as he stands 'midst the host of Odin in the Day of Doom', and later it is claimed that the earth will remember the deeds of Sigurd and Brynhild until 'the new sun shines on Baldur, and the happy sea-less shore', the Norse apocalypse acts predominantly as a culturally defining element (*CW*, xii, pp. 7, 244). Even those references in *Sigurd* that allude to a future utopia after *ragnarök*, such as Regin's prophecy that 'the new light as yet undreamed of shall shine o'er earth and sea', essentially work within the internal reality of the poem without suggesting political allegory (*CW*, xii, p. 77).

In his correspondence and speeches from 1877 onwards, however, Morris began to draw on cataclysmic imagery that potentially recalls *ragnarök* when he was highlighting the necessity for a rejuvenation of the arts and, later, of the structure of society as a whole. In the 1877 lecture 'The Lesser Arts', he expressed the need for art and poetry to descend into a 'dead blank of the arts' that will permit 'a burning up of gathered weeds, so that the field may bear more abundantly' (*CW*, xxii, p. 11), while in July 1881 he wrote to Georgiana Burne-Jones that 'the last struggle' will need to be 'mingled with violence and madness'.[9] Two years later, in August 1883, after he had become a socialist, he wrote to her again, maintaining that 'the arts have got to die, what is left of them, before they can be born again,'[10] and, in the 1886 lecture 'Architecture and History', he exclaimed 'Destruction is, alas! one of the forms of growth!' (*CW*,

---

[6] Quoted in Litzenberg, 'Doom', p. 192.

[7] Quoted in Litzenberg, 'Doom', p. 193.

[8] Ibid.

[9] Letter to Georgiana Burne-Jones, probably dated 2 July 1881, Kelvin, iiA, p. 51.

[10] Letter to Georgiana Burne-Jones, dated 21 August 1883, Kelvin, iiA, p. 217.

XXII, p. 299). Although these instances show that Morris was drawing on imagery of apocalypse and regeneration to evoke the changes that he deemed crucial to righting the wrongs of contemporary society, it does not necessarily follow that his knowledge of *ragnarök* directly inspired this desire for a renewal of the arts or the political system. The lack of any political tone to the *ragnarök* references that preceded his post-1876 campaigning suggest that the myth did not begin as a source of allegory but that, once certain social issues became more of an urgent priority to him, he turned to Norse mythology as a rich source of imagery that could convey a great transformation and the rebirth of the current order.

In addition to these general cataclysmic intimations, there are two instances in his extant writing in which Morris invokes *ragnarök* explicitly in relation to contemporary British society. The first is contained in a letter that he wrote in August 1874 in which he bemoaned the blindness of modern tradesmen to beauty, wondering 'perhaps the Gods are preparing troubles and terrors for the world (or our small corner of it) again that it may once again become beautiful and dramatic withal'.[11] The date of this comment is so early in the development of his political thought that it seems unlikely that he was alluding to a socialist revolution here. Moreover, earlier in the letter when he predicts, somewhat hazily, that blindness to beauty will 'draw down a kind of revenge one day', he seems to be expressing wistful dismay at the current state of society rather than explicitly auguring popular revolt.[12] The way in which this imagery pits the power of the natural law embodied in the gods against the meek humility of 'our small corner' of the world also suggests that, at this stage, Morris was operating on more of an intuitive hunch than a political hypothesis that what he perceived as an aberrant way of life in the present could not endure long before a more authentic way reasserted itself.

The second instance in his extant writing in which Morris explicitly relates *ragnarök* to contemporary society appears in a curious manuscript, now at the William Morris Gallery, that contains notes in Morris's hand of unclear purpose or date; perhaps part of a lecture in the post-1876 period, or else some kind of extended explanation of Old Norse mythology written between 1868 and 1876. Whitla believes that these notes formed part of the lecture Morris gave on 14 September 1884 to

---

[11] Letter to Rosalind Frances Howard, dated 20 August 1874, in Kelvin, I, p. 230.
[12] Ibid.

the Sheffield Secular Society entitled 'Iceland, Its Ancient Literature and Mythology', which has not survived in its entirety.[13] By contrast, Litzenberg maintains that the notes were written much earlier around the time that *Sigurd* was published at the end of 1876.[14] Whatever the truth of the matter, they provide perhaps the most explicit explanation that Morris ever gave of his understanding of the ideal of heroism that he had discovered in Old Norse literature, and culminate with him elaborating on how this ideal relates to the imagery of *ragnarök*:

> So comes the great strife: [...] here also shall the Gods die [...] till at last the great destruction [...] breaks out over all things, and the old Earth and Heavens are gone. And then a new Heavens and Earth [...] And what shall be our share in it? Well, sometimes, we yet alive in the unregenerate earth, must needs think that we shall live again in the regenerate one [...] yet if that were not, would it not be enough that we helped to make this unnameable glory and lived not altogether deedless?
>
> These things being so let us live joyously while we can, fearlessly at the least; [...] There is no defeat possible to a brave man [...] Think of the joy we have in praising great men and how we turn their stories over and over and fashion their lives for our joy – and this we ourselves may give to the world.
>
> [...] This seems to me pretty much the religion of the Northmen. I think one would be a happy man if one could hold it, in spite of the wild dreams and dreadful imaginings that hung about it here and there.[15]

Fundamentally a form of stoicism, for Morris, the heathen religion held that despite the vulnerability of our lives and the fact that we may have no part in the new order after the known world ends, it is fitting to make the best of our current circumstances by being 'deedful' in a life of worthwhile action, embracing our small but integral place in the great ongoing pattern of things. In a kind of reinvented version of the Carlylean ultimate reality (see Chapter 1, pp. 33–34), Morris calls the overarching totality of the great ongoing pattern 'this unnameable glory', implying that it is our supreme calling to grasp firmly our part in the continuing story but that simultaneously what is unnameable and glorious is the earthly totality

---

[13] See Whitla, p. 99; LeMire, p. 301.

[14] Litzenberg, 'Doom', p. 197.

[15] From 'The Mythology and Religion of the North', p. 2; quoted in *LWM*, I, p. 334; also in Zironi, pp. 232–33. I have cut down this text considerably for the purpose of concise presentation.

of the tale, rather than any transcendent reality beyond it. Morris's focus here on the heroic attitude of the religion corresponds to (and is, thus, in my view, possibly contemporary with) his focus in *Sigurd*. This factor, coupled with the fact that there is nothing in these notes to suggest that Morris was intending to create a political allegory, also suggests that this text was not inspired by Morris's socialism. Indeed, taken together, none of the references to *ragnarök* in his extant writing suggest that the Norse apocalypse motivated his political views. Rather, they show that Morris drew on the imagery of *ragnarök* at different times for different purposes, perhaps most significantly in explaining that ideal of heroism that he had discerned through his engagement with Old Norse literature.

If *ragnarök* did not inspire Morris's socialism, did Iceland itself? MacCarthy has implied that it did, suggesting that 'in Iceland [...] Morris learned the lesson he turned into a tenet of political intransigence over the next decade' (*LOT*, p. 278), while Linda Parry maintains that 'his comparison of the simplicity of life there and so-called civilised sophisticated British society roused in him his first political yearnings'.[16] This belief that Morris's socialist views of the 1880s had their roots in the voyages to Iceland of the early 1870s has arisen principally from two sources: a comment that he made in a letter to Andreas Scheu in September 1883, the year he joined the Democratic Federation, and certain points that he made in the lecture 'The Early Literature of the North – Iceland', which he delivered four years later at Kelmscott House, Hammersmith.[17] With regard to Iceland's influence on the development of Morris's politics, in my opinion, both texts should be read with a degree of scepticism.

In the letter to Scheu, Morris implies that, despite the considerable hardship of life in Iceland, he had witnessed a healthier society during his time there than existed in contemporary Britain because the Icelanders' class system was less demarcated: 'I learned one lesson there, thoroughly I hope, that the most grinding poverty is a trifling evil compared with the inequality of classes.'[18] While it true that in the 1868–76 'Old Norse period' Morris was struck by the arduousness of the lives of the medieval Icelanders (in poems such as the sonnet that prefaces his translation of *Grettis saga*, for instance, he called medieval Iceland 'a wretched land |

[16] *William Morris*, ed. Linda Parry (London: Philip Wilson in association with the Victoria and Albert Museum, 1996), p. 18.

[17] See LeMire, p. 179.

[18] Letter to Scheu, dated 15 September 1883, see Introduction, footnote 2.

Where fear and pain go upon either hand') (*CW*, VII, p. xxxvi), it is equally true that nowhere in his Icelandic journals does Morris seem to be deliberating the relative strength of the country's social structure in relation to the starkly obvious poverty around him. Indeed, as Wawn has highlighted, Morris's entries make 'no substantive' reference 'to the "trifling evil" of poverty' but instead highlight his 'obsession with lice' whenever he enters a farmhouse, and are organised around sojourns with a string of upper-class 'merchants, sheriffs, well-situated priests, doctors, and friends of Eiríkur Magnússon' behind whom hover the faceless throng of a 'nameless peasantry'.[19] Considered in this light, Morris's comment to Scheu, made a decade after he had last set foot in Iceland, seems to reflect a reimagined account of the summer treks that, in Waithe's words, may have 'evolved in his mind' in the intervening years of social engagement.[20]

Morris implicitly linked Iceland and socialism again in October 1887 when he gave the lecture 'The Early Literature of the North – Iceland'. Throughout it, he strongly suggests that aspects of life in both medieval and modern Iceland were congruent with his model of socialism. The early Icelandic political system, he explains, was originally based 'on the equal personal rights of all freedmen' and medieval Icelanders held in high esteem the ability to be versatile in their labour, with the heroes often winning renown as much from 'their skill as weapon-smiths as for their fighting qualities'.[21] Women, he maintains, also enjoyed a more egalitarian position in early Iceland, being able to declare themselves divorced 'for some insult or offense, a blow being considered enough excuse'.[22] Moreover, for Morris, the contemporary Icelanders of the 1880s are only a stone's throw from enjoying a socialist system since they could 'live very comfortably if they were to extinguish individualism' and 'the simplest possible form of co-operative commonwealth [...] ought not to be hard to establish' there.[23]

Despite his obvious sincerity, however, there is something sanitised about Morris's allusions in this lecture to an egalitarian society in Iceland. While it true that a wide range of skills are prized by the saga heroes, and women in the narratives appear to enjoy a degree of autonomy in marriage that is unusual in medieval literature, the sagas of Icelanders,

---

[19] Wawn, *Vikings*, pp. 276–77; *CW*, VIII, pp. 44, 81.
[20] Waithe, p. 75.
[21] From 'The Early Literature of the North – Iceland', in LeMire, p. 184.
[22] From 'The Early Literature of the North – Iceland', in LeMire, p. 185.
[23] From 'The Early Literature of the North – Iceland', in LeMire, p. 198.

even through Morris's eyes, can hardly be said to portray a classless utopia. Indeed, many of their plots revolve around the manoeuvrings of the most powerful regional leaders and the bloodshed across classes that ensues. Far from being classless, there is a clearly demarcated social hierarchy in the sagas with slaves at the bottom, and influential chieftains (in Iceland) and royalty (abroad) at the top. In addition, the very fact that Morris draws attention to the potential for a socialist society in contemporary Iceland is a tacit acknowledgement that it does not currently exist. Read together, his reinvention of the Icelandic journeys in his 1883 letter to Scheu, and the particularly idealised version of Icelandic society he depicts in the 1887 lecture, appear to confirm Wawn's candid view that, at the peak of Morris's social campaigning of the 1880s, he sometimes used Iceland and its literature to create 'self-authenticating political testimonies' built on 'brittle memories and undernourished understandings'.[24]

Other than Morris's politics, a second area of his post-1876 activities that critics have argued was influenced by his engagement with Old Norse literature between 1868 and 1876 are the 'late' romances, which consist of the two 'Germanic' romances, *The House of the Wolfings* (1889) and *The Roots of the Mountains* (1890), and the five subsequent fantasy novels that were mostly published contemporaneously with The Saga Library in the first half of the 1890s. Together *Wolfings* and *Roots* present an idealised view of the lives of early Germanic tribes who Morris imagined living in the central forests of Europe, while *The Story of the Glittering Plain* (1891), *The Wood Beyond the World* (1894), *Child Christopher and Goldilind the Fair* (1895), *The Well at the World's End* (1896), *The Water of the Wondrous Isles* (1897) and *The Sundering Flood* (1897) are fantastical adventures set in entirely imaginary worlds. *Wolfings* is the story of a hard-working tribe who, while inhabiting a Continental area called the Mark around the second or third century ad, are forced to defend their liberty from the Romans. Set about 100 years later, *Roots* explains how the Dalemen, Woodlanders and Shepherds who live around a valley called Burgdale are threatened by encroachments from Wolfing descendants as they are pushed back by Hun-like invaders.[25] In Salmon's view, the two novels present what Morris saw as 'the progressive development of barbarism',

[24] Wawn, *Vikings*, p. 277.
[25] Nicholas Salmon, 'A Study in Victorian Historiography: William Morris's Germanic Romances', *The Journal of the William Morris Society*, 14.2 (2001), 59–89 (pp. 69–70).

which entailed 'the gradual association of the tribes into a people'[26] as they were steadily obliged to abandon traditions of communal living for the institution of private property.[27] Through these narratives, Salmon argues, Morris infers that the ancient ideals of the Germanic peoples have been corrupted 'under conditions of modern capitalism'.[28]

Those who have connected Morris's knowledge of Old Norse litera-ture to *Wolfings* and *Roots* have sometimes anticipated the priorities of the novels in the earlier Norse-inspired works, and sometimes detected vestiges of the translations from Old Norse and saga adaptations in the later novels. May Morris, for example, suggests that in *Wolfings* and *Roots* her father 'seems to have got back to the atmosphere of the *Sagas*' (*CW*, XIV, p. xxv), while Kocmanová implies that, as in the later novels, in *Sigurd* and his saga translations Morris wished 'to show the kindred or *gens* society as possessing values more lasting than those of Victo-rian capitalism'.[29] Other scholars have stressed the way in the which the 'Germanic' romances particularly emphasise community in a way that Morris's explicitly saga-inspired work does not. Boos has underlined the 'more egalitarian' characteristic of the societies portrayed in them, especially highlighting the fact that in the imaginary 'folk moots' of both romances, each male has the vote and right to speak, regardless of wealth or social status.[30]

It is true that the 'folk moots' of *Wolfings* and *Roots* depict a classless, collective and dignified society but this is neither portrayed in the sagas nor in Morris's adaptations of them. In the chapter 'Of the Great Folk-mote: Atonements Given, and Men Made Sackless' in *Roots*, for example, the equality and decorousness of the early Germanic political system is evident when the Alderman convenes the assembly:

> Herewith I hallow-in this Folk-mote of the Men of the Dale and the Sheep-cotes and the Woodland, in the name of the Warrior and the Earth-god and the Fathers of the kindreds. Now let not the peace of the Mote be broken. Let not man rise against man, or bear blade of hand, or stick or stone against any. If any man break the Peace of the Holy Mote, let him be a man accursed, a wild-beast in the Holy Places. (*CW*, XV, p. 279)

[26] Salmon, 'Germanic Romances', p. 71.
[27] Salmon, 'Germanic Romances', p. 67.
[28] Salmon, 'Germanic Romances', p. 73.
[29] Kocmanová, p. 83.
[30] Florence Saunders Boos, 'Morris's German Romances as Socialist History', *Victorian Studies*, 27 (1984), 321–42 (pp. 334–35).

Though the 'Great Folk-mote' in this scene recalls the *Alþingi* (literally 'All Thing' but meaning 'General Assembly') of the sagas of Icelanders, and the fields in which it is held are reminiscent of Þingvellir ('Assembly Fields') in Iceland (which Morris had visited in August 1871 and July 1873),[31] the mood of sanctity, cooperation and fellowship suggested in this passage in *Roots* is worlds apart from the mood of the assemblies in the sagas, which are often dominated by dramatic conflicts that advance the plot. Morris's 'folk moot', by contrast, depicts what Waithe has called 'a Teutonic tradition of liberty and equality' that is barely evident in the sagas and certainly not communicated by the legal cases brought to the assemblies that they describe.[32]

In my view, the most significant factor that distinguishes the story-worlds of *Wolfings* and *Roots* from Morris's Norse-inspired works is how they emphasise the community over the individual. Though the Sigurðr legend arguably originates from the period of 'barbarism' in which the communal tales of the 'Germanic' romances are set (see Chapter 5, p. 152), in *Sigurd*, Morris is fundamentally interested in each hero's distinct attitudes and actions, while in *Wolfings* and *Roots*, it is the individual's interrelation with the community that he continuously stresses. In contrast to Sigurd, heroes like the Wolfing leader Thiodolf are portrayed as exemplary, interconnected constituents of their society. In a moment during a battle with the Romans, for example, Thiodolf acts altruistically immediately that he sees fire rising from the hall, a sign that he knows augurs imminent defeat for his people:

> From the West gate Thiodolf the War-duke gave one mighty cry like the roar of the angry lion, and cleared a space before him for the wielding of Ivar's blade; for that moment he had looked up to the Roof of the Kindred and had beheld a little stream of smoke curling blue out of a window thereof, and he knew what had betided, and how short was the time before them. (*CW*, XIV, p. 189)

There is little sense of individual agency, complexity or interiority in Thiodolf's response here. The sight of the smoke immediately reinforces his responsibility to the community, which is highlighted by the fact that it emanates from the 'Roof of the Kindred', and he acts accordingly with spirited commitment. Though Morris was attracted to the unquestioning conviction that the saga heroes have in the need to uphold honour (see

[31] See *CW*, VIII, pp. 164–77, 188–89; *CW*, XV, pp. 273–74.
[32] Waithe, p. 77.

Chapter 2, p. 80), in the 'late' romances he portrays characters who are operating on another level altogether of intuitive selflessness.

Such explicitly exemplary conduct means that it is possible to read the 'Germanic' romances as allegories, despite Morris's protests that they were only stories: 'Doesn't the fool realise that it's a romance, a work of fiction - that it's all LIES!'[33] In *Wolfings*, the Romans (and, with them, classical civilization) embody egocentric individualistic values, whereas the Germanic (or 'Gothic') tribes embody cooperative communal ones. The two novels, therefore, portray both what has been lost (how, as Waithe explains, 'traditional ideas of community [have] been systematically replaced by individualism')[34] and what might be gained if this vision of Britain's political heritage were to become a prototype for 'the organisation of post-capitalist society.'[35] Though *Sigurd* can be read as a paradigm of heroic values and action (as I argued in Chapter 5, p. 155), in no way can it be read as a model for organising society, as *Wolfings* and *Roots* can.

Where it seems clear that Morris's 'Old Norse project' (and his work on *Sigurd*, in particular) did influence the 'Germanic' romances and fantasy novels that followed them is in the aesthetic of their language and fictional worlds. Morris employs a diction for these romances throughout that is remarkably similar to the style he used in his translations from Old Norse. In the following sentence from *Wolfings*, for example, the archaic-sounding pronominal adverb 'Therewith' and the inversion of subject 'their talk' and verb 'fell' are familiar from his saga style (see Chapter 4, pp. 114–19): 'Therewith fell their talk awhile, and as they rode they came to where the wood drew nigher to the river, and thus the Mid-mark had an end' (*CW*, xiv, p. 48). In addition, the choice of 'nigher' rather than *nearer* and 'had' rather than *came to* or *reached* adds to the quality of archaism, rendering the register more measured (see Chapter 3, pp. 85–88). However, unlike the saga translations, this style does not arise from the syntax of the source text that Morris is translating. He employs these features in these romances purely for the sake of it, perhaps with the intention of evoking a 'pure' Germanic language before it became degraded by French (see Chapter 4, pp. 154–55). He also emulates the 'prosimetric' character of the Icelandic sagas, by interspersing his prose with verse quotations.

---

[33] Quoted in Henry Halliday Sparling, *The Kelmscott Press and William Morris Master-Craftsman* (London: Macmillan, 1924), p. 50.
[34] Waithe, p. 78
[35] Waithe, p. 74.

In *Wolfings*, for example, the heroine named the Hall-Sun speaks large sections in the 'epic' hexameters that Morris chose for *Sigurd*, possibly reflecting a primitivist notion that the early Germanic peoples enjoyed less fettered access to poetic genius (see *CW*, xv, p. xi).

As well as influencing the language of the 'late' romances, Morris's Norse-inspired work appears to have influenced the physical reality of their fictional worlds. As Jane S. Cooper has remarked, there are distinct similarities between the wildernesses described in his fantasy novels and the descriptions of the landscape of Iceland in Morris's Icelandic journals, as well as in his letters and lectures. Mountains described in *The Well at the World's End* (*CW*, xix, p. 43) evoke the 'horrible black mountains of the waste' described in the journals (*CW*, viii, p. 79),[36] and the 'little grass growing in hollows, and here and there a dreary mire where the white-tufted rushes shook in the wind, and here and there stretches of moss blended with red-blossomed sengreen' in *The Story of the Glittering Plain* (*CW*, xiv, p. 228) recall the 'favoured spots' where 'a little short grass grows, sweet on the hill slopes, on the low ground, boggy and sour, dominated by that most grievously melancholy of all plants the cotton rush' mentioned in 'The Early Literature of the North – Iceland'.[37]

Such visually evocative passages in the entirely imagined immersive story-worlds of the 'late' romances are integral to why critics have often regarded them as the first modern fantasy novels in English.[38] Morris frequently describes with a high degree of aesthetic detail the material or cultural artefacts that he includes in them. In *The Water of the Wondrous Isles*, for example, the hall in the fantastical house of the witch-wife's sister is depicted particularly vividly:

> So came they at last to the very house, and whereas it stood high on the bent, a great stair or perron of stone went up to it, and was of such majesty. They went through the porch, which was pillared and lovely, and came into a great hall most nobly builded, and at the other end thereof, on a golden throne raised upon a dais, sat a big woman clad in red scarlet [...] on the right and left the tall pillars going up gleaming toward the roof, and about

---

[36] See Jane S. Cooper, 'The Iceland Journeys and the Late Romances', *The Journal of the William Morris Society*, 5.4 (1983–84), 40–59, (p. 41); *LWM*, I, p. 266.

[37] From 'The Early Literature of the North – Iceland', in LeMire, p. 180. See also Jane S. Cooper, pp. 43–44.

[38] See Introduction to Gardner Dozois, *Modern Classics of Fantasy* (New York: St. Martin's Press, 1997), pp. xvi–xvii.

her feet the dark polished pavement, with the wallowing of strange beasts and great serpents and dragons all done on the coal-blue ground. (*CW*, xx, p. 58)

While it is true that the degree of detail here that is marvellous to our eyes, but nevertheless simultaneously self-consistent and substantive within the reality of the novel, immediately suggests the genre of modern fantasy, the 'late' romances do not contain the earliest examples in Morris's writing of what O'Donoghue calls 'a fully rounded (and indeed seductively detailed) material world'.[39] Indeed, in creating the fictional world of *Sigurd*, Morris invented an almost immeasurable amount of aesthetic detail that is not contained in its sources. The following section in *Sigurd*, for example, simply has no corresponding passage in *Völsunga saga*:

> There was a dwelling of Kings ere the world was waxen old;
> Dukes were the door-wards there, and the roofs were thatched
> with gold;
> Earls were the wrights that wrought it, and silver nailed its
> doors;
> Earls' wives were the weaving-women, queens' daughters
> strewed its floors,
> And the masters of its song-craft were the mightiest men that
> cast
> The sails of the storm of battle adown the bickering blast [...]
> Thus was the dwelling of Volsung, the King of the Midworld's
> Mark,
> As a rose in the winter season, a candle in the dark;
> So therein withal was a marvel and a glorious thing to see,
> For amidst of its midmost hall-floor sprang up a mighty tree,
> That reared its blessings roofward, and wreathed the roof-tree
> dear
> With the glory of the summer and the garland of the year [...]
> So there was the throne of Volsung beneath its blossoming
> bower,
> But high o'er the roof-crest red it rose 'twixt tower and tower,
> And therein were the wild hawks dwelling, abiding the dole of
> their lord;
> And they wailed high over the wine, and laughed to the waking
> sword. (*CW*, xii, pp. 1–2)

[39] O'Donoghue, *Old Norse-Icelandic Literature*, p. 171.

From an aesthetic perspective, the degree of invented detail in the imagined reality of *Sigurd* that Morris created for passages such as this one can be seen as a stepping stone between the legend cycle of the Old Norse sources and the fully formed secondary worlds of the 'late' romances that would go on to influence authors such as Tolkien and C. S. Lewis.[40] In considering the influence of the 1868–76 'Old Norse period' (and Morris's engagement with the Sigurðr stories in particular) on the work that came after 1876, the quality of vividly imagined visual authenticity that Morris achieved in *Sigurd* may have become the most enduring legacy of his Norse-related work. While the heroic ideal that he gradually envisioned through his engagement with the sagas no doubt stimulated his contribution to 'the Unnameable Glory' of existence, via a model of action that grew into the social and political campaigning for which he is still undoubtedly remembered, the acutely realised fictional world that he first achieved in *Sigurd*, and subsequently cultivated in the 'late' romances, laid a major portion of the foundation for twentieth- and twenty-first-century fantasy fiction.

---

[40] See Gary K. Wolfe, 'Fantasy from Dryden to Dunsany', in *The Cambridge Companion to Fantasy Literature*, ed. Edward James and Farah Mendlesohn (Cambridge: Cambridge University Press, 2012), pp. 7–20 (p. 19).

Conclusion

OVER THE COURSE of this book, I have had to base a number of points regarding Morris's motivations on reasonable surmise. It is, for example, impossible to know to what extent he intended the style of his translations and *Sigurd* to be a literary device of alienation or whether the alienating effect was the result of a lack of sensitivity on his part to his audience, though his belief that his saga translations were 'in English idiom' points towards the latter (see Chapter 4, p. 114). In addition, while I hope I have successfully called into question the commonly repeated assumption that Jane Morris's relationship with Rossetti lay at the heart of her husband's engagement with Old Norse literature, Morris's true feelings about the affair and the state of his marriage are also ultimately unknowable, so it is difficult to ascertain with confidence how they did or did not motivate him. Nevertheless, it seems unlikely, even ridiculous, that such a sustained and passionate interest as the one that Morris possessed in Old Norse literature was motivated primarily by his marital difficulties, not least because the interest appears to have outlasted Jane's affairs with both Rossetti and Blunt (and, indeed, in its earliest phase, preceded his meeting Jane in the first place).

As I see it, though the Icelandic trips and, perhaps more pertinently, Morris's desire to test his own sense of inadequacy, coincided with the period in which he was depressed about his personal life (see Introduction, pp. 19–20), the ontological reflection that caused him to redefine his model of heroism when he read and translated Old Norse literature was simply part of the lifelong impulse for inquiry and learning that motivated almost all of his personal endeavours outside of 'the Firm'. This is not to say that his interest in medieval Icelandic literature did not interact with his personal life. The second trip to Iceland of 1873 seems to have confirmed a sense of self-assurance in him that led to his almost immediately restructuring Morris, Marshall, Faulkner, & Co. into Morris & Co., and the code of secular action that he laid out in *Sigurd* correlates conspicuously with the crusade of social campaigning that he embraced immediately after its publication.

Having compared Morris's translations and Norse-inspired poetry against a more detailed analysis of the Old Norse sources than has previously been performed, this book has uncovered areas of research that could prove fertile for future scholars. At the moment, for instance, there is a lack of detailed scholarship on how Morris's and Eiríkur Magnússon's work influenced the development of Old Norse studies in Britain. Though scholars have made general reference to 'Gudrun' and *Sigurd* playing a significant role in popularising *Laxdæla saga* and *Völsunga saga*, the size and make-up of Morris's and Eiríkur's audience has never been clearly established. Wawn's feeling that their 'philologically-alert' translations may have 'preached to the converted rather than won a wide new readership'[1] could be tested by researching the composition of the readers of the reviews, as well as the reasons behind Bernard Quaritch agreeing to fund The Saga Library to begin with (which by focusing on the sagas of Icelanders and kings' sagas, represents a shift away from the nineteenth-century proclivity for eddic myths).[2] The extent to which Eiríkur's legacy as a scholar – and the first lecturer in Icelandic at the University of Cambridge – rests on his collaboration with Morris could also be examined.

A great deal more work could be done on the personal library that Morris possessed at the different stages of his life and what it can tell us about his background knowledge during the phases of his engagement with Old Norse literature.[3] Similarly, there is room for more research on differentiating Morris's earlier Norse project from his 'late' romances of the 1880s and 1890s. Though I have given some opinions on this topic in the final chapter of this book, more attention could be given on how, for example, the content and style of the saga translations, *Sigurd*, and the myth of the accursed ring went on to influence the secondary worlds of his fantasy novels and the work of those twentieth-century writers who were subsequently inspired by them. Another, as yet, unanswered question is whether Morris's approach to translating from Old English in

---

[1] Email to the author from Andrew Wawn entitled 'History of ON Studies', 5 January 2015.

[2] See letters to Bernard Quaritch, dated 2 July 1890, 15 November 1890 and probably 16 November 1890, in Kelvin, III, pp. 172, 229–30.

[3] For information on Morris's library over his lifetime, see Author's Note, footnote 5, above.

the 1895 translation of *Beowulf* differed substantially from his approach to translating from Old Norse. In addition, the unique wording of the saga translations contained in calligraphic manuscripts that are dispersed amongst several archives (including those of the Society of Antiquaries, London; the Fitzwilliam Museum, Cambridge; the Bodleian Library, Oxford; and the Museum & Art Gallery, Birmingham) could be studied to expand on the points that I have made in Chapters 1–3 of this book on how Morris characterised the heroes in his translations.

Further research into the early translation method employed by Morris and Eiríkur might also shed light on the extent to which Eiríkur shaped Morris's tendency to repress and exaggerate certain qualities in the sagas through the initial translations that he provided him, especially in those that preceded the publication of Cleasby's and Guðbrandur Vigfússon's dictionary in 1874. One way to assess how much Eiríkur anticipated Morris's preferred diction in the translations that he provided him would be to compare Eiríkur's style in the manuscripts that he prepared for Morris to the style of his translation of *Hávarðar saga Ísfirðings* (renamed *The Story of Havardr the Lame*) that he prepared for Powell in the mid-1860s (currently in The National Library of Wales, Aberystwyth). Such a comparison might establish whether the always pragmatic Icelander adjusted his translation style to fit the taste of each of his two collaborators, each of whom began as his employer.

In the introduction to this book I suggested that a thorough study of the relationship between Morris's rearticulation of the sagas and the medieval Icelandic texts on which they were based was warranted, because of a history of conflicting scholarly opinions on what Old Norse literature meant to Morris. In providing this study, this book has shown that Morris's engagement with Old Norse literature between 1868 and 1876 coincided with a shift in his worldview away from a Carlylean paradigm that celebrated the attempt to transcend the mundane towards an outlook that embraced the need to make the best of earthly conditions boldly and actively. Morris deemed this outlook to be fundamentally heroic and epitomised by the heroes portrayed in the sagas. Partly to minimise the conflict between the heroic attitude he increasingly celebrated and the ethos that the sagas actually portray, in his translations and saga-inspired poetry, he simultaneously exaggerated and repressed certain impulses that are integral to a great deal of medieval Icelandic literature. Though contemporary legislation on obscenity certainly affected what he was able to publish, Morris transmuted behaviour that was cruel, crude, overtly sexual or nakedly competitive and, at the same time, accentuated other characteristics such as dignity, benevolence and humanity, as well as the capacity for a man to embrace vulnerability as part of a process of maturation.

As his intimacy with Old Norse literature grew and the ideal that he perceived in it became clearer, Morris moved towards a literal style of translation that forged linguistic bridges between Old Norse and Modern English, through which his British audience might encounter that vestige of early Gothic consciousness that he believed still endured in them. Similarly, with *Sigurd*, he offered them an epitome of their originating cultural consciousness by reforging what was, in his view, the founding myth of Northern Europe, and articulating the heroic expression of 'deedfulness' in every line of the poem. However, while the work that he undertook in the late 1870s, throughout the 1880s, and up until his death in 1896 was doubtless informed by this attitude of what it meant to live heroically (or 'deedfully'), it is a mistake to think that his experience of Iceland and the sagas led directly to the expressions of socialist revolution and post-revolutionary utopias that frequently dominate his later writing. Rather, the earlier engagement with Old Norse literature led to a redefined ideal of heroism, and the redefined ideal of heroism eventually influenced his particular brand of socialism and the disposition of his final novels.

In considering *William Morris and the Icelandic Sagas* it has become clear that, in Harold Bloom's definition of the word, Morris *misread* Old Norse literature by continually performing acts of 'creative correction' in his saga translations and Norse-inspired poetry that were 'actually and necessarily a misinterpretation'.[4] Though Litzenberg was right when he maintained that Morris attempted to '*preserve* the medieval spirit which the documents already had'[5] and that this 'belief that such a preservation of spirit was necessary' became 'in effect, *his* theory of translation',[6] the spirit that Morris communicated in his versions of the sagas was often quite different to the one that is actually there. By repressing qualities that were base or grasping, swelling others that showed self-possession and endurance, and all the while pursuing a literal style and 'deedful' ethos that he believed would communicate to his audience the culture of their forbears, he may, in fact, have alienated them. Even if one considers

    [4] Harold Bloom, *The Anxiety of Influence: A Theory of Poetry*, 2nd edn (Oxford: Oxford University Press, 1997), p. 30.
    [5] Litzenberg, 'Diction', p. 331.
    [6] Litzenberg, 'Diction', pp. 362–63.

it possible to liberate the cultural values of an earlier time for the present through translation, Morris frequently translated narratives that, in fact, *problematise* the very culture that he wished to resuscitate, portraying the strife intrinsic to honour-based societies, rather than the glory. For Hoare, it was this blindness to the problems presented by the sagas that in the end makes the style of his translations so stilted: 'His faults in manner [...] may ultimately be reduced to the same first cause, the idea that the life dealt with was heroic in the ideal sense, a kind of earthly paradise [...] This pre-misconception is what makes his style pitched up, and hollowly dignified.'[7]

Overall, this book demonstrates that between 1868 and 1876 Morris redefined an ideal of heroism that was heavily influenced by his engagement with the Icelandic sagas but that, in doing so, he selectively altered his translations and adaptations of the literature to meet it. Having become sceptical of the possibility of earthly transcendence during the 1860s, on meeting Eiríkur in 1868 he encountered in its original language a medieval literature whose apparent realism seemed to offer an ethos of worldly tenacity. If, in 'Gudrun' Morris posed the question of how best we should proceed in an indifferent, godless universe, then by translating the sagas, testing himself in Iceland and communing with the Icelandic heroes he gradually provided an answer. In *Sigurd*, he was able to articulate a positive secular ideal of unyielding action for the sake of the world that, in his eyes, allowed mankind to 'live joyously while we can, fearlessly at the least' (see Chapter 6, p. 161).

Once Morris had fully articulated this ideal, it seems that he was able to apply it to his own life – to see, in his words, 'the play played out fairly'[8] – in a phase of social engagement that led to him explicitly articulating his views on art, craft and design, society and government, cultural history and its preservation, as well as creating forms of popular myth in the 'late' romances that, to a large extent, portray societies with values that he endorsed. As Salmon has emphasised, it was his 'formulation of modes of practical action' that distinguishes Morris from the other Victorian moralists whom he admired, such as Carlyle and Ruskin. If his contemporaries were mostly 'content to criticise and not act', as a practical man Morris felt that 'thought without action was self-indulgence'.[9] Old Norse

---

[7] Hoare, pp. 54–55.
[8] Letter to Jane Morris, possibly dated 3 December 1870, in Kelvin, I, p. 128.
[9] Salmon, 'Pre-Socialist Ideology', p. 35.

literature helped him to define this attitude. As Oberg argued, the sagas came to mean more to Morris than a source of literary inspiration. For him, they contained within them a tangible ethos for living and, after he had read and translated them with Eiríkur Magnússon, he endeavoured for the rest of his life to emulate their great heroes whose 'lives and deeds', he felt, 'attest the efficacy, the divine sanction, of action'.[10]

[10] Oberg, p. 93.

Bibliography

Aho, Gary L., 'William Morris in Iceland', *Kairos*, 1 (1982), 102–33

Alderson, David, *Mansex Fine: Religion, Manliness and Imperialism in Nine-teenth-Century British Culture* (Manchester: Manchester University Press, 1998)

Anderson, Karl O. E., 'Scandinavian Elements in the Works of William Morris' (unpublished Ph.D., Harvard University, 1940)

Arnot, Robert Page, *William Morris: The Man and the Myth* (London: Lawrence and Wishart, 1964)

Ashton, Rosemary, *The German Idea: Four English Writers and the Reception of German Thought, 1800–1860* (Cambridge: Cambridge University Press, 1980)

Ashurst, David, 'Wagner, Morris and the Sigurd Figure: Confronting Freedom and Uncertainty', in *Revisiting the Poetic Edda: Essays on Old Norse Heroic Legend*, ed. Paul Acker, Carolyne Larrington and T. A. Shippey (New York: Routledge, 2012), pp. 219–37

——, 'William Morris and the Volsungs', in *Old Norse Made New: Essays on the Post-Medieval Reception of Old Norse Literature and Culture*, ed. David Clark and Carl Phelpstead (London: Viking Society for Northern Research, 2007), pp. 43–61

Barnhart, Robert K., ed., *Chambers Dictionary of Etymology* (Edinburgh: Chambers, 1988)

Barribeau, James Leigh, 'The Vikings and England: The Ninth and the Nineteenth Centuries' (unpublished Ph.D., Cornell, 1982)

——, 'William Morris and Saga-Translation: "The Story of King Magnus, Son of Erling"', in *The Vikings*, ed. R. Farrell (Ithaca: Cornell University Press, 1983), pp. 239–55

Beer, Gillian, *The Romance* (London: Methuen, 1970)

Bezzola, Reto R., *Le sens de l'aventure et de l'amour (Chrétien de Troyes)* (Paris: La Jeune Parque, 1947)

Bloom, Harold, *The Anxiety of Influence: A Theory of Poetry*, 2nd edn (Oxford: Oxford University Press, 1997)

Boos, Florence Saunders, 'Morris' Radical Revisions of the "Laxdaela Saga"', *Victorian Poetry*, 21 (1983), 415–20

——, 'Morris's German Romances as Socialist History', *Victorian Studies*, 27 (1984), 321–42

———, *The Design of William Morris' The Earthly Paradise*, Studies in British Literature, 6 (Lewiston: Mellen, 1990)

———, 'Victorian Response to *Earthly Paradise* Tales', *The Journal of the William Morris Society*, 5.4 (1983–84), 16–29

Briggs, Katharine M., *A Dictionary of British Folk Tales in the English Language*, 2 vols (London: Routledge and Paul, 1970)

Bullen, J. B., *The Pre-Raphaelite Body: Fear and Desire in Painting, Poetry, and Criticism* (Oxford: Clarendon Press, 1998)

Byock, Jesse, trans., *The Saga of the Volsungs: The Norse Epic of Sigurd the Dragon Slayer* (London: Penguin, 1999)

Byock, Jesse and Russell Poole, trans., *Grettir's Saga* (Oxford: Oxford University Press, 2009)

Carlyle, Thomas, *Chartism*, 2nd edn (London: Fraser, 1840)

———, *On Heroes, Hero-Worship & the Heroic in History*, ed. Michael K. Goldberg, Joel J. Brattin and Mark Engel, The Norman and Charlotte Strouse Edition of the Writings of Thomas Carlyle (Berkeley: University of California Press, 1993)

———, *On Heroes, Hero-Worship and the Heroic in History: Six Lectures* (London: Fraser, 1841)

———, *Past and Present*, ed. Chris Vanden Bossche, Joel J. Brattin and D. J. Trela, The Norman and Charlotte Strouse Edition of the Writings of Thomas Carlyle (Berkeley: University of California Press, 2005)

———, *Past and Present* (London: Chapman and Hall, 1843)

———, *Sartor Resartus: The Life and Opinions of Herr Teufelsdröckh in Three Books*, ed. Rodger L. Tarr and Mark Engel, The Norman and Charlotte Strouse Edition of the Writings of Thomas Carlyle (Berkeley: University of California Press, 2000)

———, *Sartor Resartus: The Life and Opinions of Herr Teufelsdröckh; In Three Books* (London: Saunders and Otley, 1838)

'Catalogue of a Portion of the Valuable Collection of Manuscripts, Early Printed Books, etc. of the late William Morris' (Sotheby, Wilkinson and Hogg, 1898), BIBL/SOT(O), (London: William Morris Society Library)

Chase, Philip, 'William Morris and Germanic Language and Legend: A Communal Ideal' (unpublished Ph.D., Drew University, 2002)

Chisholm, Hugh, ed., *The Encyclopædia Britannica*, 11th edn, 29 vols (Cambridge: Cambridge University Press, 1910–11)

Cleasby, Richard and Gudbrand Vigfusson, *An Icelandic-English Dictionary Based on the MS Collections of Richard Cleasby, Enlarged and Completed by Gudbrand Vigfusson; with an Introduction and Life of Richard Cleasby by George Webbe Dasent* (Oxford: Clarendon Press, 1874)

Clover, Carol J., 'Regardless of Sex: Men, Women, and Power in Early Northern Europe', *Speculum*, 68 (1993), 363–87

Clunies Ross, Margaret, *The Cambridge Introduction to the Old Norse-Icelandic Saga* (Cambridge: Cambridge University Press, 2010)

Colligan, Colette, *The Traffic in Obscenity from Byron to Beardsley: Sexuality and Exoticism in Nineteenth-Century Print Culture* (Basingstoke: Palgrave Macmillan, 2006)

Cook, Robert, trans., *Njal's Saga* (London: Penguin, 2001)

Cooper, Helen, *The Romance in Time: Transforming Motifs from Geoffrey of Monmouth to the Death of Shakespeare* (Oxford: Oxford University Press, 2004)

Cooper, Jane S., 'The Iceland Journeys and the Late Romances', *The Journal of the William Morris Society*, 5.4 (1983–84), 40–59

Coote, Stephen, *William Morris: His Life and Work* (London: Garamond, 1990)

Cottle, Amos Simon, trans., *Icelandic Poetry, or The Edda of Sæmund* (Bristol: Briggs, 1797)

D'Arcy, Julian and Kirsten Wolf, 'Sir Walter Scott and *Eyrbyggja Saga*', *Studies in Scottish Literature*, 22 (1987), 30–43

Dasent, George Webbe, 'The Norsemen in Iceland', in *Oxford Essays, Contributed by the Members of the University* (London: Parker, 1858)

——, trans., *The Prose or Younger Edda, Commonly Ascribed to Snorri Sturluson* (London: Pickering, 1842)

——, trans., *The Story of Burnt Njal; or, Life in Iceland at the End of the Tenth Century*, 2 vols (Edinburgh: Edmonston and Douglas, 1861)

——, trans., *The Story of Gisli the Outlaw* (Edinburgh: Edmonston and Douglas, 1866)

Dawson, Gowan, *Darwin, Literature and Victorian Respectability* (Cambridge: Cambridge University Press, 2007)

Dentith, Simon, *Epic and Empire in Nineteenth-Century Britain*, Cambridge Studies in Nineteenth-Century Literature and Culture, 52 (Cambridge: Cambridge University Press, 2006)

——, 'Morris, "The Great Story of the North", and the Barbaric Past', *Journal of Victorian Culture*, 14 (2009), 238–54

——, 'Sigurd the Volsung: Heroic Poetry in an Unheroic Age', in *William Morris: Centenary Essays. Papers from the Morris Centenary Conference Organized by the William Morris Society at Exeter College Oxford, 30 June–3 July 1996*, ed. Peter Faulkner and Peter Preston (Exeter: University of Exeter Press, 1999), pp. 60–69

Dodds, E. R., *The Greeks and the Irrational* (Berkeley: University of California Press, 1951)

Donald, James, ed., *Chambers's English Dictionary* (London: Chambers, 1872)

Dozois, Gardner, *Modern Classics of Fantasy* (New York: St Martin's Press, 1997)

Durrenberger, E. Paul and Dorothy Durrenberger, trans., *The Saga of Gunnlaugur Snake's Tongue with an Essay on the Structure and Translation of the Saga* (Rutherford: Farleigh Dickinson University Press, 1992)

Eddison, E. R., trans., *Egil's Saga Done into English Out of the Icelandic with an Introduction, Notes, and an Essay on Some Principles of Translation* (Cambridge: Cambridge University Press, 1930)

Einar Ól. Sveinsson, ed., *Vatnsdæla saga; Hallfreðar saga; Kormáks saga; Hrómundar þáttr halta; Hrafns þáttr Guðrúnarsonar*, Íslenzk Fornrit, 8 (Reykjavík: Hið íslenzka fornritafélag, 1939)

Eiríkr Magnússon, ed., *Biblía það er Heilög Ritníng*, British and Foreign Bible Society (Oxford: Oxford University Press, 1866)

——, ed., *Hið nýa testamenti drottins vors Jesú Krists, ásamt með Davíds Sálmum*, trans. Pétur Pétursson and Sigurður Melsteð, British and Foreign Bible Society (Oxford: Oxford University Press, 1863)

Ellison, Ruth, 'Icelandic Obituaries of William Morris', *The Journal of the William Morris Society*, 8.1 (1988), 35–41

——, '"The Undying Glory of Dreams": William Morris and the "Northland of Old"', in *Victorian Poetry*, ed. Malcolm Bradbury and David Palmer (London: Arnold, 1972), pp. 138–75

Eysteinn Ásgrímsson, *Lilja (The Lily): An Icelandic Religious Poem of the Fourteenth Century*, ed. Eiríkr Magnússon (London: Williams & Norgate, 1870)

Fairbank, Alfred, 'A Note on the Manuscript Work of William Morris', in *The Story of Kormak the Son of Ogmund* (London: William Morris Society, 1970), pp. 53–72

Faulkner, Peter, ed., *William Morris: The Critical Heritage* (London: Routledge, 1973)

Finnur Jónsson, *Historia Ecclesiastica Islandiae*, 4 vols (Copenhagen: Salicath, 1772)

Finnur Magnússon and Þorgeir Guðmundsson, eds., *Kormaks saga: sive, Kormaki Oegmundi filii vita, ex manuscriptis legati Magnæani cum interpretatione latina, dispersis Kormaki carminibus ad calcem adjectis et indicibus, personarum, locorum ac vocum rariorum* (Copenhagen: Thiele, 1832)

Frawley, Maria H., *Invalidism and Identity in Nineteenth-Century Britain* (Chicago: University of Chicago Press, 2004)

Frith, Richard, '"Honorable and Notable Adventures": Courtly and Chivalric Idealism in Morris's Froissartian Poems', *The Journal of the William Morris Society*, 17.3 (2007), 13–29

Frye, Northrop, *Anatomy of Criticism: Four Essays* (Princeton, NJ: Princeton University Press, 1957)

——, *The Secular Scripture: A Study of the Structure of Romance* (Cambridge, MA: Harvard University Press, 1976)

Geir T. Zoëga, *A Concise Dictionary of Old Norse*, Medieval Academy Reprints for Teaching (London: University of Toronto Press, 1910; repr. 2004)

G. Magnússon, and G. Thordarson, eds., *Grettis saga*, Nordiske oldskrifter udgivne af det Nordiske Literatur-Sámfund, 16 (Copenhagen: Berling, 1853)

G. Thordarson, ed., *Vápnfirðinga saga; Þáttr af Þorsteini hvíta; Þáttr af Þorsteini stangarhögg; Brandkossa þáttr*, Nordiske Oldskrifter udgivne af det Nordiske Literatur-Sámfund, 5 (Copenhagen: Berling, 1848)

Grant, Ben, 'Translating/"The" Kama Sutra', *Third World Quarterly*, 26 (2005), 509–16

Grundtvig, Svend, ed., *Sæmundar Edda hins fróða. Den ældre Edda* (Copenhagen: Gyldendal, 1868)

Gunnlaugur Oddsson and Hans Evertsson Wium, eds., *Laxdæla-saga: sive, Historia de rebus gestis Laxdölensium*, trans. Þorleifur Guðmundsson Repp (Copenhagen: Popp, 1826)

Guðbrandr Vigfússon, ed., *Eyrbyggja Saga* (Leipzig: Vogel, 1864)

Guðni Jónsson, ed., *Grettis saga Ásmundarsonar; Bandamanna saga; Odds þáttr Ófeigssonar*, Íslenzk fornrit, 7 (Reykjavík: Hið íslenzka fornritafélag, 1936)

Guðni Thorlacius Jóhannesson, *The History of Iceland* (Oxford: Greenwood, 2013)

Hallberg, Peter, *Old Norse Poetry: Eddic Lay and Skaldic Verse* (Lincoln: University of Nebraska Press, 1975)

Halliday Sparling, Henry, *The Kelmscott Press and William Morris Master-Craftsman*, (London: Macmillan, 1924)

Hanson, Ingrid, *William Morris and the Uses of Violence, 1856–1890* (London: Anthem Press, 2013)

Harris, Richard L., 'William Morris, Eiríkur Magnússon, and Iceland: A Survey of Correspondence', *Victorian Poetry*, 13 (1975), 119–30

Harvey, Charles and Jon Press, *Art, Enterprise and Ethics: The Life and Works of William Morris* (London: Cass, 1996)

Hascall, Dudley L., '"Volsungasaga" and Two Transformations', *The Journal of the William Morris Society*, 2.3 (1968), 18–23

Henderson, Philip, *William Morris: His Life, Work and Friends* (Harmondsworth: Penguin, 1973)

Hermann Pálsson and Paul Edwards, trans., *Egil's Saga* (Harmondsworth: Penguin, 1976)

Hight, G. A., trans., *The Saga of Grettir the Strong: A Story of the Eleventh Century* (London: Dent, 1914)

Hoare, Dorothy M., *The Works of Morris and Yeats in Relation to Early Saga Literature* (Cambridge: Cambridge University Press, 1937)

Hodges, Kenneth, 'Wounded Masculinity: Injury Gender in Sir Thomas Malory's "Le Morte Darthur"', *Studies in Philology*, 106 (2009), 14–31

Hodgson, Amanda, *The Romances of William Morris* (Cambridge: Cambridge University Press, 1987)

Horwood, William, ed., *The Complete Works of Shakespeare* (London: Murdoch, 1880)

Jackson, Rosemary, *Fantasy: The Literature of Subversion* (London: Methuen, 1981)

James, Henry, 'The Picture Season in London, 1877', in *The Painter's Eye: Notes and Essays on the Pictorial Arts*, ed. John L. Sweeney (London: Hart-Davis, 1956), pp. 130–51

Johnson, Samuel, George Steevens and Isaac Reed, eds., *Complete Works of W. Shakespeare* (Edinburgh: Nimmo, 1864)

Johnston, George, 'On Translation — II', *Saga-Book of the Viking Society for Northern Research*, 15 (1957), 394–402

Jón Árnason, ed., *Icelandic Legends*, trans. George E. J. Powell and Eiríkr Magnússon (London: Bentley, 1864)

——, ed., *Icelandic Legends: Second Series*, trans. George E. J. Powell and Eiríkr Magnússon (London: Longmans, Green, 1866)

——, ed., *Íslenzkar þjóðsögur og æfintýri*, 2 vols (Leipzig: Hinrich, 1862)

Jón R. Hjálmarsson, *A Short History of Iceland* (Reykjavík: Almenna bókafélagið, 1988)

Jones, Gwyn, ed., *Eirik the Red and Other Icelandic Sagas* (Oxford: Oxford University Press, 1980)

Julian, Linda, '*Laxdaela Saga* and "The Lovers of Gudrun": Morris' Poetic Vision', *Victorian Poetry*, 34 (1996), 355–71

Keary, Annie, *The Heroes of Asgard and the Giants of Jötunheim, Or, The Week and Its Story* (London: Bogue, 1857)

Keightley, Thomas, ed., *The Plays and Poems of William Shakespeare* (London: Bell and Daldy, 1865)

Kelvin, Norman, ed., *The Collected Letters of William Morris*, 5 vols (Princeton, NJ: Princeton University Press, 1984)

Kingsley, Charles, *Three Lectures Delivered at the Royal Institution, on the Ancien Régime as it Existed on the Continent before the French Revolution* (London: Macmillan, 1867)

Kinna, Ruth, *William Morris: The Art of Socialism* (Cardiff: University of Wales Press, 2000)

Kirchhoff, Frederick, *William Morris: The Construction of a Male Self, 1856–1872* (Athens: Ohio University Press, 1990)

Kocmanová, Jessie, *The Poetic Maturing of William Morris: From the Earthly Paradise to the Pilgrims of Hope* (Prague: Státni Pedagogické Nakladatelství, 1964)

Kristján Kristjánsson, 'Liberating Moral Traditions: Saga Morality and Aristotle's Megalopsychia', *Ethical Theory & Moral Practice*, 1 (1998), 397–422

Larrington, Carolyne, trans., *The Poetic Edda* (Oxford: Oxford University Press, 1996)

LeMire, Eugene D., *The Unpublished Lectures of William Morris* (Detroit: Wayne State University Press, 1969)

Lindsay, Jack, *William Morris, Writer: A Lecture Given to the William Morris Society on the 14th November 1958 at Caxton Hall, London* (London: William Morris Society, 1961)

——, *William Morris: His Life and Work* (London: Constable, 1975)

Litzenberg, Karl, 'The Diction of William Morris: A Discussion of His Translations from the Old Norse with Particular Reference to His "Pseudo-English" Vocabulary', *Arkiv för Nordisk Filologi*, 53 (1937), 327–63

——, 'The Social Philosophy of William Morris and the Doom of the Gods', *Essays and Studies in English and Comparative Literature*, 24 (1933), 183–203

——, *The Victorians and the Vikings: A Bibliographical Essay on Anglo-Norse*

Literary Relations, Contributions in Modern Philology, 3 (Ann Arbor: University of Michigan Press, 1947)

——, 'William Morris and the Reviews: A Study in the Fame of the Poet', *The Review of English Studies*, 12 (1936), 413–28

Lushington, Vernon, 'Carlyle: Chapt. 1 – His "I Believe"', *The Oxford & Cambridge Magazine, Conducted by Members of the Two Universities*, April 1856, pp. 193–211

MacCarthy, Fiona, *William Morris: A Life for Our Time* (London: Faber and Faber, 1994)

Mackail, J. W., *The Life of William Morris*, 2 vols (London: Longmans, Green, 1899)

Magnusson, Magnus and Hermann Pálsson, trans., *Laxdaela Saga* (Harmondsworth: Penguin, 1969)

Major, Albany F., review of *The Saga Library. 6 Vols. London: Bernard Quaritch*, by William Morris and Eiríkr Magnússon, *Saga-Book of the Viking Society for Northern Research*, 4 (1904), 468–70

Mallet, Paul Henri, *Northern Antiquities; or, An Historical Account of the Manners, Customs, Religion and Laws, Maritime Expeditions and Discoveries, Language and Literature of the Ancient Scandinavians*, ed. I. A. Blackwell, trans. Thomas Percy (London: Bohn, 1847)

Malory, Thomas, *Le Morte Darthur*, ed. Robert Southey, 2 vols (London: Longman, Hurst, Rees, Orme and Brown, 1817)

Mancoff, Debra N., *Jane Morris: The Pre-Raphaelite Model of Beauty* (San Francisco: Pomegranate, 2000)

Marsh, Jan, *Pre-Raphaelite Women: Images of Femininity in Pre-Raphaelite Art* (London: Phoenix Illustrated, 1998)

Marshall, Roderick, *William Morris and His Earthly Paradises* (Tisbury: Compton Press, 1979)

Mauer, Oscar, 'William Morris and *Laxdœla Saga*', *Texas Studies in Literature and Language*, 5 (1963), 422–37

Metcalfe, Frederick, *The Englishman and the Scandinavian; or, A Comparison of Anglo-Saxon and Old Norse Literature* (London: Trübner, 1880)

Meulengracht Sørensen, Preben, *The Unmanly Man: Concepts of Sexual Defamation in Early Northern Society*, The Viking Collection, 1 (Odense: Odense University Press, 1983)

Miller, William Ian, *Bloodtaking and Peacemaking: Feud, Law, and Society in Saga Iceland* (Chicago: University of Chicago Press, 1990)

Morris, May, ed., *The Collected Works of William Morris*, 24 vols (London: Longmans, Green, 1910–15)

——, *William Morris: Artist, Writer, Socialist*, 2 vols (Oxford: Blackwell, 1936)

Morris, William, *A Book of Verse: A Facsimile of the Manuscript Written in 1870* (London: Scolar, 1980)

——, 'A Dream', *The Oxford & Cambridge Magazine, Conducted by Members of the Two Universities*, March 1856, pp. 146–55

——, *A Tale of the House of the Wolfings and All the Kindreds of the Mark* (London: Reeves and Turner, 1889)

——, 'B. L. Add. MS 45,318' (British Library, London, [n. d.])

——, *Child Christopher and Goldilind the Fair* (London: Kelmscott, 1895)

——, *Icelandic Journals*, ed. James Morris (Fontwell: Centaur Press, 1969)

——, 'Lindenborg Pool', *The Oxford & Cambridge Magazine, Conducted by Members of the Two Universities*, September 1856, 530–34

——, *Love Is Enough, Or, The Freeing of Pharamond: A Morality* (London: Ellis and White, 1873)

——, *Poems by the Way* (London: Kelmscott Press, 1891)

——, trans., *The Aeneids of Virgil* (London: Ellis and White, 1876)

——, *The Defence of Guenevere, and Other Poems* (London: Bell and Daldy, 1858)

——, *The Earthly Paradise: A Poem*, 3 vols (London: Ellis, 1868)

——, *The Earthly Paradise*, ed. Florence Saunders Boos, 2 vols (London: Routledge, 2002)

——, 'The Hollow Land: A Tale', *The Oxford & Cambridge Magazine, Conducted by Members of the Two Universities*, October 1856, 632–41

——, *The Life and Death of Jason: A Poem* (London: Bell and Daldy, 1868)

——, trans., *The Odyssey of Homer* (London: Longmans, Green, 1896)

——, 'The Mythology and Religion of the North' (William Morris Gallery, London, [n. d.]), MS J 146

——, *The Roots of the Mountains: Wherein is Told Somewhat of the Lives of the Men of Burgdale, their Friends, their Neighbours, their Foemen and their Fellows in Arms* (London: Reeves and Turner, 1890)

——, trans., 'The Story of Frithiof the Bold', *The Dark Blue*, 1 (1871), 42–58, 176–82

——, *The Story of Sigurd the Volsung and the Fall of the Niblungs* (London: Ellis and White, 1876)

——, *The Story of the Glittering Plain: which has been also called the Land of Living Men or the Acre of the Undying* (London: Kelmscott Press, 1891)

——, *The Sundering Flood* (London: Kelmscott Press, 1897)

——, *The Water of the Wondrous Isles* (London: Kelmscott Press, 1897)

——, *The Well at the World's End* (London: Kelmscott Press, 1896)

——, *The Wood Beyond the World* (London: Kelmscott Press, 1894)

Morris, William and Alfred John Wyatt, trans., *The Tale of Beowulf* (London: Kelmscott Press, 1895)

Morris, William and Eiríkr Magnússon, trans., 'Eyrbyggia Saga' (Fitzwilliam Museum, Cambridge, 1868), Morris/Eyrbyggia, William Morris Collection

——, trans., *Grettis Saga: The Story of Grettir the Strong* (London: Ellis and White, 1869)

——, eds., *The Saga Library*, 6 vols (London: Quaritch, 1891–1905)

——, trans., 'The Saga of Gunnlaug the Worm-Tongue and Rafn the Skald', *Fortnightly Review*, January 1869, 27–56

——, trans., 'The Story of Hen Thorir; The Story of the Banded Men; The Story of Haward the Halt' (Fitzwilliam Museum, Cambridge, [n.d.]), Morris/ Icelandic, William Morris Collection

——, trans., *The Story of Kormak the Son of Ogmund* (London: William Morris Society, 1970)

——, trans., *Three Northern Love Stories and Other Tales*, William Morris Library, 11 (Bristol: Thoemmes, 1996)

——, trans., *Three Northern Love Stories, and Other Tales* (London: Ellis and White, 1875)

——, trans., *Völsunga Saga: The Story of the Volsungs & Niblungs, with Certain Songs from the Elder Edda* (London: Ellis and White, 1870)

Morris, William and May Morris, 'Partial Catalogue of William Morris's Library' (Library of the Society of Antiquaries, London, 1876), MS 860

Nead, Lynda, 'Bodies of Judgement: Art, Obscenity and the Connoisseur', in *Law and the Image: The Authority of Art and the Aesthetics of Law*, ed. Costas Douzinas and Lynda Nead (Chicago: University of Chicago Press, 1999), pp. 203–25

——, *Victorian Babylon: People, Streets and Images in Nineteenth-Century London* (New Haven: Yale University Press, 2000)

Nordby, Conrad Hjalmar, *The Influence of Old Norse Literature on English Literature*, Columbia University Germanic Studies, 3 (New York: Columbia University Press, 1901)

O'Donoghue, Heather, *English Poetry and Old Norse Myth: A History* (Oxford: Oxford University Press, 2014)

——, *Old Norse-Icelandic Literature: An Introduction* (Cambridge: Blackwell, 2004)

——, *The Genesis of a Saga Narrative: Verse and Prose in Kormaks Saga* (Oxford: Clarendon Press, 1991)

Oberg, Charlotte H., *A Pagan Prophet: William Morris* (Charlottesville: University Press of Virginia, 1978)

Olaus Olavius, ed., *Sagan af Niáli Þorgeirssyni ok sonvm hans &c* (Copenhagen: Thiele, 1772)

Parry, Linda, ed., *William Morris* (London: Philip Wilson in association with the Victoria and Albert Museum, 1996)

Percy, Thomas, trans., *Five Pieces of Runic Poetry Translated from the Islandic Language* (London: Dodsley, 1763)

Powell, George E. J. and Eiríkr Magnússon, trans., 'The Story of Havardr the Lame' (The National Library of Wales, Aberystwyth), Music MSS, Snell and Sons Collection

Preston, Peter, '"The North Begins Inside": Morris and Trollope in Iceland', *The Journal of the William Morris Society*, 14.2 (2001), 8–28

Purkis, John, *The Icelandic Jaunt: A Study of the Expeditions Made by Morris in 1871 and 1873* (Dublin: Dolmen Press, 1962)

Quirk, Randolph, 'Dasent, Morris, and Problems of Translation', *Saga-Book of the Viking Society for Northern Research*, 14 (1955), 64–77

Rafn, Carl Christian, ed., *Fornaldar sögur nordrlanda*, 3 vols (Copenhagen: Popp, 1829)

Rafn, Carl Christian, Jón Sigurðsson and Finnur Magnússon, eds., *Íslendinga sögur: udgivne efter gamle haandskrifter af det Kongelige Nordiske Oldskrift-Selskab*, 2 vols (Copenhagen: Möller, 1847)

Regal, Martin S. and Judy Quinn, trans., *Gisli Sursson's Saga and The Saga of the People of Eyri* (London: Penguin, 2003)

Riddehough, Geoffrey B., 'William Morris's Translation of the "Aeneid"', *The Journal of English and Germanic Philology*, 36 (1937), 338–46

Roberts, M. J. D., 'Making Victorian Morals? The Society for the Suppression of Vice and its Critics, 1802–1886', *Historical Studies*, 21 (1984), 157–73

——, 'Morals, Art, and the Law: The Passing of the Obscene Publications Act, 1857', *Victorian Studies*, 28 (1985), 609–29

Robertson, Geoffrey, *Obscenity: An Account of Censorship Laws and Their Enforcement in England and Wales* (London: Weidenfeld and Nicolson, 1979)

Roget, Peter Mark, *Thesaurus of English Words and Phrases*, 1st edn (London: Longman, Brown, Green and Longmans, 1852)

Ruskin, John, *The Stones of Venice*, 3 vols (London: Smith and Elder, 1851–53)

Sagas of Warrior-Poets: Kormak's saga; The Saga of Hallfred Troublesome-poet; The Saga of Gunnlaug Serpent-tongue; The Saga of Bjorn, Champion of the Hitardal People; Viglund's saga [with and Introduction and Notes by Diana Whaley] (London: Penguin, 2002)

Salmon, Nicholas, '"The Down-Trodden Radical": William Morris's Pre-Socialist Ideology', *The Journal of the William Morris Society*, 13.3 (1999), 26–43

——, 'A Study in Victorian Historiography: William Morris's Germanic Romances', *The Journal of the William Morris Society*, 14.2 (2001), 59–89

Schlegel, Johan Frederik Vilhelm and Jean-Marie Pardessus, eds., *Hin forna lögbók islendínga sem nefnist Grágás: Codex juris Islandorum antiqvissimus, qvi nominatur Grágás*, trans. Þórður Sveinbjørnsson, 2 vols (Copenhagen: Thiele, 1829)

Sigurður Gylfi Magnússon, *Wasteland with Words: A Social History of Iceland* (London: Reaktion, 2010)

Sigurður Nordal and Guðni Jónsson, eds., *Borgfirðinga sögur: Hœnsa-Þóris saga; Gunnlaugs saga ormstungu; Bjarnar saga Hítdœlakappa; Heiðarvíga saga; Gísls þáttr Illugasonar*, Íslenzk fornrit, 3 (Reykjavík: Hið íslenzka fornritafélag, 1938)

Silver, Carole G., 'The Earthly Paradise: Lost', *Victorian Poetry*, 13 (1975), 27–42

Simpson, John M., 'Eyrbyggja Saga and Nineteenth Century Scholarship', in *Proceedings of the First International Saga Conference. Edinburgh, 1971* (Viking Society for Northern Research: London, 1973), pp. 360–94

Skoblow, Jeffrey, *Paradise Dislocated: Morris, Politics, Art* (London: University Press of Virginia, 1993)

Snorre Sturlassøn, *Heimskringla eller norges kongesagaer*, ed. C. R. Unger (Oslo: Brögger and Christie, 1868)

Snorre Sturlesson, *Norske Kongers sagaer*, ed. Jacob Aall (Oslo: Guldberg and Dzwonkowski, 1838)

Snorri Sturluson, *Edda*, trans. Anthony Faulkes (London: Dent, 1987)

——, *Heimskringla: History of the Kings of Norway*, trans. Lee M. Hollander (Austin: University of Texas Press, 1964)

——, 'Story of Olaf the Holy', trans. Eiríkr Magnússon and William Morris (Leeds University Library, 1891), MS C19 Morris, Brotherton Collection

——, *The Heimskringla: or, Chronicle of the Kings of Norway*, trans. Samuel Laing, 3 vols (London: Longman, Brown, Green and Longmans, 1844)

——, 'The Story of Harald Greycloak and Earl Hakon', trans. William Morris and Eiríkr Magnússon (Huntington Library, San Marino [n. d.]), Huntington Manuscript 6428

Spatt, Hartley S., 'Morrissaga: *Sigurd the Volsung*', *ELH: A Journal of English Literary History*, 44 (1977), 355–75

Stefán Einarsson, 'Eiríkr Magnússon and his Saga-Translations', *Scandinavian Studies*, 13 (1933), 17–32

——, 'Eiríkur Magnússon – The Forgotten Pioneer', in *Studia Centenalia in Honorem Memoriae Benedikt S. Þórarinsson*, ed. Benedikt S. Benedikz (Reykjavík: Ísafoldarprentsmiðja, 1961), pp. 3–50

——, *Saga Eiríks Magnússonar* (Reykjavík: Ísafoldarprentsmiðja, 1933)

Stevenson, Robert Louis, 'Health and Mountains', in *Sketches, Criticisms: Lay Morals, and Other Essays* (London: Heineman, 1923), pp. 473–79

Ström, Folke, *Níð, Ergi and Old Norse Moral Attitudes*, The Dorothea Coke Memorial Lecture in Northern Studies (London: Viking Society for Northern Research, 1974)

Svavar Hrafn Svavarsson, 'Honour and Shame: Comparing Medieval Iceland and Ancient Greece', ed. Vésteinn Ólason, *Gripla*, 20 (2009), 241–56

Swannell, J. N., *William Morris & Old Norse Literature: A Lecture Given by J. N. Swannell on 18th December 1958 in Prince Henry's Room Fleet Street London* (London: William Morris Society, 1961)

——, 'William Morris as an Interpreter of Old Norse', *Saga Book of the Viking Society for Northern Research*, 15 (1957), 365–82

Tägil, Sven, *Ethnicity and Nation Building in the Nordic World* (London: Hurst, 1995)

Tegnér, Esaias, *Frithiofs Saga: A Legend of the North*, trans. George Stephens (London: Black and Armstrong, 1839)

——, *Frithiofs saga* (Stockholm: Nordström, 1825)

The Complete Works of Shakspere: With a Memoir (London: Dicks, 1868)

The Sagas of Icelanders: A Selection (London: Penguin, 2001)

The Works of William Shakespeare, Complete. With Life and Glossary (London: Ward, Lock and Tyler, 1877)

Thomas, R. G., 'George E. J. Powell, Eiríkr Magnússon and Jón Sigurðsson: A Chapter in Icelandic Literary History', *Saga-Book of the Viking Society for Northern Research*, 14 (1953), 113–30

Thompson, E. P., *William Morris: Romantic to Revolutionary* (London: Lawrence and Wishart, 1955)

Thompson, Paul, *The Work of William Morris* (London: Heinemann, 1967)

Thorpe, Benjamin, trans., *Edda Sæmundar hinns fróða: The Edda of Sæmund the Learned from the Old Norse or Icelandic, with a Mythological Index* (London: Trübner, 1866)

——, trans., *Northern Mythology: Comprising the Principal Popular Traditions and Superstitions of Scandinavia, North Germany, and the Netherlands*, 3 vols (London: Lumley, 1851)

——, trans., *Yule-Tide Stories: A Collection of Scandinavian and North German Popular Tales and Traditions, from the Swedish, Danish, and German* (London: Bohn, 1853)

Timo, Helen, 'A Church without God: William Morris's "A Night in a Cathedral"', *The Journal of the William Morris Society*, 4.2 (1980), 24–31

Todorov, Tzvetan, *The Fantastic: A Structural Approach to a Literary Genre*, trans. Richard Howard (Cleveland: Case Western Reserve University Press, 1973)

Tolkien, J. R. R., 'Beowulf: The Monsters and the Critics', *Proceedings of the British Academy*, 22 (1936), 245–95

——, *Tree and Leaf* (London: Allen and Unwin, 1964)

Tompkins, J. M. S., *William Morris: An Approach to the Poetry* (London: Woolf, 1988)

Townend, Matthew, *The Vikings and Victorian Lakeland: The Norse Medievalism of W. G. Collingwood and His Contemporaries*, Extra Series, 34 (Kendal: Cumberland and Westmorland Antiquarian and Archaeological Society, 2009)

——, 'Victorian Medievalisms', in *The Oxford Handbook of Victorian Poetry*, ed. Matthew Bevis (Oxford: Oxford University Press, 2013), pp. 166–83

Tucker, Herbert F., 'All for the Tale: The Epic Macropoetics of Morris' *Sigurd the Volsung*', *Victorian Poetry*, 34 (1996), 373–96

——, *Epic: Britain's Heroic Muse 1790–1910* (Oxford: Oxford University Press, 2008)

Upstone, Robert, *The Pre-Raphaelite Dream: Paintings and Drawings from the Tate Collection* (London: Tate, 2003)

Venuti, Lawrence, *The Translator's Invisibility: A History of Translation* (London: Routledge, 1995)

Vigfusson, Gudbrand and F. York Powell, eds., *Corpus Poeticum Boreale: The Poetry of the Old Northern Tongue from the Earliest Times to the Thirteenth Century*, 2 vols (Oxford: Clarendon Press, 1883)

Vilhjálmur Árnason, 'An Ethos in Transformation: Conflicting Values in the Sagas', ed. Vésteinn Ólason, *Gripla*, 20 (2009), 217–40

——, 'Morality and Social Structure in Icelandic Sagas', in *The Journal of English and Germanic Philology*, 90 (1990), 157–74

Wahl, Robert, 'The Mood of Energy and the Mood of Idleness: A Note on "The Earthly Paradise"', *English Studies in Africa*, 2 (1959), 90–97

Waithe, Marcus, *William Morris's Utopia of Strangers: Victorian Medievalism and the Ideal of Hospitality* (Cambridge: D. S. Brewer, 2006)

Wawn, Andrew, 'History of ON Studies', 5 January 2015

——, *The Vikings and the Victorians: Inventing the Old North in Nineteenth-Century Britain* (Cambridge: D. S. Brewer, 2000)

Webster, Noah, *A Complete Dictionary of the English Language*, rev. C. A. Goodrich and N. Porter, (London: Bell and Daldy, 1865)

Weeks, Jeffrey, *Coming Out: Homosexual Politics in Britain, from the Nineteenth Century to the Present* (London: Quartet, 1977)

Whitla, William, '"Sympathetic Translation" and the "Scribe's Capacity": Morris's Calligraphy and the Icelandic Sagas', *The Journal of Pre-Raphaelite Studies*, 10 (2001), 27–108

Wiener, Martin J., *Men of Blood: Violence, Manliness, and Criminal Justice in Victorian England* (Cambridge: Cambridge University Press, 2006)

Wiens, Pamela Bracken, 'Fire and Ice: Clashing Visions of Iceland in the Travel Narratives of Morris and Burton', *The Journal of the William Morris Society*, 11.4 (1996), 12–18

Wilmer, Clive, 'Dreaming Reality: The Poetry of William Morris', in *The Oxford Handbook of Victorian Poetry*, ed. Matthew Bevis (Oxford: Oxford University Press, 2013), pp. 475–91

——, 'Maundering Medievalism: D. G. Rossetti and William Morris as Poets', *PN Review (Manchester)*, 29 (2003), 69–74

Wolfe, Gary K., 'Fantasy from Dryden to Dunsany', in *The Cambridge Companion to Fantasy Literature*, ed. Edward James and Farah Mendlesohn (Cambridge: Cambridge University Press, 2012), pp. 7–20

Wright, Joseph, *The English Dialect Dictionary*, 6 vols (London: Frowde, 1898–1905)

Zironi, Alessandro, 'William Morris and the *Poetic Edda*', in *The Hyperborean Muse: Studies in the Transmission and Reception of Old Norse Literature*, ed. Judy Quinn and Adele Cipolla, Acta Scandinavica, 6 (Turnhout: Brepols, 2016), 211–37

Index

Medievalism

I
Anglo-Saxon Culture and the Modern Imagination
edited by David Clark and Nicholas Perkins

II
Medievalist Enlightenment:
From Charles Perrault to Jean-Jacques Rousseau
Alicia C. Montoya

III
Memory and Myths of the Norman Conquest
Siobhan Brownlie

IV
Comic Medievalism: Laughing at the Middle Ages
Louise D'Arcens

V
Medievalism: Key Critical Terms
edited by Elizabeth Emery and Richard Utz

VI
Medievalism: A Critical History
David Matthews

VII
Chivalry and the Medieval Past
edited by Katie Stevenson and Barbara Gribling

VIII
Georgian Gothic:
Medievalist Architecture, Furniture and Interiors, 1730–1840
Peter N. Lindfield

IX
Petrarch and the Literary Culture of Nineteenth-Century France:
Translation, Appropriation, Transformation
Jennifer Rushworth

X
Medievalism, Politics and Mass Media:
Appropriating the Middle Ages in the Twenty-First Century
Andrew B.R. Elliott